100 Years of Pragmatism

100 Years of Pragmatism

· · · · · · · · · · · · · · · · · · · ·

William James's
Revolutionary Philosophy

Edited by John J. Stuhr

Indiana University Press | BLOOMINGTON AND INDIANAPOLIS

This book is a publication of

Indiana University Press
601 North Morton Street
Bloomington, IN 47404-3797 USA

www.iupress.indiana.edu

Telephone orders   800-842-6796
Fax orders   812-855-7931
Orders by e-mail   iuporder@indiana.edu

Library of Congress Cataloging-in-Publication Data

100 years of pragmatism : William James's revolutionary
philosophy / edited by John J. Stuhr.
    p. cm. — (American philosophy)
  Includes bibliographical references and index.
  ISBN 978-0-253-35387-0 (cloth : alk. paper) — ISBN 978-0-
253-22142-1 (pbk. : alk. paper) 1. James, William, 1842–1910.
Pragmatism. 2. James, William, 1842–1910. 3. Pragmatism. I.
Stuhr, John J. II. Title: One hundred years of pragmatism.
  B945.J23P735 2010
  144'.3—dc22

                                              2009025717

1 2 3 4 5 15 14 13 12 11 10

CONTENTS

ACKNOWLEDGMENTS

Dee Mortensen at Indiana University Press provided unwavering enthusiasm for this project, as well as good judgment and substantial patience.

Jason Aleksander's research and bibliographical assistance and attention to manuscript details were first-rate and nothing short of astonishing.

Emory College of Arts and Sciences deans Robert A. Paul and Cristine Levenduski provided crucial institutional support.

And, thanks, above all, to my fellow contributors to this volume. Its strengths are a function of their deep knowledge, personal commitment, and creative ideas and original voices.

ABBREVIATIONS

Citations of the writings of William James are included in an abbreviated format in all chapters for ease of reference and flow of text. (Citations of, and references to, other authors, as well as more substantial notes, are included in the footnotes in all chapters.) All abbreviated citations and references are to *The Works of William James,* published by Harvard University Press (Frederick Burkhardt, general editor, and Fredson Bowers, textual editor; Cambridge, Massachusetts and London, England), or to *The Correspondence of William James,* published by the University Press of Virginia (Ignas K. Skrupelis and Elizabeth M. Berkeley, eds.; Charlottesville, Va., and London, England). The abbreviations and full references (including original publication dates) are as follows:

APU	*A Pluralistic Universe* (1977 [1909])
CWJ	*The Correspondence of William James* (1992–2004 [1861–1910]; 12 vols.)
ECR	*Essays, Comments, and Reviews* (1987 [1865–1909])
ERE	*Essays in Radical Empiricism* (1976 [1912])
ERM	*Essays in Religion and Morality* (1982 [1884–1910])
EP	*Essays in Philosophy* (1978 [1876–1910])
MEN	*Manuscript Essays and Notes* (1988 [1872–1910])
MT	*The Meaning of Truth* (1975 [1909])
P	*Pragmatism: A New Name for Some Old Ways of Thinking* (1975 [1907])
PP	*The Principles of Psychology* (1981 [1890]; 2 vols.)
SPP	*Some Problems of Philosophy* (1979 [1910])
TT	*Talks to Teachers on Psychology* (1983 [1899])
VRE	*The Varieties of Religious Experience* (1985 [1902])
WB	*The Will to Believe and Other Essays in Popular Philosophy* (1979 [1897])

100 Years of Pragmatism

Introduction:
100 Years of Pragmatism

JOHN J. STUHR

I.

In 1907, William James published *Pragmatism*. The book was based most directly on public lectures at the Lowell Institute and Columbia University, but its major ideas and lines of thought had been evident in James's lectures and publications, and in debates and discussion in philosophy journals, for some three decades. James dedicated the book to John Stuart Mill, "from whom I first learned the pragmatic openness of mind and whom my fancy likes to picture as our leader were he alive today," and he added a characteristically pluralistic subtitle—*Pragmatism: A New Name for Some Old Ways of Thinking*—that suggests anything but genuine originality, conceptual sea change, and revolution in philosophy (*P*, 3, 1). James added, early in the book, that "there is absolutely nothing new in the pragmatic method" and located its earlier if more fragmentary use in philosophers such as Aristotle, Locke, Berkeley, Hume, and Hodgson, in addition to Mill (*P*, 30).

Still, James referred to pragmatism as a "conquering destiny" with "universal mission" (*P*, 30), and it is clear that he viewed it as original and highly important. Writing that same year to his brother, Henry, he claimed, "I shouldn't be surprised if ten years hence it should be rated as 'epoch-making,' for of the definitive triumph of that general way of thinking I can entertain no doubt whatever—I believe it to be something quite like the protestant reformation" (*CWJ*, III, 339). James described this general way of thinking as a "turn away from abstraction and insufficiency, from verbal solutions, from bad a priori reasons, from fixed principles, closed systems, and pretended absolutes and origins" and a "turn towards concreteness and adequacy, towards facts, towards action, and towards power" (*P*, 31). It is, he added, "the attitude of looking away from first things, principles, 'categories,' supposed necessities; and of looking towards last things, fruits, consequences, facts" (*P*, 32).

Today, more than a century after the publication of James's *Pragmatism*, has pragmatism's general way of thinking been triumphant, even epoch-making? What has been the pragmatic impact of pragmatism? What is its pragmatic meaning today? What are its pragmatic possibilities for tomorrow?

This volume addresses these questions. In substance, it is neither an introduction to, nor an explication of, James's philosophy. Rather, it is an original engagement with the major ways in which James himself understood pragmatism. In orientation, it takes up the spirit of neither closed-minded cheerleading nor closed-minded refutation. Rather, it is a critical assessment of pragmatism in light of more than a century of its facts, consequences, fruits, and last things.

Four overlapping issues and clusters of questions constitute the focus of this volume. First, beginning with James's own projection of the historical importance of his work, attention is focused on the impact of pragmatism in the United States and in the world, both backward in terms of the century after *Pragmatism* and forward in terms of its present and future potential. In so doing, pragmatism also is situated in contexts that outstrip national boundaries—contexts of modernism and postmodernism, democratic movements and totalitarian regimes, and issues of race, gender, class, and globalization.

James characterized pragmatism as a method, as a theory of truth, and as an attitude, each serving as a point of focus here. So, second, consider pragmatism as a method—a method for settling otherwise interminable metaphysical problems, a method for philosophers (finally) to make progress, a method that would "unstiffen our theories" and render philosophy radically experiential and, if those experiences are irreducibly plural, radically pluralistic. Has this method succeeded? Has it achieved a wholesale reconstruction in philosophy by undercutting the assumptions of traditional problems? If pragmatism has not triumphed, how and why has it failed or stumbled? If it has succeeded, how, and how is any such triumph consistent with the seemingly interminable continuation of metaphysical problems and intellectualist tendencies? And can pragmatism really be, as James sometimes squarely says, a method only that "does not stand for any special results?"

Third, James set forth his pragmatism as a theory of truth. In his view, truth is an instrument for getting us into satisfactory relations with experiences, an expedient in our way of thinking, a marrying function between old beliefs and new experiences, and something made rather than found. Is this account of truth true? Does it square with science, including science since James's day? And if truth is bound up with notions of what works and satisfaction of purposes, what are the implications of this for different persons and different types of persons? Does James's pluralism about truth lead to multiculturalism and a philosophy that takes seriously differences among individuals? Does it lead to relativism or nihilism? If so, is that bad?

James also identified pragmatism as an attitude or spirit or temperament, as a way of feeling or mood. A hundred years after *Pragmatism,* has this attitude been sustained, nurtured, or expanded? Or has it become constricted, overwhelmed, or undone? What is the proper place, if any, of personal temperament in philosophy, particularly in a diverse, global world? Is this some kind of irrationalism? And, given the horrors of the past one hundred years, must pragmatism still today incline toward meliorism?

In chapter 1, James T. Kloppenberg examines in detail the influence, both in the early twentieth century and at the beginning of the twenty-first century, of James's pragmatism and "ceaseless experimentation" on American history and American thought in areas of life such as politics, law, business, architecture and urban planning, medicine, education, and the environment, and across matters of gender, race, and ethnicity. This influence of pragmatism is, of course, complex, and it has usually been opposed and contested. But it is also, Kloppenberg demonstrates, unmistakable, having "filtered down into many corners of practical life" and, just as important, still providing critical leverage on those dogmatic, self-righteous, and arrogant parts of culture that it has not yet transformed.

Pragmatism's emergence as a transforming cultural force, Mark Bauerlein documents in chapter 2, is rooted to a large extent in "more immediate influences, arguments, and adversaries," "in a local, unfolding, and piecemeal setting: the philosophy periodicals circa 1905" that typically scooped book publication. Journals, Bauerlein shows, played essential functions in the development of pragmatism—spreading pragmatic views, sharp criticism of them, competition from other points of view, and sharpened and improved reformulations. Pragmatism's content turned on intellectual points, Bauerlein observes, but other messy factors, from individual personalities to institutional politics, also shaped the articulation of pragmatism by James and Dewey.

Efforts to ignore or escape the "messily human" factors in order to forge a refined and fully mature philosophy are rejected by James (who "seizes the low ground"), as Ross Posnock explains in chapter 3. Recalling Whitman, Emerson, and Thoreau, Posnock makes clear James's horizontal transvaluation of values, in which, as James put it, "the earth of things . . . must resume its rights." Posnock illustrates the vitality of James's thought by means of a genealogy extending from ancient Greek thinkers to earlier American writers to twentieth-century modernists in literature, painting, and philosophy (including Wittgenstein), a genealogy that illuminates James's "massive recovery of experience" as an antidote to absolute certitude and the barbarism that certitude enables.

In *Pragmatism,* this recovery of experience, William J. Gavin shows in chapter 4, takes place in the context of death. Through this context, Gavin examines James's focus on temperament rather than objective reason, his use of metaphor and his rejection of philosophy as mere description, and the role of will in the choice between tragedy and hope—a choice Gavin characterizes as one between partial tragedy and complete tragedy. This choice is not a problem that James, the pragmatist, solves or resolves. Rather, it is a site at which James attests to a particular attitude—meliorism—and simultaneously signals the limits of that attitude—individual death.

In chapter 5, Bruce Wilshire begins by calling James "a tragic philosopher" and then asserts that in *Pragmatism* his "hold on the manifoldness of experience comes partially undone" by being "heavy on ever ongoing experiencing and light on the integrity of the experienced." Connecting James's pragmatic theory of truth with his radically empirical metaphysics, Wilshire finds too little attention (perhaps due to desire for approval by the masses) in the former to the ways in which ideas are discovered and not merely made, the ways in which ideas are constrained by what just is the case and by obdurate realities (stressed in James's 1878 "Remarks on Spencer's Definition of Mind as Correspondence"). But if James did not always keep his balance, Wilshire concludes that his "thoughtful balancing act over the abyss" deserves our serious reconsideration.

This reconsideration, Richard Gale claims in chapter 6, reveals major shortcomings in James's pragmatic theory of meaning—a theory that commits James, Gale argues, to an in-principle private language. These shortcomings, Gale continues, doom James's and other pragmatists' attempts to deconstruct traditional debates in the history of philosophy by applying this pragmatic theory of meaning to them. There is nothing special here: Gale asserts that all attempts to deconstruct traditional philosophy, "thank God," are complete failures. Happily, Gale concludes, James's actual philosophical practice violated his own pragmatic metaphilosophical principles and strictures against hard-core traditional philosophy.

Stressing James's pragmatism as a kind of multiple relationalism rather than traditional relativism, in which truth functions as a value, José Medina in chapter 7 uses James's conception of truth to connect epistemic reconstructions of belief with political reconstructions of ways of life. Analyzing the normative dimension and the performative renegotiations of truth, Medina argues that James's pluralistic conception of truth accounts for both objectivity and justice, and so constitutes more than a century later an immense resource for a critical epistemology attuned to difference and critical social thought attuned to specificity and a view of solidarity as shared commitments held in light of irreducible diversity.

In chapter 8, James Livingston also finds pragmatism not only an immense resource but more useful to philosophers in an age of globalization (rather than artisanal labor) than Nietzsche, Heidegger, or critical theorists such as Horkheimer, Adorno, and Habermas. In the metaphors of cash-value, money, business, credit, and such that run through James's pragmatism and radical empiricism, Livingston locates crucial resources for avoiding the "pathos of authenticity" and for understanding commodity universalization "as both an impediment to and the condition of democracy" at the end of modernity and its myth of subjectivity. James wants to overthrow traditional philosophy and "to rewrite philosophy as history," just as exchange value has overthrown use value. We should follow this lead, Livingston concludes.

Can we, or should we, follow someone's lead if we think of philosophy as inextricably bound to personality and individual temperament? If so, how does pragmatism account for, or apply to, "the myriad varieties of individual perspectives?" Linda Simon addresses these questions in chapter 9, explaining pragmatism not simply as a philosophy that highlights personal temperament but as a philosophy of a personal temperament—William James's temperament—attuned to moments of "thrilling aliveness" brought about by the need to make a decision and act on an outcome in question, and by moments brought about by the need to understand others and to sustain community. Interweaving James's life and his philosophy, *Pragmatism*'s legacy, Simon concludes, lies in the ways it allows us to ask these questions, not in any final or universal answers to them.

In a parallel way, Ruth Anna Putnam in chapter 10 identifies pragmatism in terms of a meliorist attitude marked by an "agent point of view" rather than by any system of propositions or school of thought. This attitude, Putnam "audaciously maintains," has enduring value—perhaps even particularly timely value today. This pragmatist attitude, Putnam continues, is the basic "attitude of any scientist" and is "alive and well among scientists and a large majority of the general population." Is pragmatism alive in philosophy? Putnam answers that it is, no matter what it may be named, whenever philosophy understands itself as public in character, as inevitably multiply perspectival, and as involved in social ferment and "tolerance for the alien point of view."

Has this pragmatic philosophy been epoch-making, as James expected? And, how and for whom does this matter? John J. Stuhr addresses these questions in chapter 11, beginning with an account of pragmatism as: a method for settling some problems, with science settling others; a theory of truth as the product of verifying processes and a branch of a revolutionary pluralistic, tragic account of values akin to relativity theory in physics; and, an attitude of looking toward last things. Stuhr argues that the success of this philosophy depends ultimately upon one's temperament, and that, accordingly, in the next one hundred years pragmatists would do best to focus practically on securing and expanding the cultural conditions that sustain this temperament.

"It is high time to urge the use of a little imagination in philosophy" (*P*, 112) James wrote. This volume is one effort by its many authors to respond to that urging. More than one hundred years after the publication of *Pragmatism*, in critically assessing its consequences and impact, this volume, like pragmatism, "faces forward to the future" (*P*, 108). The guiding hope here is that it will help its readers do just that.

"You see how differently people take things," James observed (*P*, 126).

1. James's *Pragmatism* and American Culture, 1907–2007

JAMES T. KLOPPENBERG

William James usually tended more toward self-deprecation than self-aggrandizement. In a letter to his brother Henry dated May 4, 1907, however, William characterized his new book *Pragmatism* with uncharacteristic enthusiasm. It was "an unconventional utterance," William conceded, but after the passage of a mere ten years, he wrote, it might be considered "epoch-making." Even more boldly, he predicted "the definitive triumph" of the "general way of thinking" laid out in the book, and he characterized the overall cultural change as "something quite like the protestant reformation" (*LWJ*, III, 337–40). What did he mean? How does his prophecy look a century after the publication of *Pragmatism*? Did the twentieth century witness the change he anticipated?

A decade ago, scholars were attempting to make sense of the unquestionable presence of pragmatism in American intellectual life at the close of the twentieth century. In my own contribution to this conversation, I asked readers to consider which aspects of contemporary pragmatism preserved the central ideas of James and his colleague John Dewey, which aspects constituted new departures, and what difference the controversies made in our understanding of twentieth-century American intellectual history.[1] The essay attracted some attention, particularly from those whom I characterized as having left behind James's and Dewey's crucial commitments to experience and democratic culture.[2] The essay was also criticized from a different angle, by the philosopher Elizabeth Minnich, for having paid insufficient attention to the importance of social action.[3] Since the article stressed my conviction that the truth-testing envisioned by James and Dewey requires democratic forms of cultural experimentation, at first I considered Minnich's criticism surprising, but I do see her point. Inasmuch as I focused on the controversies over how we should understand James's and Dewey's ideas and those of their successors in the multifaceted and diverse traditions of pragmatism, I did pay less attention to social practices than I did to the ideas themselves. In part in response to that observation and in part in response to the division of labor for this volume envisioned by the editor, in this essay I concentrate less on how intellectual historians should interpret pragmatism old and new and more on the influence of James's (and, to a lesser extent, Dewey's) ideas on American history.[4] But my focus will remain on the consequences of pragmatism for American thought, because I share James's own conviction that thinking itself constitutes a kind of action and that ideas make a difference.

I will discuss a number of different domains, including politics, law, race and ethnicity, gender, business management, architecture and urban planning, medicine, law, education, and environmentalism, and two different eras, the early twentieth century and the turn of the twenty-first. My goal in this essay is to sketch—because in the space of an essay it is not possible to do more than that—some indications of the immediate impact of pragmatism in the first half of the last century and some signs of its longer-term legacies as manifested in various contemporary practices.

Two further introductory notes: First, James's *Pragmatism* marked the blossoming of ideas germinating for thirty years, ideas first advanced in his 1878 essay "Remarks on Spencer's Definition of Mind as Correspondence." There James observed that thinking begins with "mental interests," emotional or practical reasons that propel individuals to act and thereby "help to *make* the truth which they declare." Already advancing a crucial argument that he believed would distinguish his pragmatism from wishful thinking, an argument his critics then and ever since have persistently misunderstood, James insisted in the essay, in the *Journal of Speculative Philosophy*, that "the only objective criterion of reality is coerciveness, in the long run, over thought" (*EP*, 21).[5] In a later essay of 1885, "The Function of Cognition," which James described to C. A. Strong in 1907 as the "fons et origo of all *my* pragmatism,"[6] an essay he later reprinted as chapter 1 of *The Meaning of Truth*, James contended that theoretical speculation is idle unless it can be tested in the world beyond the mind. "These *termini*, these sensible things," he wrote in an article from an 1885 issue of *Mind* titled "The Function of Cognition," "are the only realities we ever directly know," so disagreements about ideas should be settled according to their "practical issue" (*MT*, 31). James continued refining the lectures eventually published as *Pragmatism* in presentations given before various audiences in places from Berkeley to Rome, and in his Harvard courses, during the years 1898–1907. Because the argument of *Pragmatism* itself is best understood as the product of a very lengthy process that began several decades before the book appeared, it is no surprise that some signs of the ideas' impact predate publication of the book.

Second, when James invoked the Protestant Reformation in his letter to his brother Henry, he had in mind a particular kind of cultural transformation. In *Pragmatism* he characterized the Reformation as a shift in the "centre of gravity" and "an alteration in 'the seat of authority'" away from "the upper ether" to the "facts themselves." Just as Protestantism had seemed "to papal minds" nothing more than "a mere mess of anarchy and confusion," so would his pragmatism strike "ultrarationalist minds in philosophy" as "so much sheer trash." But "to minds more scientific and individualistic in their tone yet not irreligious either," James sought to show the value of shifting attention from abstract principles to "the really vital question for us all," namely, "What is life eventually to make of itself?" As the first Protestants splintered into rival sects, some early challengers to orthodoxy worried that individual congregations, or even individual believers, might take it upon themselves to answer such questions on their own, interpreting scripture according to their own lights and deciding for themselves how to live their lives. Such anxieties prompted some Protestants to circumscribe the boundaries of legitimate experimentation, whereas others ventured so far beyond those limits that they eventually constituted communities of their own and governed themselves independent of any other authority. It was that spirit of ceaseless experimentation, not the quest to replace one orthodoxy with another, that prompted James to compare his pragmatism to the Protestant Reformation (*P*, 62). For that reason the myriad claimants to the pragmatist mantle throughout the last century have been acting very much in the spirit of James's own understanding of what pragmatism means, and my own sketches of forms of pragmatist experimentation are intended to suggest some of its many dimensions rather than to define or delimit it. Nor will I discuss here pragmatism in literature or the arts, even though many of the most important writers and artists of the last century have expressed their debts to pragmatism. That is a story for another time.

Evidence indicating the influence of pragmatism on American politics in the early decades of the twentieth century is complex but unmistakable.[7] In the presidential election of 1912, both the platforms of the Progressive Party of Theodore Roosevelt and the Democratic Party of Woodrow Wilson reflected the impact of James's ideas. James and Roosevelt had a history. They became acquainted during TR's sophomore year at Harvard in 1877–78, when he studied comparative anatomy and physiology of vertebrates with James as part of his plan for a career in science. During that year, when his father's death plunged TR into a depression that he worked through with outbursts of various kinds, he engaged in spirited exchanges with James of the sort for which he later became famous. TR's pugnacity initially amused James, but when it matured into bellicose imperialism he denounced his former student.

James's anti-imperialism deserves our attention now, at a time when our nation is wrestling with the agonizing consequences of another war justified in terms reminiscent of those used a century ago. In a letter to the *Boston Evening Transcript* on March 1, 1899, James condemned his nation for suppressing indigenous forces in the Philippines at the end of the Spanish-American War. "We are now openly engaged in crushing out the sacredest thing in this great human world—the attempt of a people long enslaved to attain to the possession of itself, to organize its laws and government, to be free to follow its internal destinies according to its own ideals." James concluded with a stinging attack on everyone involved: "Could there be a more damning indictment of that whole bloated idol termed 'modern civilization' than this amounts to? Civilization is, then, the big, hollow, resounding, corrupting, sophisticating, confusing torrent of mere brutal momentum and irrationality that brings forth fruits like this." After TR delivered a defense of American policy a month later in his speech "The Strenuous Life," James wrote a reply in the *Boston Evening Transcript* on April 15, 1899, that can be read as an early draft of *Pragmatism*. American imperialism, he wrote, was born of an abstract doctrine of national strength conceived without ever taking into account the people of the Philippines themselves "face to face as a concrete reality." It illustrated just the sort of thinking James decried in *Pragmatism*. "Of all the naked abstractions that were ever applied to human affairs, the outpourings of Governor Roosevelt's soul in this speech would seem the very nakedest." TR, James wrote, seemed frozen in "early adolescence"—the state in which James had first encountered him. He "gushes over war as the ideal condition of human society, for the manly strenuousness which it involves, and treats peace as a condition of blubberlike and swollen ignobility." Why? TR never felt the need to explain: "Not a word of the cause,—one foe is as good as another, for aught he tells us; not a word of the conditions of success." James's fury seethed through his concluding words. "To enslave a weak but heroic people, or to brazen out a blunder, is a good enough cause, it appears, for Colonel Roosevelt. To us Massachusetts anti-imperialists, who have fought in better causes, it is not quite good enough."[8] Having delivered a speech in 1897 at the dedication of the monument to Robert Gould Shaw and the Massachusetts 54th, the regiment of African American soldiers that included among its officers James's younger brother Wilky, the regiment that was sacrificed in the bloody and futile battle of Fort Wagner, James was sickened by TR's glorification of war for no purpose other than the "hollow abstractions" of national greatness. The nation needed no such pointless displays; it needed instead the "civic courage" of those who could put the common good above their own self-interest, the sensibility that fueled progressivism at its best.[9]

By 1912, however, through James's student Herbert Croly, whose book *The Promise of American Life* shaped TR's Bull Moose campaign, and through Wilson's adviser Louis Brandeis, a legal pragmatist known as "the people's lawyer," James's social and political sensibility was helping to set the tone of domestic political debates during the crucial years before America's entry into World War I. From its origins in "the Wisconsin idea" of consumer protection, economic regulation, and a graduated income tax, the progressive reform movement that transformed public life at the local, the state, and eventually the national level represented a deliberate departure from the dogmatic claims of laissez-faire and Marxist-inspired ideologies and a conscious commitment to incremental reform and democratically guided experimentation in public policy. When Croly joined the economist Walter Weyl and another of James's students, Walter Lippmann, in 1914 as founding editors of *The New Republic,* they made no secret of their commitment to pragmatism, a commitment that Croly himself made even more explicit in *Progressive Democracy* (1914). They urged discarding inherited formulas and testing proposals in practice, thereby transmitting to a wider public the radical ideas advanced by the precocious Lippmann in the most Jamesian of his books, *A Preface to Politics* (1913) and *Drift and Mastery* (1914).

As Lippmann explained to his English friend Graham Wallas, whose Fabian socialism appealed to him as much because of its eclecticism as its radicalism, his aim in *A Preface to Politics* was to demonstrate the fruitfulness for politics of James's idea of uncertainty. Paraphrasing James, Lippmann contended that the "great difficulty in all complicated thinking" is "to understand that the concept is a rough instrument" that we use when we lack "adequate perception." "James always felt," Lippmann continued in his letter to Wallas, that "the epistemological problem, especially," has "tremendous consequences" for political practice. As Lippmann put it in *A Preface to Politics,* we can no longer "expect to meet our problems with a few inherited ideas" and "uncriticized assumptions." Instead "our primary care must be to keep the habits of mind flexible and adapted to the movement of real life," precisely the argument at the center of *Pragmatism.*[10]

Drift and Mastery was Lippmann's plea for using the capacities of government to investigate and solve problems rather than shackling it according to the dictates of left- or right-wing ideologies. Scientific research could generate reliable information, and educated public servants attuned to Jamesian ideas might apply that knowledge to experiments designed to ameliorate the unprecedented problems facing a culture undergoing urbanization and industrialization. "Rightly understood science is the culture under which people can live forward in the midst of complexity, and treat life not as something given but as something to be shaped." Although Lippmann later came to doubt the capacity of the people to think either pragmatically or even responsibly, in his youth he had greater confidence in democracy because he equated it with science: "There is nothing accidental then in the fact that democracy in politics is the twin-brother of scientific thinking. They had to come together. As absolutism falls, science arises. It *is* self-government. For when the impulse which overthrows kings and priests and unquestioned creeds becomes self-conscious we call it science." Lippmann did not promise easy answers. To the contrary, he urged pragmatic experimentation. "The only rule to follow," he wrote, "is that of James: 'Use concepts when they help, and drop them when they hinder understanding.'" In other words, "Mastery in our world cannot mean any single, neat, and absolute line of procedure."[11]

Croly and Lippmann preferred Roosevelt to Wilson in 1912. They judged Wilson a less attractive candidate because they worried that his apparent commitment to small government might rule out some of the experiments Roosevelt seemed eager to try. For that reason their shift to Wilson after his election surprised many of those who knew them or read them. But consistent with their pragmatism, the editors of *The New Republic* turned enthusiastic when Wilson proved much more willing to explore unconventional pathways than they had anticipated. In fact, Wilson's domestic policies during his first term in office came closer to the programs of the Progressive Party platform than to the Jeffersonian shibboleths of many of the Democrats he courted to win his party's nomination. As president of Princeton Wilson had attacked numerous old-boy traditions, ranging from the shape of the curriculum to the centrality of Presbyterianism and the social clout of the undergraduate eating clubs. He appointed the first Jew and the first Catholic to the Princeton faculty. He described his approach as academic reformer in a single word: "expediency."[12] As governor of New Jersey he had instituted a direct primary to challenge the power of political machines, and he had created a public utilities commission to identify and protect the public interest. Given that background, Wilson's commitment as president to the quintessential progressive reforms, a graduated income tax and independent regulatory agencies such as the Federal Trade Commission, should not have come as a surprise. Wilson's record of innovation first brought him to prominence in the academy and in state politics, and that willingness to experiment likewise manifested itself in his domestic agenda as president.

Wilson's debts to James are only now coming to light. From Wilson's days as a graduate student at Johns Hopkins, when he read and responded enthusiastically to the radical social democratic writings of the economist Richard T. Ely, through his own writings about American government and his terms as president of Princeton and as governor of New Jersey, Wilson showed a growing interest in experimentation masked by his respect for thinkers such as Walter Bagehot and Edmund Burke. Most commentators have missed the precise contours of Wilson's admiration for such thinkers, whose interest in moderate reform has been eclipsed by their opposition to revolution. Just as his teacher Ely defended himself from accusations of socialism in Wisconsin during the 1890s by differentiating his interest in progressive reforms from the revolutionary slogans and strategies of American Marxists, so Wilson could simultaneously value Burke's interest in organic change and nevertheless advocate significant transformations in American democratic government. Wilson's familiarity with James's ideas has escaped the attention of historians more interested in dissecting Wilson's political maneuverings than in understanding the ideas that shaped his sensibility.

Wilson cited James's "will to believe" in his own public addresses. His correspondence with his fiancée Ellen Axson, who became not only his wife but the center of his emotional life until her tragic death in 1914, reveals their intimate acquaintance with James's crucial essays "What Makes a Life Significant?" and "On a Certain Blindness in Human Beings," essays that exerted a lasting influence on both of them. If Wilson's own ethics owed a debt to Ellen, as his biographers have noted, both of them clearly owed a debt to James, whose emphasis on the importance of yoking strenuous effort to ethical ideals—and whose acute awareness of the tragic incompatibility of competing moral principles—manifested themselves in Wilson's campaigns for political and economic reform. Wilson started out as a champion of laissez faire, and when circumstances required it (as in Democratic Party primary campaigns) he could still sing hymns to competition. But from the time he entered Johns Hopkins until his death, Wilson showed increasing appreciation of the distance his nation had traveled from its agrarian origins and of the consequences of that journey for social and economic policy. Democracy in an urban industrial age, Wilson came to realize, required active intervention by government both through taxation and through regulation. His operating principles as governor and president were those he had followed at Princeton, weighing what was desirable—in this case intervention in the economy to bring about greater equality—against what was possible politically. In politics and economics he became increasingly impatient with inherited formulas and increasingly committed to the pragmatist principle of experimentation. The same qualities that attracted James's personal friend Louis Brandeis to Wilson, his rigorous mind, his uneasiness with the shibboleths of backward-looking agrarians within the Democratic Party, and his passion for exposing the excessive power of big business, ultimately won him the support of other self-proclaimed Jamesians such as Croly and Lippmann and America's most prominent pragmatist philosopher (after James's death in 1910), John Dewey.[13]

Wilson's commitment to such an experimental politics, fully consistent with the arguments that progressives such as Brandeis, Croly, and Lippmann derived from James and Dewey, is seldom acknowledged today primarily because the popular image of Wilson has been so powerfully shaped by his disastrous failures in foreign policy. First in his ham-handed dealings with Mexico, Haiti, Santo Domingo, and the Russian Revolution, then in his final tragedy after he returned from Versailles, Wilson failed to follow or secure the principles of democracy for which he claimed the United States was going to war in 1917. The reasons for his dramatic change from flexible experimentation at home to unyielding dogmatism concerning the rest of the world remain a puzzle. They involve political, psychological, and (late in his life) even physiological factors too intricate to discuss here. But the doctrinaire, unsuccessful, and unwell Wilson of the post-stroke period should not cause us to lose sight of the pragmatist Wilson who inspired Brandeis, Croly, Lippmann, and Dewey during the first six years of his presidency. Reading history backward makes it easy to miss the dimensions of Wilson's presidency that the pragmatists among his contemporaries recognized and admired. From the perspective of 1917, however, it was much less clear than it became later that Wilson's plans for "peace without victory" and a world "safe for democracy," plans fully consistent with the ideas of other American pragmatist progressives such as those clustered around the then-progressive *New Republic*, would vanish in the smoke of resurgent nationalism in Europe and the fog of isolationism at home. Randolph Bourne's now-celebrated critique of Dewey, who endorsed Wilson's rationale for entering World War I because of the effects Dewey thought likely to result from American participation, looks persuasive to us now for the same reasons it persuaded Dewey after Wilson's plans had failed.[14]

But that outcome was hardly inevitable. Consider a modest counterfactual hypothesis. Had Wilson remained a pragmatist before leaving for France, he might have worked to bring along his Republican critics as shrewdly as Franklin Roosevelt was later to do before and during World War II. Had Wilson remained a pragmatist in Paris and when he returned to negotiate with the Senate in Washington, he might have persuaded both his European allies that "peace without victory" was a better strategy for them in the long term and his critics at home that joining the League of Nations would contribute to America's national security. Had Wilson shown the same commitment to pragmatism in foreign policy after 1918 that he had shown in domestic politics (although not in his dealings with Latin America) up to that point, and had a vigorous League of Nations succeeded in preventing the tragic spiral that brought Hitler to power, Wilson's legacy would look very different indeed.[15]

Self-proclaimed pragmatists could reach opposite conclusions concerning the meaning of pragmatism for politics, as the Bourne-Dewey debate illustrates. So does the difference between the positions on the war taken by two other influential and equally self-conscious pragmatists, James's and Dewey's close friend Jane Addams and James's student W. E. B. Du Bois. Addams earned considerable notoriety (and, eventually, a Nobel Peace Prize) for opposing American participation in WWI and advocating international cooperation afterward, whereas Du Bois judged the war as Dewey did and argued, moreover, that honorable military service in the war might enable African Americans to escape the opprobrium of racism.[16] Although of course no single individuals can be considered emblematic of social movements as multifaceted as those advocating equal rights for women and blacks, the pragmatists Addams and Du Bois played central roles in those movements.

Addams frequently invoked the importance of pragmatism for her life and work. She emphasized the role Dewey played in shaping the programs and sensibilities of Hull House, the first and most influential of the many settlement houses that emerged during the progressive reform era. Such settlements served a variety of purposes. Not only did they offer alternative social services to those provided by Democratic Party machines and access to education, health care, and recreation for recent immigrants to American cities, they also offered employment and career paths to many members of the first generation of college-educated American women.

The lines of influence between pragmatism and the founder of Hull House ran in both directions. Visits to Hull House helped Dewey decide he should accept a professorship at the University of Chicago, frequent lectures there helped him hone his ideas about schools and social psychology, and he often cited the educational programs of Hull House as models of pragmatist education. From 1897 until he left for New York in 1904, Dewey served on the board of trustees of Hull House, and Addams cited both his ideas and his personal influence in many of her speeches and writings.[17]

Addams's relation to James was marked by a similar reciprocity of influence, although it began somewhat later and focused primarily on questions of war and peace. In response to the U.S. suppression of the indigenous efforts at self-government in the Philippines at the end of the Spanish-American War, James and Addams both developed arguments concerning the injustice of imperialism and the need to redirect bellicose human impulses toward less destructive ends. In *Twenty Years at Hull House,* Addams explained her hope that the interaction of different immigrant communities in American cities would breed a cosmopolitan sensibility that might make outbreaks of war less likely. In Chicago in 1898 and in Boston in 1904, Addams and James appeared on the same platform to advance that argument, and both of them understood that they shared a common conception of the reasons for opposing war. In her introduction to *Newer Ideals of Peace,* a book that James greeted with admiration, she contrasted the reasons for her aversion to war with what she called "the older, dovelike ideal." She championed peace for explicitly pragmatist reasons: she believed "the newer, more aggressive ideals of peace" would be embraced not because of a basic commitment to the principles of pacifism but because of the positive results of developing what she called "a moral substitute for war." Although James provided a more dramatic formulation of their common argument in the lecture he published as "The Moral Equivalent of War," they articulated versions of the same pragmatist position: given the increasingly devastating destructiveness of warfare and the apparently ineradicable human inclination toward conflict, twentieth-century Americans must find an alternative outlet.[18]

W. E. B. Du Bois played a role in the twentieth-century struggle for black equality no less central than that of Addams in the settlement house movement, and he too explicitly credited James with shaping his sensibility. While a student at Harvard, Du Bois later wrote, he was "a devoted follower of James at the time he was developing his pragmatic philosophy," and he credited James with converting him from "the sterilities of scholastic philosophy to realist pragmatism." Du Bois decided to devote his own talents to the social sciences and to journalism, becoming the first African American to earn a Ph.D. at Harvard, the only African American among the founders of the NAACP, and the first editor of that organization's journal, *The Crisis*. Whereas many members of his generation derived from Darwin's followers the lesson that whites and blacks were categorically different, Du Bois took a different path. He reasoned, drawing on James and his other teachers, including the Harvard historian Albert Bushnell Hart and the German historical economists with whom Du Bois studied in Berlin, that all cultural forms and judgments—including race consciousness—emerge from historical processes. For that reason all cultural norms should be subjected to critical scrutiny, as James urged in *Pragmatism*, without preconceived or inherited notions about the nature, let alone the superiority, of any one nation, creed, or race.[19] Although Du Bois, like Addams, drew on multiple sources, and although the experiences that radicalized him after WWI carried him away from pragmatism and toward Marxism, there is clear and convincing evidence that his influential early writings and political engagement reflected the ideas he learned from James.

James's pragmatism was equally decisive in the emergence of a multi-stranded discourse about racial and ethnic identity and cultural pluralism that has persisted into the present. From his 1890 *Principles of Psychology* through his Hibbert Lectures at Oxford in 1908, later published as *A Pluralistic Universe*, James insisted that experience is inescapably relational and value-laden. Although those ideas did not come into focus in *Pragmatism*, and James even contended that his philosophy of radical empiricism was distinct from his pragmatism, his phenomenological conception of immediate experience underlay everything he wrote. It figured especially prominently in the writings of his students who addressed issues of color and culture, notably Robert Park, Alain Locke, and Horace Kallen, whose writings helped set the terms of debate on these issues throughout the interwar period. James claimed that selves are constituted, within particular cultural matrices marked by particular constellations of values, through interactions with other similarly constituted individuals. In essays such as "On a Certain Blindness in Human Beings" and "The Moral Philosopher and the Moral Life," James traced the significance of those insights for America's diverse and democratic culture. Robert Park, after working as a muckraking journalist in Chicago and joining with Dewey on the short-lived progressive periodical *Thought News,* enrolled at Harvard in 1898 to study with James. In class one day Park heard James read a draft of "On a Certain Blindness," which made such a powerful impression that Park quoted it repeatedly in his own writing and teaching and recommended, "in preference to anything else that James or anyone else has written," that it be required reading "for sociologists and for teachers." Park later wrote that "On a Certain Blindness" was "the most radical statement of the difficulty and necessity" of overcoming the inability to see the significance of others' lives. Achieving mutual "recognition," Park wrote, is a prerequisite to "communication in a society composed of individuals as egocentric as most of us naturally are."[20]

After Park completed his studies in Germany, he returned to serve as James's assistant for a year before spending ten years working at the institution that Park considered a radical pragmatist educational experiment, Booker T. Washington's Tuskegee Institute. Park then joined the Department of Sociology at the University of Chicago, where he worked to collect and disseminate data concerning American cities that he believed prerequisite to social policies conceived pragmatically and democratically. Among the many students he and the other Chicago sociologists trained were notable African Americans such as Charles C. Johnson, who completed most of the work that went into *The Negro in Chicago* before moving to New York, where he became the editor of the magazine *Opportunity* and one of the most influential figures in the Harlem Renaissance. In his teaching Park had emphasized the unique role of the arts, particularly novels, in awakening the sympathetic identification with others that James had identified in "On a Certain Blindness." In an obituary he wrote when Park died in 1944, Johnson recalled Park's insistence that his students understand—and work to overcome—"that blindness to the meaning of other people's lives to which James referred." Johnson carried that confidence concerning the democratic reformist potential of aesthetic experience with him to *Opportunity* and sustained it as president of Fisk University. Johnson later wrote approvingly that Dewey, to whose work Park had first introduced him, "redefines faith in terms of attitudes, as 'tendency toward action.'" Paraphrasing James's argument in *Pragmatism,* Johnson proclaimed that "adherence to any body of doctrines and dogmas, based upon a specific authority, as adherence to any set of beliefs, signifies distrust in the power of experience to provide in its own on-going movement, the needed principles of belief and action." The pragmatists, in Johnson's words, urged instead "a new faith in experience itself as the sole ultimate authority," a commitment to flexibility that had already proven problematical in debates concerning the relation between white and African American culture.[21]

The pragmatists' perspectives on experience and the power of art—not only to help awaken sympathy but to fuel democratic social change and erode racial and ethnic enmity—also surfaced in the work of other writers directly influenced by James. Horace Kallen, a rabbi's son who served as James's teaching assistant at Harvard two years after Park departed, became well acquainted with one of the students in James's class, Alain Locke, an African American who insisted to the skeptical Kallen that their racial difference should make no difference. Two years later Kallen and Locke, on fellowships at Oxford, forged a friendship from their shared animosity toward the white American Southerners who refused to include their fellow Rhodes scholar, Locke, in their Thanksgiving celebration. Kallen and Locke were together in Oxford when James delivered the Hibbert Lectures there; his own pluralism clearly shaped their ideas. Consider a metaphor James employed in an essay published in a 1904 issue of *The Journal of Philosophy, Psychology, and Scientific Methods* under the title "A World of Pure Experience" (*ERE*, 21–44) in which he termed his position "a mosaic philosophy." He then noted that whereas in "actual mosaics the pieces are held together by their bedding," in his "radical empiricism there is no bedding; it is as if the pieces clung together by their edges, the transitions experienced between them forming their cement." So, thinking in terms of the distinct groups comprising American culture, one could reason (as Kallen and Locke, if in somewhat different ways, both did) that the edges, the transitions, and the clinging together do the work. Yet James conceded that the metaphor is misleading, "for in actual experience the more substantive and the more transitive parts run into each other continuously, there is in general no separateness needing to be overcome." In the hybridities of ethnic and racial interaction, James's students could infer, lies the possibility for "Experience itself," as James put it, "to grow by its edges." Just as "one moment proliferates into the next," so "Life is in the transitions as much as in the terms of connection; often, indeed, it seems to be there more emphatically." Whereas most early twentieth-century American writers upheld a more or less static and vaguely Anglo-Protestant norm as the standard according to which all immigrant groups should be judged and toward which all Americans should aspire (the "melting pot" model), Kallen, Locke, and Du Bois all followed their mentor James in challenging that image. They urged Americans to view identity as more fluid and the United States as the product of a distinctive—and incessant—juxtaposition, jostling, and mixture of diverse races, religions, ethnicities, and nationalities.[22]

The term "cultural pluralism" itself entered American discourse through the efforts of Kallen, who was born in Germany and raised in an orthodox Jewish household, and whose consciousness of his own ethnic and religious identity is usually identified as the source of his insights. But from Kallen's perspective his ideas originated in the "commingling" of the ideas of two of his Harvard mentors: on the one hand, the Anglophile literary critic Barrett Wendell, who alerted the assimilated and non-practicing Kallen to the richness of his Jewish cultural tradition; and on the other, the hero of Kallen's first book, *William James and Henri Bergson: A Study in Contrasting Theories of Life* (1914). Kallen adopted James's philosophical ideas of consciousness, experience, toleration, pluralism, and experimentation, from which he forged the theory of cultural pluralism with which he became identified. Rather than insisting that one's identity is always fixed by one's grandparents, to use a formulation often associated with Kallen, or offering his now equally familiar image of American society as a symphony in which various ethnic groups represent different groups of instruments, Kallen at first sought merely to emphasize the distinctive cultural resources available to individuals from different backgrounds as they shape their own lives and help shape the culture in which they live. Far from essentializing ethnicity, in other words, Kallen viewed it pragmatically, as his later critiques of Zionism made clear. Although he endorsed the idea of a Jewish homeland, Kallen bristled when he saw Zionism applied as a litmus test (or wielded as a club) by those with less flexible or pragmatic conceptions of the idea. Locke, although he remained "a reluctant race man," gradually grew to share Kallen's appreciation of the particularities of individual racial and ethnic traditions. Indeed, whereas Kallen's model remained Eurocentric, Locke joined with other contributors to the landmark volume he edited, *The New Negro: An Interpretation* (1925), to celebrate the distinctive contributions of African Americans to the culture of the United States. Although sharp disagreements concerning the singularity of the black experience and the relative insularity of African American culture marked the debates among both blacks and whites during the 1920s (as of course they have ever since), the contributions of Du Bois, Johnson, and Locke—all fueled by pragmatism—inaugurated the twentieth-century African American challenge to previous assumptions concerning the inferiority of African American culture. Together with arguments from anthropology advanced by Dewey's Columbia colleague and ally Franz Boas and their students Ruth Benedict and Randolph Bourne, these writers used James's ideas of experience and pluralism to unsettle prevailing assumptions about race and ethnicity.

Since the 1960s Bourne has often been cited for his critique of the "war intellectuals" Dewey and Lippmann, who supported Wilson's policies in World War I, but he was equally well known during his brief life for his contributions to other debates concerning American culture. In his brilliant essay "Trans-national America" (1916), Bourne cited Kallen's work and presented himself as an ally in the struggle against forced assimilation of immigrants into a preexisting American mold. But the thrust of his essay differed from the cultural pluralism Kallen advocated. Bourne contrasted the cosmopolitan sensibility available to individuals who shrugged off a single ethnic or cultural background to the provincialism of those locked in a single enclave or simple way of thinking—those whose identity was fixed by their grandparents or who played but a single instrument in the American symphony. Two decades of sharp ideological debates over multiculturalism have made the cultural pluralist Kallen and the cosmopolitan Bourne seem quite distinct to us. In the context of early twentieth-century American culture, however, their shared respect for cultural diversity and for the plasticity of identity and culture—as well as their shared debts to pragmatism—made their similarities appear far more significant than their differences. Although other routes besides the one that Kallen and Bourne followed led to an appreciation of cultural difference, it is undeniable that they—like Park and Johnson, Du Bois and Locke—chose to emphasize the debts they owed to James's pragmatism.[23]

During the 1920s James's version of pragmatism, like many other aspects of prewar culture, faded from the spotlight. Lippmann began his steady march away from James toward Aquinas, and Du Bois from James toward Marx. Dewey emerged as the most prominent pragmatist philosopher and the most steadfast champion of democracy. Yet pragmatism remained an important influence in politics and loomed even larger in law during the interwar period. The next Democratic Party nominee to be elected president after Wilson, Franklin D. Roosevelt, learned from Wilson's successes and from his failures. FDR shared Wilson's preference for piecemeal experimentation over rigid doctrine; the eclecticism of the New Deal has earned FDR both admiration and ridicule as a "pragmatist" from many writers who would not know William from Jesse James or John from Thomas Dewey. But the evidence is now clear that from his election in 1932 until his death in 1945, FDR developed a firm commitment to plans and programs that emerged from the work of professional social scientists in his administration whose familiarity with and allegiance to pragmatist philosophy is not in doubt. Dewey in particular was widely admired by some influential members of FDR's inner circle and by less prominent members of New Deal agencies, particularly those on the National Resources Planning Board. Dewey's arguments for experimenting with radical democratic decision making filtered into some of the programs that took shape and many of the more ambitious plans that Congress refused to adopt during the 1930s and 1940s. The failure of FDR's 1944 plan for a Second Bill of Rights, which would have committed the United States to policies of full employment, public housing, national health care, and other aspects of what has come to be known as "the welfare state," is clear. The reasons for its failure are complex. There is little agreement concerning what such programs would have accomplished, or why they were not adopted in the United States, especially since the G.I. Bill did institute precisely such programs for returning veterans, and most European nations moved rapidly after WWII to secure just such guarantees for all citizens. As political scientists, legal scholars, and historians now scrutinize FDR's proposals for the postwar period with greater care, it has become clear that some of his closest advisers were led to their distinctive approach to these thorny issues because of the influence of James's, and especially Dewey's, pragmatism.[24]

Some of the most prominent champions of the New Deal came from the legal community, where legal realism became particularly influential during the 1930s. Usually associated with the jurisprudence of Roscoe Pound, Learned Hand, and Felix Frankfurter, legal realism descended directly from the writings of James's friends Oliver Wendell Holmes Jr. and Louis Brandeis, the latter of whom Wilson nominated for the US Supreme Court in 1916 in a very controversial appointment. Legal pragmatists denied that the law conforms to reason, to morality, or to any unchanging principles. They insisted that it must change with changing conditions and changing expectations. In other words, law should be a flexible tool adapted to addressing new challenges, an experimental form of problem solving fully consistent with James's recommendations in *Pragmatism*. Brandeis and his protégé Frankfurter were the most visible proponents of a pragmatist jurisprudence on the Supreme Court, but different versions of legal pragmatism had been worked out long before, first by the cynical anti-democrat Holmes, then by the unwavering democrat Brandeis, and afterward by other less widely known judges and legal scholars.[25]

The philosophical dimensions of the legal realist critique were most fully elaborated in the interwar writings of law professors at Yale and Columbia. Scholars such as Karl Llewellyn, Jerome Frank, Thurman Arnold, William O. Douglas, Felix Cohen, Adolf Berle, Robert Lee Hale, Walter Hamilton, and James Landis challenged the legal formalism still being taught in many law schools and still being practiced on the bench. These legal pragmatists directed their fire particularly against the sacred status of property and contract, which they insisted were contingent on public policy rather than protected by the Constitution against any legislative challenges. Some legal realists remained in law schools. Others ended up in New Deal agencies, where they translated their ideas into practice. Still others, most notably Douglas, continued the assault on fixed legal ideas by working as judges to extend legal pragmatism from administrative law and economic regulation to the domains of conservation, civil liberties, and civil rights.[26]

But of course pragmatism in politics and law did not go unchallenged. To the contrary. Particularly with the rise of communism and fascism, critics of pragmatism charged that the flexibility pragmatists prized opened the door to a pernicious relativism that made impossible the principled resistance to evil. James's death in 1910 removed his voice from these debates, but many critics on the right and the left charged his allies and heirs—especially Dewey, the most visible and prolific pragmatist—with having sapped the vital strength of American democratic culture. Whereas pragmatists questioned dogmatism and urged experimentation, the struggles against fascism and communism persuaded many Americans that a dangerous world requires vigilant fidelity to fixed truths. Although through the 1950s many prominent intellectuals, from Reinhold Niebuhr and David Riesman to C. Wright Mills and Richard Hofstadter, continued to invoke James's ideas in relation to everything from religious faith to anti-intellectualism, pragmatism became increasingly suspect as the demand for certainty became increasingly urgent.[27]

In the four decades since the late 1960s, when so many aspects of American culture came under attack, the yearning for certitude and the accompanying temptations of self-righteousness have been particularly strong in U.S. politics. The early student radicalism that emerged with the manifesto known as the Port Huron Statement showed signs of a significant debt to pragmatism. The faculty members and graduate students at the University of Michigan who most directly influenced Tom Hayden and his fellow founders of Students for a Democratic Society were steeped in the democratic radicalism of John Dewey; the aversion to dogma and the commitment to experimentation manifested in the Port Huron Statement extended the central arguments of the early twentieth-century pragmatists into the post-WWII world.[28]

But that radical political sensibility from the outset stood in tension with a different set of impulses, a defiant repudiation of authority and an enthusiastic embrace of authenticity understood as the satisfaction of individual desires. The counterculture thus contained the potential for renewing the crusades of progressive pragmatists focused on the ideal of egalitarian social justice, on the one hand, and the strikingly different emphasis of the catch phrase "if it feels good, do it," on the other. That latter formula not only parodied the strenuous ethics of James and Dewey but substituted the escape from discipline for the longer-term project of validating hypotheses against the resistant stuff of the world, the bar against which James insisted from the beginning to the end of his writings that all truth claims must be tested.[29] Neither the Freudian left drawn to Herbert Marcuse or Norman O. Brown nor the varieties of the Civil Rights movement drawn to Martin Luther King Jr. or Malcolm X, thinkers who had little in common with each other, showed any evidence of having been shaped by James's or Dewey's pragmatism. Even so, the backlash against a now legendary, larger-than-life army of cultural revolutionaries has set the terms of recent American public debate. In the stylized framework of the post-1960s culture wars, the early pragmatists have been recast as cultural relativists who undermined the core values of American life. Whereas James and Dewey saw themselves as contributing to the fulfillment of the American democratic project as they understood it, their critiques of dogma and their embrace of experimentation rendered pragmatism subversive in the eyes of those who prized fixed standards and stable authority.

On the right, the reassertion of unchanging truths in the realms of politics and culture meant an emphatic rejection of pragmatism. The unprecedentedly doctrinaire form of recent American conservatism that emerged with Barry Goldwater's 1964 candidacy for president, picked up momentum with Ronald Reagan's election as governor of California, and first crested with Reagan's election to the presidency in 1980, has been surging forward ever since. In the two terms of the presidency of George W. Bush, particularly since the bombing of the World Trade Center in 2001, we have witnessed the almost complete repudiation of evidence-based reasoning and the scientific model of trial and error, perhaps because such trials can indeed provide evidence of errors, which only the weak admit. In place of experimentation stands an increasingly brittle reliance on dogmas such as cutting taxes at home and slogans such as "staying the course" in the "war against terror" abroad—regardless of the consequences of turning a police action against renegade Islamists into a replay of the Cold War—doctrines that cannot be challenged without eliciting charges of allegedly un-American class warfare, cowardice, or treason.

In short, during the past three decades there have been few echoes of James's *Pragmatism* in the increasingly polarized world of American public life. Efforts to criticize the status quo on pragmatist grounds tend to be met with shrill responses from the extreme right and sometimes from the extreme left, neither of which shows much interest in the strategies recommended by pragmatists: the frank admission of uncertainty and the testing of hypotheses by trial and error. Modesty, tentativeness, and acknowledgment of the provisionality of all social policies have become endangered species in American politics. Those few politicians who have invoked the pragmatists explicitly, such as former New Jersey senator Bill Bradley, and those reformers and writers who have stressed the need to revitalize civil society have been maligned as temporizers by critics on both ends of the political spectrum. The doctrinaire right is locked into rigid commitments to the rewards of a so-called free market and a tightly regulated culture—except where economic activity is concerned. One part of the left, almost equally doctrinaire, seems locked almost as tightly into defending problematic social programs such as public assistance and public schools, and committed to rights-based, liberationist mantras at a time when increasingly large numbers of people lack the moral principles necessary to deal responsibly with others and the basic skills necessary to cope with the bewildering world they confront. Echoes of James's advice about cultivating respect for those with whom one disagrees, or trying to understand how one's opponents see the world, grow ever fainter in the escalating shrillness of political debate.[30]

For all those reasons, as well as for all the reasons having to do with the transformation of academic disciplines from philosophy to cultural studies, which I have discussed elsewhere and which are discussed in other essays in this volume, the resurgence of pragmatism in the late twentieth century came as a surprise. Early in that resurgence, I and others hoped that the return of a pragmatist sensibility in the academic community might signal a new progressive movement. Such hope has become much harder to sustain. Perhaps just as significant as the return of pragmatism in academic disciplines such as philosophy, however, has been the proliferation of pragmatisms in different domains of American life. In the remainder of this essay I will briefly survey six areas in which forms of pragmatism have shown signs of life in recent years. Some of the people involved explicitly invoke James, others Dewey, and others contemporary pragmatists such as Richard Rorty, Richard Bernstein, Hilary Putnam, or Cornel West. But all of them nevertheless claim the mantle, and show clear signs of the continuing influence, of the founders of the tradition; a brief glance at them should suggest how vibrant varieties of American pragmatism remain outside the realm of philosophy a century after the publication of *Pragmatism*.

I embark on this survey of current uses of pragmatism with misgivings. In another letter William wrote to his brother Henry, this one on September 8, 1907, he complained about some of the early responses to *Pragmatism*. Many readers seemed to assume that the book was "got up for the use of engineers, electricians and doctors, whereas it really grew up from a more subtle and delicate theoretic analysis of the function of knowing, than previous philosophers had been willing to make" (*CWJ*, III, 343–44).[31] It is a cliché that Americans are a "pragmatic people," and I do not want to be understood as claiming that James's direct influence has ever been decisive in any of these areas. But neither should it be assumed that outside the small community of academic philosophers all references to James are uninformed or meaningless. Having myself written elsewhere about the philosophical issues involved in the resurgence of pragmatism, and confident that those issues will receive appropriate attention elsewhere in this volume, I will proceed to assess some of the other uses to which pragmatism has been put.

It might seem self-evident that in fields such as business, architecture, medicine, law, education, and environmentalism, a pragmatist sensibility understood as the testing of results in practice would be commonplace; the principles of James's pragmatism should be everywhere. According to prominent practitioners in each of those professions, however, the opposite is true. There are two reasons:

First, for reasons that will become apparent, there are serious questions involved in deciding what it means for ideas to "work" in each of these domains. Second, pragmatism has always appealed above all to mavericks, to those like James and Dewey who stood outside the mainstream and raised critical questions about standard practices. Were pragmatism ever to become orthodoxy, it might cease to serve the purpose its founders had in mind, its potential as a lever for unsettling conventional wisdom.[32]

Invocations of pragmatism in the realm of corporate management are nothing new. Ever since, to use the image of labor historian David Montgomery, a manager first tried to insert his own brain under the workman's cap, consultants have been aiming to improve the efficiency of corporations. Historians have disagreed about whether Frederick Winslow Taylor's time-management studies were intended to streamline production and save needless effort or merely to control those at the bottom of the pecking order. But there is little doubt that Brandeis advocated "scientific management" because he thought everyone involved would benefit from the careful application of pragmatist methods to the organization of labor. Although some thought behaviorist psychology marked the flowering of James's insights into the link between physical and emotional responses, the cynical application of such insights only to manipulate workers more effectively betrayed James's underlying purpose. So varied were the uses to which techniques of business management were put that generalizing is impossible. Suffice to say that by the time Peter Drucker wrote *The Practice of Management* in 1954, many critics viewed strategies of "democratic leadership" and "participative management" that can be traced to Deweyan social democratic impulses as oxymoronic within the framework of corporate culture.[33]

More recently, Nitin Nohria of the Harvard Business School has contrasted the recommendations James offered in *Pragmatism* to the standard—and distinctly non-pragmatic—practices of most U.S. corporations. From Nohria's perspective, the recent lagging performance of the American economy, the widely acknowledged "competitive decline" of American firms, stems from "the failure of U.S. management to address its most serious problem: a lack of pragmatic judgment." Nohria skewers managers' tendency to rely uncritically on "ready-made answers instead of searching for creative solutions"; he offers James's pragmatism as the antidote to this serious condition. Managers of American companies, according to Nohria, frequently fall for three faulty strategies. First, they tinker with familiar "off-the-shelf" approaches that have already proven to be failures. Second, managers adopt the latest fad, the "flavor of the month" that promises immediate results although it has never been tested. Finally, other companies decide to try all available options at once, an eclectic approach almost guaranteed to end in chaos rather than coherent management. Nohria recommends instead "a return to pragmatism as espoused by the nineteenth-century American pragmatists: to judge any idea by its practical consequences, by seeing what it allows you to do, rather than by chasing after an elusive notion of truth." He quotes James's observation that "[t]heories are instruments, not answers to enigmas in which we can rest," and he urges managers to adopt that "pragmatic attitude" toward the problems they confront. Nohria points out that James considered all problem-solving strategies context-specific rather than universal in their applicability, and he recommends that managers must be alert to "both the macro and micro—from the cultural milieu of a host country, for example, to the personalities of employees on a management team." Pragmatist managers "have a keen sense of the company's history, including the successes and failures of past management programs," knowledge that enables them to avoid the three sorts of failure noted above. They know well the entire range of a company's resources, from "physical assets to human capital, which gives them the ability to judge what is possible in addition to what they might consider desirable in the abstract." Moreover, strategies adopted according to these pragmatist principles must constantly be reevaluated to measure their continuing adequacy as circumstances change. Nohria cites the success some firms have experienced with "town-meeting-like settings" that "fostered a sense of community while ensuring the visibility of individual contributions." Such public settings not only generated new ideas that could be discussed and evaluated, they also "forced reticent managers to face up to pressures for change," thereby nudging those reluctant to adopt pragmatist strategies to see their value rather than dismissing them out of hand as challenges to their own authority.

Pragmatist managers are resourceful improvisers, whom Nohria characterizes by invoking Claude Lévi-Strauss's concept of the *bricoleur,* who reasons inductively from day-to-day experience and experiments creatively rather than attempting to apply abstract principles to concrete problems. For such pragmatist bricoleurs, "solutions are never fixed or final." Nohria offers several examples of such managerial approaches, including Shikhar Ghosh, a partner at the Boston Consulting Group who is a "self-avowed pragmatist" and sees the principal difficulty of using management theory as the inability of most managers to act flexibly and adapt to changing conditions instead of getting stuck in comfortable but unsuccessful patterns. In Ghosh's words, "Managing is a matter of constantly looking at the way you do things and adjusting the process to reflect your goals and resources. That's pragmatism. You use the resources you have to get where you need to go." Although it would be a wild exaggeration to contend that James's pragmatism is pervasive in American business, because in many corporate cultures the bottom lines of profit and shareholder value are the only measures that matter, the awareness of at least some prominent practitioners of its persistent value as a critical tool seems clear enough.[34]

The notoriety of pragmatism at the turn of the twenty-first century also led to its discussion among architects and urban planners. But for reasons difficult to discern, it seems to me less clear that any of them has shown a sophisticated understanding of what the application of pragmatism to such domains might entail. Of course architects throughout the twentieth century experimented with styles that diverged from the standard repertoire descending from the classical, gothic, renaissance, and baroque vocabularies. Whether such innovative architects as Louis Sullivan and Frank Lloyd Wright actually drew valuable ideas from James and Dewey is less clear than that they tried to break the molds they were given. Mid-century architects such as Bruce Goff and Herbert Greene did invoke James explicitly as a source of ideas in their critiques of the formulaic, unimaginative buildings springing up around America after WWII. One could argue that Greene in particular, by taking into account not only the site, materials, and functions of a building but also the character and aspirations of those who would occupy it, and by trying consciously to construct environments that make possible both expected and unexpected experiences of space, tried deliberately to design buildings that embodied James's ideas of truth testing. But of course people and their needs and desires change constantly, in rhythms that even the most dynamic buildings cannot match; efforts to find architectural versions of the dynamism of music or of life necessarily encounter obstacles.

Buildings, like cities, emerge from the interactions between architects, engineers, funding sources, and those who will inhabit them. Inasmuch as architects seek to inform themselves about and incorporate the myriad and changing lives and values of all those who will experience what they create rather than designing according to a priori ideas or predetermined patterns, they can be seen, and have seen themselves, as operating in a Jamesian spirit.[35] But the method of truth testing that James addressed in *Pragmatism* cannot very easily be translated into the more or less fixed forms that buildings and cities assume. Of course architecture and urban planning more nearly embody pragmatist principles when conceived as a dynamic, integrative, and participatory process, as the influential developer James Rouse tried to do. But whether, to what extent, and for what reasons the products of that process themselves ought to be called "pragmatist" is another question.[36]

Pragmatism shows more promise as a method of critical analysis when wielded by physicians. Although James himself was trained at the Harvard Medical School, he never practiced medicine, in part because he found the primitive diagnostic techniques and even more primitive remedies available to physicians in the late nineteenth century so distant from the methods of science. According to psychiatrists such as David Brendel, the medical profession today still needs an injection of James's pragmatism. Doctors tend to rely on "outmoded" ideas of evidence that draw a rigid distinction between human subjectivity and the natural world, an inclination that results in the formulaic application of prescribed cures, most often chemical, without paying sufficient attention to the phenomenology of health. Instead, Brendel argues in *Healing Psychiatry: Bridging the Science/ Humanism Divide*, the medical profession needs to embrace what he calls "clinical pragmatism," an approach resting on four pillars—practical, pluralistic, provisional, and participatory—all of which descend directly from the insights of the founders of pragmatism. First, rather than bull-headedly prescribing standard treatments in all cases, psychiatrists should concentrate on practical results for individual patients and acknowledge that the same approach does not work in all cases. Second, they should remain alert to the wide variety of options available rather than depending too heavily on common medications. Third, evidence from even the most rigorous double-blind tests should be seen as provisional rather than fixed, both because the tests are usually devised for certain purposes, with certain outcomes in mind, and because further testing or experimentation with alternatives might always yield different results. Finally, patients should be invited to become active participants in devising their own treatments rather than subjected to the wisdom of omniscient clinicians. Medical science, according to Brendel, has tended to adopt "the mythology that we can observe the world independently of our own values," and as a result there has been too much reliance on the supposedly objective facts of biochemistry and insufficient attention paid to the particular experience of each individual. Although Brendel cautions that "we need to be able to apply the science, of course," he believes that renewed attention to James's concept of pragmatic tests of truth can improve clinical training and practice.[37]

Arthur Kleinman, another psychiatrist involved with training physicians at the Harvard Medical School, likewise invokes James's *Pragmatism* in his diagnosis of what ails medicine. In his eloquent study *What Really Matters: Living a Moral Life amidst Uncertainty and Danger,* Kleinman recounts the stories of individuals whose life experiences illustrate the ways in which wrenching choices shape sensibilities that cannot simply be "cured" by psychiatry but are instead constituted by the pain occasioned by tragic outcomes. Like Brendel, Kleinman cautions his fellow physicians against assuming that the standard repertoire of medical responses can be more effective in dealing with such individuals than resources drawn from the traditions of religion and moral philosophy. In the chapter of *Pragmatism* in which James addressed religious faith—and of course in his *Varieties of Religious Experience*—he argued that scientists should pay less attention to interrogating evidence concerning the existence of the supernatural and more attention to evidence of the consequences of faith for believers. As Kleinman puts it, "The passion-laden, practical self is caught up in what I have called our local moral worlds, what William James called genuine reality. The reflective self is caught up in ethical deliberation and aspiration." Bridging that gap, which Kleinman sees as the pragmatist strategy for coping with an intransigent and often tragic reality, requires understanding how selves negotiate the differences between the realm of abstraction and the "practical tasks of living." For Kleinman, accomplishing this task no more involves the warm bath of wishful thinking than it did for James; instead it requires the hard work of acknowledging that "suffering, well-being, and the ethical practices that respond to human problems are constantly changing as local worlds change and as do we, the people in them, become something new and different." Kleinman concludes, as Brendel does, that "simplistic distinctions between the objective and the subjective, the absolute and the relative, the right and the wrong, are no help and may even get us into deeper trouble." Yet neither "is it at all sufficient to take up a position in which complexity, uncertainty, and undecidability negate the vexing questions themselves, covering over our own weaknesses and self-serving willingness to comply as long as we are comfortable and protected." That Nietzschean path leads only to "cynicism and nihilism, and ultimately disables us and denies us the capability to change ourselves and our world." Kleinman sees, as James did, that the search for answers involves the activity of living and choosing rather than merely the activity of contemplation or theorizing. It is in the realm of individuals' lived experience, with awareness of the range of meanings that they impute to their lives and to the cultures they inhabit rather than merely a sophisticated understanding of pharmaceuticals, that medicine in a pragmatist spirit is to be practiced.[38]

The fields in which pragmatism has had, and continues to have, the deepest impact are law and education, yet those are also among the fields in which the meaning of pragmatism has been most fiercely contested. Pragmatism been such an important factor in so many of the landmark judicial decisions of the twentieth century, including *West Coast Hotel v. Parrish* (1937) and *Brown v. Board of Education* (1954), and it plays such an important part in legal education at leading law schools today, that it is difficult to decide how to focus a brief discussion of its contemporary significance. Perhaps it is sufficient to note that across the spectrum of opinion within the law, from figures such as Duncan Kennedy in critical legal studies and Margaret Jane Radin in feminist jurisprudence on the left to Cass Sunstein and Akhil Amar in the center and Richard Posner on the right, many of the most prominent and influential participants in legal discourse emphasize the shaping role of pragmatism in American law throughout the twentieth century. The question in the law is not whether pragmatism matters, the question is what it means. For Sunstein, for example, pragmatism authorizes Deweyan deliberative democracy. That means in practice that judges should often exercise restraint. They should allow legislatures to experiment with diverse solutions whenever social disagreements are deep and unresolved and clear guidance from the Constitution is unavailable—as it so often is concerning issues that did not arise in eighteenth-century America. For Posner, by contrast, the pragmatic test of truth boils down to economic efficiency as determined in the unfettered marketplace through bargains struck by self-interested individuals.[39]

Instead of surveying rival forms of legal pragmatism, I want to focus on the practical consequences of dual commitments to pragmatism and feminism in the work of Joan Williams, a legal scholar who has become the most visible figure in the WorkLifeLaw (WLL) movement. This organization, born at American University in Washington, D.C., and now located at the University of California Hastings College of the Law, has developed from the growing awareness of an increasing number of scholars, lawyers, and ordinary working Americans that the workplace has become incompatible with the requirements of family life. Whereas the demands placed on exemplary employees, whose existences are thought to revolve around their jobs, have long been considerable, the intensification of those demands in recent decades has sparked a response. In her book *Unbending Gender: Why Family and Work Conflict and What To Do about It*, Williams dissected "the ideal worker model" and demonstrated the ways in which it systematically disadvantages those workers—usually but not always women in their childbearing years—with family responsibilities that conflict with devotion to the demands of high-pressure jobs. The Center for WorkLifeLaw is a clearinghouse and a resource for those interested in filing lawsuits in those cases in which unavoidable conflicts between work and family responsibilities cause workers to be penalized or fired. Such cases, reflecting "family responsibilities discrimination," have increased nearly 400 percent in the last decade. The WLL report "Litigating the Maternal Wall: U.S. Lawsuits Charging Discrimination against Workers with Family Responsibilities," documents more than six hundred cases over three decades. Although many of the workers involved are mothers, other suits have been filed by males responsible for the care of children, parents, or spouses.[40]

This approach to sex discrimination, explicitly inspired by James's *Pragmatism*, is something new. In the 1960s many women lawyers adopted the stance of Ruth Bader Ginsburg. Despite having finished at the top of her class at Harvard and Columbia Law Schools, Ginsburg was denied a clerkship and was unable to find a job. Nevertheless, speaking for a generation of women, Ginsburg declared in her confirmation hearings for the U.S. Supreme Court that a person's sex is rarely relevant to job performance. Thus, Ginsburg argued, treating women as equal to men would solve the problem of discrimination. The WLL position is less committed to the abstract ideal of equality and more pragmatist. Finding that fealty to the principle of anti-discrimination failed to address the problems women continue to face in the work place, and finding that not all men and not even all women—not even all working women—share the conviction that the differences between men and women are insignificant or irrelevant, Williams and the other legal activists at WLL have discovered that focusing on the consequences for men as well as women of the "ideal worker model" more effectively enables them to address the challenges of balancing work and family duties. The new policies concerning family leave now being instituted in many workplaces, ranging from elite law firms to discount stores, not only reflect changes in federal legislation. They also reflect the success of WLL in litigating cases of family responsibilities discrimination. In a self-conscious turn toward James's conception of truth in *Pragmatism*, Williams declares that "feminism does not represent a commitment to 'discover' eternal truths whose blinding light will persuade everyone." Instead, as James argued in his analysis of religion, wherever the evidence does not yield a definitive answer, we should be content to remain open to new evidence. In such domains, different people's experiences yield different truths. From a pragmatist perspective, it makes better sense to acknowledge that a plurality of truths (concerning the existence of God, for James, or concerning the essential quality or sameness of men and women, for Williams and WLL) exist than to declare categorically that the experiences of some people are simply false. To the extent that WLL succeeds over time in breaking down the "maternal wall" that keeps employers from extending to women the opportunities and the rewards available to "ideal workers" who happen to be men, particularly men who happen to be unburdened by family duties, the consequences of that change will provide particularly powerful evidence of the role pragmatism continues to play in twenty-first-century American life.[41]

The field of education has been no less contentious than the law and no less clearly shaped by pragmatism. James as well as Dewey wrote influential guides to education; both lectured extensively to teachers about translating their philosophical ideas into a new form of teaching. Dewey's tireless efforts, first at the University of Chicago, then at Columbia University, spawned generations of teachers and administrators committed to varieties of "progressive education" as they understood it. Many studies have shown what went wrong. Dewey's own emphasis on rigor and his insistence on balancing the transmission of information—or "content"—with the training of skills was lost when his ideas about teaching, ideas that he shared with James, escaped from the classrooms of exceptional, and exceptionally well-trained, teachers into the classrooms of the often unimaginative and ill-prepared cadres who fanned out into America's schools. Debates about the adequacy of pragmatist education resemble debates about the adequacy of Christian ethics: neither has been tried outside a few select and usually short-lived experiments. We know that virtuoso teachers, such as those with whom Dewey worked at the laboratory school in Chicago, can bring to equally exceptional students the demanding, energizing, and all-absorbing experience that Dewey believed every school should provide. But just as Dewey believed that democracy could stave off the pressures that Max Weber identified—bureaucratization, rationalization, and disenchantment—so he believed that small-scale, well-funded, locally controlled schools could engage parents as well as students in shared educational endeavors that would give teachers the chance as well as the incentive to bring pragmatism into the classroom. When instead school systems consolidated, when some children were channeled into more "academic" and others into "vocational" tracks, when professionalizing educators increasingly monopolized decisions about methods and curricula and spawned a distinct class of administrators, and especially when taxpayers decided they would prefer to buy bigger cars and houses for themselves instead of paying for smaller classes and better-compensated teachers for their children, almost all the characteristics necessary for pragmatist education vanished. Yet the ideal of the student as an energetic, teacher-directed problem solver, like the ideal of the child-centered school as a place of teacher-led critical inquiry, survives; in the best public and private schools, it is even practiced.[42]

I can testify that pragmatism is as vibrant a presence in debates about higher education as it is in the fields of early-childhood, elementary, and secondary education. In the mid-1990s I took part in a lively conference at Rollins College that spawned a valuable book, *Education and Democracy: Re-imagining Liberal Learning in America*.[43] Since then I have participated in conversations sponsored by the Carnegie Foundation for the Advancement of Teaching, the American Historical Association, Harvard's Graduate School of Education, Brandeis University, Wellesley College, and Harvard University devoted to the question of how American colleges can meet their goals of producing well-educated citizens. Those involved in those conversations have not taken for granted that we know the meaning of "well-educated" or that there is any obvious way to go about accomplishing that goal. Instead the means and the end are subjected to critical scrutiny and careful consideration of the evidence concerning what students do and do not learn in colleges today. In one of the most widely read books of recent years on this subject, *Our Underachieving Colleges,* former and current Harvard president Derek Bok makes available to his readers the evidence about what appears to work best: small, discussion-oriented classes that engage students with demanding materials and require them both to master bodies of knowledge and to make independent, critical judgments about how to use it to solve problems on their own.[44]

In the last three years of deliberations at Harvard concerning reforms of undergraduate education, Bok's ideas and those of many others received the careful consideration of the faculty-student committees investigating different dimensions of the student experience. Nothing in Bok's book, and little in the reforms still being debated by the Harvard faculty, would have surprised William James. The principal changes are likely to include emphasis on the following: (1) balancing exposure to a wide range of disciplines with deeper learning in a particular field, the size and shape of that more focused study to be determined by faculty within departments rather than according to a single model; (2) education that occurs outside as well as inside the classroom, from off-campus service experiences and/or from intensive foreign study; (3) the active engagement of each student in shaping a program suited to his or her own goals; (4) bringing students and senior faculty together in small-group courses, beginning with freshman seminars and culminating in capstone courses of various kinds; and (5) the need to review all of these programs within five years both to reconsider our goals and to assess how our programs are working. All five of these desiderata embody the principles of pragmatism.[45]

James criticized much that was happening to American colleges during his own lifetime. He was particularly upset by professionalization and the obsession with what he termed "the Ph.D. octopus." Many features of contemporary higher education, including the hyper-specialization as well as the focus on research and graduate training of many members of the professoriate, would upset him, but James would surely recognize and applaud the conversion of many of his successors to "the general way of thinking" he announced in *Pragmatism*.[46]

Because the preservation of the natural world was a topic almost as close to James's heart as was education, it is fitting to conclude this essay with a brief discussion of pragmatism in the discourse of early twenty-first-century environmentalism. Some of James's most eloquent writing was inspired by the time he spent "tramping," as he liked to call his hikes around Keene Valley in the Adirondacks and in the Lake Chocorua region of the White Mountains where he and his family built a summer home. Despite his own rhapsodies about the wilderness, which he shared with many Progressive-era conservationists, James was acutely aware, as some of his nature-loving contemporaries were not, of the tension between his own preservationist impulses and the desire of other Americans to develop natural resources—or simply clear a few acres of forest land for farming. That tension, between the desire to exclude humans from wilderness areas and the desire to regulate land use for the public good according to principles of scientific management, persisted among environmentalists throughout the twentieth century. Environmental debates have tended to oscillate between biocentrism, or deep ecology, in which nature is considered inviolable and humans are judged intruders, and technocentrism, in which concerns with preserving scarce or endangered resources such as air, water, or non-human life forms have led scientists to work through government regulation or judicial decisions to protect the environment without much concern for public participation.

In recent decades, both wings of environmentalism have been under attack from several directions, not only the laissez-faire wing of the Republican Party. Critics opposed to some biocentrists' disregarding of what they consider the legitimate interests of humans in making use of nature have been joined by radicals opposed to some technocentrists' disregarding of democratic engagement in environmental policy. In response to these critiques, some environmental scientists have called for a new sensibility, which they term environmental pragmatism. One of these environmental pragmatists, Kelly Parker, observes that "experience" is "the most basic term in pragmatism" and that the environment is, "in the most basic sense," where "experience occurs, where my life and the lives of others arise and take place." Parker rejects as incoherent the notion that nature has "intrinsic value" that must be respected "*independent of any consciousness that might value it.*" Nature matters to humans not for its own sake, as the more extreme biocentrists contend, but because it provides "the ultimate source of our growth"; hence any heedless annihilation of nature annihilates the "places where experiences unfold." Some constructivists, who have pointed out that an environmentalist sensibility has emerged historically rather than enjoying the privileged position of transcendent truth, have challenged the claims of biocentrism without then providing a rationale for environmental protection. Environmental pragmatists argue instead that just as the field of experience for individuals is enriched by the presence of other individuals with whom they interact, so, in Parker's words, the "environment is as much a part of each of us as we are parts of the environment, and moreover, each of us is a part of the environment—a part of experience— with which other beings have to contend." Environmental destruction is to be resisted because it impoverishes the range of experiences available to all of us.[47]

Environmental pragmatists in the tradition of Deweyan democracy emphasize that such resistance should involve the participation of as many individuals as possible. Rather than relying on the technical expertise of scientists or the authority of courts simply to declare what policies should be adopted, Paul Thompson has argued that participatory democracy provides the standard by which environmental activism should be judged. Restating an argument that has echoed from James and Dewey through the progressives until today, community, in Thompson's words, "is the method of science, and the basis of a pragmatic theory of truth." Engaging as many people as possible in the process of inquiry not only provides a means for individuals to become educated about environmental issues, it generates the "common visions of life and purpose" that are the life blood of democratic culture. The warrant for pragmatism, environmental pragmatists conclude, remains what it has always been: "Communities that involve practitioners—bridge builders, farmers, policy-makers—have a reliable mechanism of self-criticism: the ideas must work."[48]

But what, it is necessary to ask, should count as "working" in a pragmatist sense? In business, should the standard be profitability or shareholder value, or are other criteria such as worker involvement, compensation, and satisfaction more important? In medicine it might seem obvious that the appropriate standard is health, but in some areas, especially in the realm of psychiatry, is the appropriate standard a drug-induced tranquility or a deeper—albeit more elusive, and sometimes even painful—degree of self-understanding? In law, is the standard of what works to be arrived at through forceful and precedent-setting judicial decision making or rather through merely structuring the terms of a conflict that must be worked out through the chaotic process of democratic wrangling? In education, is the standard higher student test scores, or is it instead inculcating in students a willingness to wrestle with ideas and an understanding of how to think critically about a whole range of problems that are not amenable to easy answers? In environmentalism, is the standard protecting the environment for its own sake, or making environmental policy through expert decisions made by scientists, or is it instead whatever decision results from the sustained and unpredictable outcomes achieved by the sustained engagement of the people?

If the answer in each case lies in the latter of these alternatives, then how is it possible to stipulate—or even imagine—a pragmatic test that adequately measures results? Some of those who invoke pragmatism in twenty-first-century America seem to think there is a "bottom line" that is easy to identify and that provides clear guidelines. Those with a more sophisticated understanding of what James meant in *Pragmatism* know that both for individuals and for the culture as a whole, the process of pragmatic inquiry is unending as a matter of principle. Finding the proper standard of measurement is an endless process for individuals, and it is even harder for different individuals to reach consensus on what those measuring sticks should be. The challenge involved in assessing the meaning and significance of pragmatism for American culture, from the time of the original pragmatists until the present, has revolved around deciding what judgments are properly to be made by individuals, independent of the judgment of others, such as questions of religious experience were for James; what questions are to be decided by highly trained experts comprising communities of inquiry, such as questions of economic and environmental regulation were for many progressives and New Dealers; and what issues are best decided by the messy, contentious, and imperfect democratic process. Clear answers to those questions remain as elusive now as they were a century ago.

One of the correspondents with whom James most often shared his thoughts on the glories of experience in the wilderness was his younger friend Pauline Goldmark, a Bryn Mawr–educated progressive activist whom he got to know, along with her sister Josephine Goldmark, on one of his many trips to the Adirondacks.[49] In a letter James wrote to her on February 4, 1904, while riding the train from Syracuse to Boston after a winter storm, he began by painting a vivid image of the landscape: "The snow is over, but the horizons disappear in the blackish grey of a frozen atmospheric jelly." After reflecting on the severe beauty of "our wild cold and snow," he expressed his happiness that he was returning to the work that would culminate in the publication of *Pragmatism*. "I am ashamed to say," he confessed, "how much interested I have become in my own system of philosophy (!) since Dewey, Schiller, a Frenchman named Bergson, and some lesser lights, have, all independently of me and of one another, struck into a similar line of ideas." James really was somewhat taken aback that not only were American, English, French (and, he might have noted, German and Italian) thinkers all developing versions of what they thought of—to his surprise—as "his" philosophy, the philosophy that would come to be known as pragmatism, but he himself was beginning to think it might amount to something over the long term. "I am persuaded that a great new philosophic movement is in the air," he wrote, anticipating three years before he finished his book the high hopes he expressed to his brother Henry when *Pragmatism* appeared. But William James already saw, as we should see when we try to assess the impact of his ideas, that tracing the influence of pragmatism is a tricky business. Although philosophical movements such as pragmatism, James continued in his letter to Pauline Goldmark, "seem ridiculously abstract in their original form," they nevertheless do "filter down into practical life through the remotest channels" (*LWJ*, X, 382–84). No one familiar with these ideas would claim the "definitive triumph" of pragmatism today, when the brittle dogma of U.S. righteousness dominates public debate and threatens to silence dissenting voices who challenge whether increasing inequality at home and increasing arrogance in the world constitute "working" by any standard consistent with our nation's democratic principles and aspirations. Yet James's ideas have indeed filtered down into many corners of practical life in America, where they continue to provide leverage for some critics as dissatisfied with reflexive celebrations of that "bitch-goddess success" as was James himself.

NOTES

1. James T. Kloppenberg, "Pragmatism: An Old Name for Some New Ways of Thinking?" *Journal of American History* 83 (June 1996): 100–138. Versions of this essay were reprinted in *The Revival of Pragmatism: New Essays on Social Thought, Law, and Culture*, ed. Morris Dickstein (Durham, N.C.: Duke University Press, 1998), pp. 83–127; in *A Pragmatist's Progress? Richard Rorty and American Intellectual History*, ed. John Pettegrew (Lanham, Md.: Rowman and Littlefield, 2000), pp. 19–60; and, in a revised form refocused on issues in higher education, under the title "Cosmopolitan Pragmatism: Deliberative Democracy and Higher Education," in *Education and Democracy: Re-imagining Liberal Learning in America*, ed. Robert Orrill (New York: College Board, 1997), pp. 69–110.

2. See for example Richard Rorty, "Dewey between Hegel and Darwin," in Rorty, *Truth and Progress, Philosophical Papers*, vol. 3 (Cambridge: Cambridge University Press, 1998), pp. 290–306, an essay marked by Rorty's characteristic civility and generosity; and cf. Stanley Fish, "Truth and Toilets: Pragmatism and the Practices of Life," in *The Revival of Pragmatism*, pp. 418–434; and Fish, "Truth but No Consequences: Why Philosophy Doesn't Matter," *Critical Inquiry* 29 (2003): 389–417.

3. Elizabeth Kamarck Minnich, "The American Tradition of Aspirational Democracy," in *Education and Democracy*, especially pp. 194–99.

4. On the impact of pragmatism on the *writing* of American history, see James T. Kloppenberg, "Objectivity and Historicism: A Century of American Historical Writ-

ing," *American Historical Review* 94 (1989): 1011–30; and Kloppenberg, "Pragmatism and the Practice of History: From Turner and Du Bois to Today," in *The Range of Pragmatism and the Limits of Philosophy,* ed. Richard Shusterman (Malden, Mass.: Blackwell, 2004), pp. 197–220.

5. See the discussion of this essay in H. S. Thayer's introduction, *P,* xii.

6. See ibid., xv.

7. On the relation between pragmatism and progressivism, see James T. Kloppenberg, *Uncertain Victory: Social Democracy and Progressivism in European and American Thought, 1870–1920* (New York: Oxford University Press, 1986); Daniel T. Rodgers, *Atlantic Crossings: Social Politics in a Progressive Age* (Cambridge, Mass.: Belknap Press of Harvard University Press, 1998); Eldon Eisenach, *The Lost Promise of Progressivism* (Lawrence: University Press of Kansas, 1994); and Axel Schäfer, *American Progressives and German Social Reform, 1875–1920: Social Ethics, Moral Control, and the Regulatory State in a Transatlantic Context* (Stuttgart: Franz Steiner Verlag, 2000). As those books make clear, neither pragmatism nor progressivism was strictly an American phenomenon. Philosophers and reformers on both sides of the Atlantic participated in a transnational process of intellectual and political change, with lines of influence running both east and west, as James himself well understood.

8. See Ralph Barton Perry, *The Thought and Character of William James,* vol. 2, *Philosophy and Psychology* (Boston: Little, Brown, 1935), pp. 310–17.

9. See "Robert Gould Shaw: Oration," in *ERM,* 64–74. This brilliant address, which deserves to be better known, makes clear why it is a mistake to argue that James's pragmatism provides no grounds for making sacrifices or gives no criteria for making political decisions.

10. Walter Lippmann to Graham Wallas, July 31 and October 30, 1912, Walter Lippmann Papers, Sterling Memorial Library, Yale University; Lippmann, *A Preface to Politics* (1913; rpt. Ann Arbor: University of Michigan Press, 1962), p. 29.

11. Walter Lippmann, *Drift and Mastery* (New York: Mitchell Kennerley, 1914), pp. 206–208, 274–75, 295, 329.

12. See the discussion of Wilson's term as president of Princeton in John Milton Cooper Jr., *The Warrior and the Priest: Woodrow Wilson and Theodore Roosevelt* (Cambridge, Mass.: Belknap Press of Harvard University Press, 1983), pp. 89–107, a chapter appropriately titled "Academic Reformer."

13. This unconventional reading of Wilson as pragmatist progressive with social democratic sympathies in the domestic sphere rests on splendid research presented in the unpublished Harvard Ph.D. dissertation of Trygve Throntveit, "Related States: Progressivism, Imperialism, and Internationalism in American Thought, 1880–1920." Historians have long doubted the existence of a unified, cohesive progressive movement, preferring instead to see progressivism as an era or, better yet, as a coalition of shifting groups with diverse and sometimes incompatible interests. Such a framework makes it possible to understand why and how some progressives were able to emphasize eugenics, immigration restriction, prohibition, and racial segregation as solutions to the problem of "corruption" as they saw it, whereas others focused on socioeconomic reforms and still others emphasized changing the mechanisms of governance. For detailed analysis of these issues, see James T. Kloppenberg, *Uncertain Victory: Social Democracy and Progressivism in European and American Thought, 1870–1920* (New York: Oxford University Press, 1986). More recent studies include Eldon Eisenach, *The Lost Promise of Progressivism* (Lawrence: University Press of Kansas, 1994); Kevin Mattson, *Creating a Democratic Public: The Struggle for Urban Participatory Democracy during the Progressive Era* (University Park: Pennsylvania State University Press, 1998); Axel Shäfer, *American Progressives and German Social Reform, 1875–1920* (Stuttgart: Franz Steiner Verlag, 2000); and Michael Willrich, "The Case for Courts: Law and Political Development in the Progressive Era," in *The Democratic Experiment: New Directions in*

American Political History, ed. Meg Jacobs, William J. Novak, and Julian Zelizer (Princeton, N.J.: Princeton University Press, 2003), pp. 198–221.

14. Four different accounts of the complex Dewey-Bourne dispute are Casey Nelson Blake, *Beloved Community: The Cultural Criticism of Randolph Bourne, Van Wyck Brooks, Waldo Frank, and the Young Intellectuals* (Chapel Hill: University of North Carolina Press, 1990); Robert B. Westbrook, *John Dewey and American Democracy* (Ithaca, N.Y.: Cornell University Press, 1991); Alan Ryan, *John Dewey and the High Tide of American Liberalism* (New York: Norton, 1995); and Jonathan M. Hansen, *The Lost Promise of Patriotism: Debating American Identity, 1890–1920* (Chicago: University of Chicago Press, 2003).

15. From the voluminous literature on the tragic failures and rarely acknowledged potential of Wilson's foreign policy, see especially Throntveit, "Related States: Progressivism, Imperialism, and Internationalism in American Thought, 1880–1920"; and Erez Manela, *The Wilsonian Moment: Self-Determination and the International Origins of Anticolonial Nationalism* (New York: Oxford University Press, 2007).

16. On the positions taken by Jane Addams and W. E. B. Du Bois before, during, and after World War I, see especially Hansen, *The Lost Promise of Patriotism.*

17. On the Addams-Dewey relationship, see Allen Davis, *American Heroine: The Life and Legend of Jane Addams* (New York: Oxford University Press, 1973); Robert B. Westbrook, *John Dewey and American Democracy;* and Louise W. Knight, *Citizen: Jane Addams and the Struggle for Democracy* (Chicago: University of Chicago Press, 2005).

18. See William James to Jane Addams, February 12, 1907, cited in Davis, *American Heroine,* p. 140. Davis points out that James began developing these ideas in his philosophy courses as early as 1888. On pp. 135–56, Davis discusses the similarities between Addams's views on war and those James began to develop in 1890s and brought to fruition in "Moral Equivalent of War," which she called the "moral substitute for war." Christopher Lasch persuasively characterizes Addams's perspective on war as pragmatist in his introductory comments to "Newer Ideals of Peace" in his collection of her writings, *The Social Thought of Jane Addams,* ed. Christopher Lasch (Indianapolis: Bobbs-Merrill, 1965), pp. 218–19; for the essay itself, see pp. 219–31. See also the incisive analysis in Hansen, *The Lost Promise of Patriotism,* pp. 128–30, 137–90, which details the ideas and interactions of James, Dewey, Addams, Du Bois, and Eugene Debs.

19. See David Levering Lewis, *W. E. B. Du Bois: Biography of a Race, 1868–1919* (New York: Henry Holt, 1993); Axel Schäfer, "W. E. B. Du Bois, German Social Thought, and the Racial Divide in American Progressivism, 1892–1909," *Journal of American History* 88 (2001): 925–49; and Richard Cullen Rath, "Echo and Narcissus: The Afrocentric Pragmatism of W. E. B. Du Bois," *Journal of American History* 84 (1997): 461–95.

20. Robert Park, "Methods of Teaching: Impressions and a Verdict," in Stanford M. Lyman, *Militarism, Imperialism, and Racial Accommodation: An Analysis and Interpretation of the Early Writings of Robert E. Park* (Fayetteville: University of Arkansas Press, 1992), p. 311.

21. Charles Johnson, "Dr. Robert E. Park: 1864–1944," *Psychiatry* 7 (1944): 107, quoted in the outstanding study by George Hutchinson, *The Harlem Renaissance in Black and White* (Cambridge, Mass.: Belknap Press of Harvard University Press, 1995), pp. 52–61.

22. The aptness of this image for the concept of cultural pluralism first came to my attention through the splendid work by Ross Posnock, *Color and Culture: Black Writers and the Making of the Modern Intellectual* (Cambridge, Mass.: Harvard University Press, 1998), pp. 189–90.

23. On Kallen's and Bourne's ideas and their influence in American debates concerning racial and ethnic identity, the place to begin is David A. Hollinger, *Postethnic America: Beyond Multiculturalism,* 2nd ed. (New York: Basic Books, 2000 [1995]), a book that brings into the present the pragmatist understanding of experience and

identity as fluid and subject to change and choice. Hollinger's pragmatist argument is as unpalatable to many rigid multiculturalists today as were the arguments of early twentieth-century pragmatists such as Du Bois, Locke, Kallen, and Bourne to many of their contemporaries. Others offering variations on these themes in contemporary discourse include Werner Sollors and Anthony Appiah, two commentators born outside the United States who see the possibilities of the cosmopolitan ideal as clearly as does Hollinger. For another statement of this position, which shows Dewey's independent statement of a position similar to that taken by his student Bourne in "Trans-national America," see Dewey, "Nationalizing Education," *Journal of Education* 84 (1916): 425–28, in Dewey, *Middle Works, 1899–1924*, vol. 10 (Carbondale: University of Southern Illinois Press, 1980), pp. 202–10; and cf. the fine discussion of this essay, along with the writings of Kallen, Locke, James, and Boas, in Hutchinson, *The Harlem Renaissance in Black and White*, pp. 86–93.

24. See Sidney Milkis, *The President and the Parties: The Transformation of the American Party System since the New Deal* (New York: Oxford University Press, 1993); James T. Kloppenberg, *The Virtues of Liberalism* (New York: Oxford University Press, 1998), pp. 100–123; Cass Sunstein, *The Second Bill of Rights: FDR's Unfinished Revolution and Why We Need It More Than Ever* (New York: Basic Books, 2004); and Elizabeth Borgwardt, *A New Deal for the World: American Vision of Human Rights* (Cambridge, Mass.: Belknap Press of Harvard University Press, 2005).

25. See Robert W. Gordon, ed., *The Legacy of Oliver Wendell Holmes, Jr.* (Stanford, Calif.: Stanford University Press, 1992); G. Edward White, *Justice Oliver Wendell Holmes: Law and the Inner Self* (New York: Oxford University Press, 1994); Thomas C. Grey, "Holmes and Legal Pragmatism," *Stanford Law Review* 41 (1989): 787–870; Philippa Strum, *Louis D. Brandeis: Justice for the People* (Cambridge, Mass.: Harvard University Press, 1984); Philippa Strum, *Brandeis: Beyond Progressivism* (Lawrence: University Press of Kansas, 1993); Barbara Fried, *The Progressive Assault on Laissez Faire: Robert Hale and the First Law and Economics Movement* (Cambridge, Mass.: Harvard University Press, 1998); Morton Horwitz, *The Transformation of American Law, 1870–1960: The Crisis of Legal Orthodoxy* (New York: Oxford University Press, 1992); and David M. Rabban, *Free Speech in Its Forgotten Years* (Cambridge: Cambridge University Press, 1997).

26. John Henry Schlegel, "American Legal Realism and Empirical Social Science: From the Yale Experience," *Buffalo Law Review* 28 (1988): 459–586; Laura Kalman, *Legal Realism at Yale, 1927–1960* (Chapel Hill: University of North Carolina Press, 1986).

27. The best study of this dynamic remains Edward Purcell, *The Crisis of Democratic Theory: Scientific Naturalism and the Problem of Value* (Lexington: University Press of Kentucky, 1973).

28. On student radicalism and its animating ideas, see James Miller, *Democracy Is in the Streets: From Port Huron to the Siege of Chicago* (New York: Simon and Schuster, 1987).

29. Some critics have argued that James's pragmatism, by making the satisfaction of the individual the ultimate test of truth, contributed to the rise of the therapeutic sensibility that has manifested itself in countless self-help programs designed to substitute high self-esteem for what James, like his contemporary Theodore Roosevelt, termed the "strenuous life." That interpretation of James could not survive the careful reading of his essays on ethics, including "The Moral Philosopher and the Moral Life," "What Makes a Life Significant?" and "On a Certain Blindness in Human Beings."

30. The relation between the increasing polarization of party politics and the decline in voting has been noticed for several decades, as has the gap separating the positions of the most strident activists of both parties from the much more moderate positions taken by most Americans. On these issues, see E. J. Dionne Jr., *Why American Hate Politics* (New York: Touchstone, 1991); Theda Skocpol, *Missing in the Middle: Working Families and the Future of American Social Policy* (New York: Norton, 2000);

Alan Wolfe, *One Nation, after All: What Americans Really Think about God, Country, Family, Racism, Welfare, Immigration, Homosexuality, Work, The Right, The Left, and Each Other* (New York: Penguin, 1999); Alan Wolfe, *Moral Freedom: The Search for Virtue in a World of Choice* (New York: Norton, 2001); and Morris Fiorina, *Culture War? The Myth of a Polarized America* (London: Longman, 2005).

31. But William remained hopeful: immediately after the passage quoted in the text, he added, "I know that it will end by winning its way & triumphing!"

32. Some critics of the idea of a pragmatist resurgence have observed that pragmatism has appealed primarily to those on the left. See for example Alan Wolfe, "The Missing Pragmatic Revival in American Social Science," in *The Resurgence of Pragmatism*, pp. 199–206. Wolfe contrasts the interest of most social scientists with "reality" to the pragmatists' alleged utopianism, a contrast that echoes the long-standing tension in social science between ostensibly value-free and self-consciously value-laden inquiries. The incoherence of the idea of value freedom, which has been insisted upon by pragmatists from the beginning, has been the subject of many studies, of which I will cite only Hilary Putnam, *The Collapse of the Fact/Value Dichotomy and Other Essays* (Cambridge, Mass.: Harvard University Press, 2002), discussed in some detail in note 36 below. Although there are notable exceptions, Wolfe is correct about the clustering of those interested in pragmatism on the left of the political spectrum. It does not follow from that observation, however, that pragmatists are unconcerned with reality.

33. Compare the critical analyses of David Montgomery, *The Fall of the House of Labor: The Workplace, The State, and American Labor Activism, 1865–1925* (Cambridge: Cambridge University Press, 1987), and David F. Noble, *America by Design: Science, Technology, and the Rise of Corporate Capitalism* (New York: Oxford University Press, 1977), with two accounts that focus on the reasons behind the rise, and the wide varieties, of managerial capitalism: Alfred D. Chandler, *The Visible Hand: The Management Revolution in American Business* (Cambridge, Mass.: Harvard University Press, 1977); and Olivier Zunz, *Making America Corporate, 1870–1920* (Chicago: University of Chicago Press, 1990). On more recent management gurus such as Peter Drucker, see Stephen P. Waring, *Taylorism Transformed: Scientific Management Theory since 1945* (Chapel Hill: University of North Carolina Press, 1991).

34. See Nitin Nohria and James D. Berkley, "Whatever Happened to the Take-Charge Manager?" *Harvard Business Review* (January–February 1994): 128–37; and the proceedings of a conference sponsored by the Harvard Business School that brought together more than two dozen prominent academics, management consultants, and practitioners, *Breaking the Code of Change*, ed. Michael Beer and Nitin Nohria (Boston: Harvard Business School Press, 2000). One of the central issues discussed in this volume, an approach to corporate management that focuses on the fair treatment of employees, worker participation, and the flexible, experimental pragmatist strategies discussed in the text, descends directly from the writings of James and Dewey. On those ideas see especially the articles by Beer and Nohria, Peter M. Senge, Larry Hirschorn, Karl E. Weick, Robert H. Schaffer, and Terry Neill and Craig Mindrum. In their epilog, Beer and Nohria note the inclination of all conference participants to envision themselves engaged in a process of scientific inquiry and, as scientists, to aspire to value-free neutrality. But, they conclude, "this value-free ideal is something we will have to reject, because it simply prevents us from having the discussion we really need to have. We must accept that part of what guides our views on organizational change is our values" (p. 475). That insight too echoes much of what James and Dewey wrote about the relation between assessments of "what works" and the underlying values that inevitably inform the answer to that question. On this pivotal issue, which I have discussed in *Uncertain Victory* and in "Pragmatism: An Old Name for Some New Ways of Thinking?" see Putnam, *The Collapse of the Fact/Value Dichotomy and Other Essays*. In his preface, Putnam states bluntly the argument of the book: "developing a less scientistic account of rationality, a account that enables us to see how reasoning, far from being

impossible in normative areas, is in fact indispensable to them, and conversely, understanding how normative judgments are presupposed in all reasoning, is important not only in economics [much of the book concerns a defense of the work of Amartya Sen], but—as Aristotle saw—in all of life" (viii). Here are just two passages in which Putnam states his position—which seems to me convincing both as a restatement of the work of the early pragmatists and as the way in which we should be thinking about pragmatism today—with particular pungency: "The classical pragmatists, Peirce, James, Dewey, and Mead, all held that value and normativity permeate *all* of experience. In the philosophy of science, what this point of view implied is that normative judgments are essential to the practice of science itself" (30); and "pragmatists in particular have always emphasized that experience *isn't* 'neutral,' that it comes to us screaming with values" (103). For similar insights from the discipline of economics, see Julie A. Nelson, "Confronting the Science/Value Split: Notes on Feminist Economics, Institutionalism, Pragmatism and Process Thought," *Cambridge Journal of Economics* 27 (2003): 49–64; and Julie A. Nelson, *Economics for Humans* (Chicago: University of Chicago Press, 2006).

35. See, on Bruce Goff and Herbert Greene in particular and on prominent twentieth-century architects more generally, Paul Heyer, *Architects on Architecture: New Directions in America* (New York: Walker, 1966); Peter Blake, *The Master Builders* (New York: Alfred A. Knopf, 1961); and Ben Allen Park, "The Architecture of Bruce Goff," *Architectural Digest,* May 1957.

36. The question of a pragmatist aesthetics, on which Richard Shusterman has done fine work and which is related more directly to works of visual art, literature, and the performing arts, seems to me separate from the more problematic question of how pragmatism relates to the realm of architecture. See Shusterman, *Pragmatist Aesthetics: Living Beauty, Rethinking Art* (Cambridge, Mass.: Blackwell, 1992). For examples of the ways in which practitioners and scholars have tried to address the relation between pragmatism and architecture, with less than striking success, see William G. Ramroth Jr., *Pragmatism and Modern Architecture,* a breezy history of modern architecture in which pragmatism generally figures not at all, only to become, in the epilog, the method of all architects, the night in which all cows are black. See also *The Pragmatist Imagination: Thinking about "Things in the Making,"* ed. Joan Ockman (New York: Princeton Architectural Press, 2000). This fascinating volume of conference proceedings concludes with a skeptical afterword, "What's Pragmatism Got To Do with It?" This essay, written by the scholar who has done more than any other to analyze the problematic relation between pragmatist ideas, democratic participation, and public art, Casey Nelson Blake, raises the questions I discuss in the text. On James Rouse, see Nicholas Dagen Bloom, *Merchant of Illusion: James Rouse, America's Salesman of the Businessman's Utopia* (Columbus: Ohio State University Press, 2004); and, more broadly, on the experimental communities of Columbia, Maryland, Reston, Virginia, and Irvine, California, and how they developed over time, Nicholas Dagen Bloom, *Suburban Alchemy: 1960s New Towns and the Transformation of the American Dream* (Columbus: Ohio State University Press, 2001). Bloom's work shows clearly the tensions bedeviling developers with democratic convictions and pragmatist methods operating within the unyielding constraints of the real estate marketplace.

37. David H. Brendel, *Healing Psychiatry: Bridging the Science/Humanism Divide* (Cambridge, Mass.: MIT Press, 2006). Brendel is quoted in "Psychiatry by Prescription," in *Harvard Magazine* (July–August 2006): 42.

38. Arthur Kleinman, *What Really Matters: Living a Moral Life amidst Uncertainty and Danger* (New York: Oxford University Press, 2006), especially pp. 219–33.

39. I have addressed these issues in several articles, including "Pragmatism: An Old Idea for Some New Ways of Thinking?"; "Deliberative Democracy and Judicial Supremacy," *Law and History Review* 13 (Fall 1995): 393–411; and "The Theory and Practice of Legal History," *Harvard Law Review* 106 (April 1993): 1332–51.

40. Joan Williams, *Unbending Gender: Why Family and Work Conflict and What*

To Do about It (New York: Oxford University Press, 2000); Mary C. Still, "Litigating the Maternal Wall: U.S. Lawsuits Charging Discrimination against Workers with Family Responsibilities," a WLL report available from the Center for WorkLifeLaw, UC Hastings College of the Law, 200 McAlister Street, San Francisco, CA 94102. Assessing James's direct influence on feminism is difficult. Some feminists, such as Williams, Margaret Radin, and Nancy Fraser, invoke pragmatism as an important source of feminist ideas. Others downplay James's significance. Charlene Seigfried, one of the most visible feminist pragmatists, credits James with acknowledging the importance of dimensions of experience, such as emotion, care, and trust, now claimed by many feminists as characteristically female, and she acknowledges that he was unusually receptive to the idea of women's education (after early misgivings about it), but she nevertheless faults James for his uncritical acceptance of paternalism, of separate spheres for men and women, and his "pervasive sexism." See Charlene Haddock Seigfried, *Pragmatism and Feminism: Reweaving the Social Fabric* (Chicago: University of Chicago Press, 1996), especially chapter 6, "The Feminine-Mystical Threat to Masculine-Scientific Order." See also the essays collected in the special issue of *Hypatia* 8 (Spring 1993) titled "Feminism and Pragmatism."

41. Williams, *Unbending Gender*, pp. 260–63. As if to confirm or illustrate the salience of these issues, during the time I was working on this article word arrived of the new family-leave policy instituted recently by Harvard University. Although perhaps as much a consequence of recent federal legislation as of the controversies at Harvard brought on by the ill-considered remarks of Lawrence Summers, former president of the university, concerning women's aptitude for science, the change in Harvard's policy—whatever the reasons for it—is fully consistent with WLL initiatives. It seems likely to make as significant a difference in the lives of many male as well as female "ideal workers" at Harvard, in the dining halls as well as the laboratories and classrooms, as any other developments in contemporary American culture.

42. By far the most widely read study of these phenomena is Diane Ravitch, *Left Back: A Century of Failed School Reforms* (New York: Simon and Schuster, 2000). To her credit, Ravitch is careful to distinguish Dewey's ideas, and his Chicago lab school, from the sins of shoddy instruction and content-free skills building committed in his name. But she conflates under the rubric "progressive education" Dewey's own commitment to well-funded schools offering rigorous instruction to all American children with the disastrous "reforms" of vocational education and life-adjustment, both of which displaced not only the rote learning that Dewey sought to replace but also the strenuous engagement with traditional subject matter that he stressed. The anti-intellectualism Ravitch properly scorns should not be confused with pragmatism. An exceptionally shrewd and informative essay on these issues is the review of *Left Back* by Alan Ryan in *New York Review of Books*, February 22, 2001, pp. 18–21. For James's ideas about how pragmatism might be translated into education, see his *Talks to Teachers on Psychology; and to Students on Some of Life's Ideals* (1899; rpt. New York: Norton, 1958); and Dewey, *The Child and the Curriculum and The School and Society* (1900, 1902; rpt. Chicago: University of Chicago Press, 1958); and the book that Dewey considered the best summary of his ideas, *Democracy and Education* (1916; rpt. New York: Free Press, 1944).

43. Robert Orrill, ed., *Education and Democracy: Re-imagining Liberal Learning in America* (New York: College Entrance Examination Board, 1997). Because singling out any of the seventeen essays in this collection might be taken as a sign of less respect for the others, I want merely to recommend the entire collection, with contributions from college presidents, scientists, social scientists, humanists, and scholars of education, as an illustration of how widespread interest remains in the resources pragmatism can offer those thinking critically about the reform of American higher education.

44. Derek Bok, *Our Underachieving Colleges: A Candid Look at How Much Students Learn and Why They Should Be Learning More* (Princeton, N.J.: Princeton University Press, 2006).

45. Because the Harvard curricular review will continue into the coming year, I cannot predict the particular shape the programs will take. I have not addressed the issues that remain most contentious, which concern the general education program to be prescribed for all students. But the characteristics of the reforms that I have identified in the text either have already been adopted or are almost certain to be adopted.

46. In this note I will cite articles in publications concerning the curricular review written by various faculty members, including in particular the essays written by Louis Menand, and the essays by Katherine De Salvo, Thomas Wolf, Emily Riehl, and John Haddock, all of whom invoke James's writings in their analyses of what needs to be done, in *Student Essays on the Purpose and Structure of a Harvard Education* (Cambridge, Mass.: Harvard College, 2005).

47. For a clear overview of these issues, see Andrew Light and Eric Katz, "Introduction: Environmental Pragmatism and Environmental Ethics as Contested Terrain," in *Environmental Pragmatism,* ed. Andrew Light and Eric Katz (London: Routledge, 1996), pp. 1–18; and cf. Kelly Parker, "Pragmatism and Environmental Thought," in *Environmental Pragmatism,* pp. 352–76; Kelly Parker, "The Values of a Habitat: *Environmental Ethics* 12 (1990): 353–68; Anthony Weston, "Beyond Intrinsic Value: Pragmatism in Environmental Ethics," *Environmental Ethics* 7 (1985): 321–39; Eric Katz, "Searching for Intrinsic Value: Pragmatism and Despair in Environmental Ethics," in *Environmental Pragmatism,* pp. 307–18; and the exchange between Weston and Katz, and the commentary by Andrew Light, in *Environmental Pragmatism,* pp. 319–38. See also Sandra B. Rosenthal and Rogene A. Buchholz, "How Pragmatism *Is* an Environmental Ethic," in *Environmental Pragmatism,* pp. 38–49; James Proctor, "A Social Construction of Nature: Relativist Accusations, Pragmatist and Critical Realist Responses," *Annals of the Association of American Geographers* 88 (1998): 352–76; Bob Pepperman Taylor, "John Dewey and Environmental Thought," *Environmental Ethics* 12 (1990); Bob Pepperman Taylor, *Our Limits Transgressed: Environmental Political Thought in America* (Lawrence: University Press of Kansas, 1992); and the critique of Taylor in Larry A. Hickman, "John Dewey's Pragmatic Naturalism," in *Environmental Pragmatism,* pp. 50–72, especially p. 70n25. For help in clarifying these issues I am indebted to Zachary Liscow, "Environmentalism versus Democracy: The Threats of Biocentrism and Technocentrism and the Promise of Environmental Pragmatism," unpublished paper, May 2005.

48. Paul Thompson, "Pragmatism and Policy: The Case of Water," in *Environmental Pragmatism,* pp. 187–208. For an ambitious analysis of the implications of pragmatism for environmental law and policy, see Daniel Farber, *Eco-Pragmatism: Making Sensible Environmental Decisions in an Uncertain World* (Chicago: University of Chicago Press, 2000); and for a history of the intersection between pragmatism and environmentalism, see Ben A. Minteer, *The Landscape of Reform: Civic Pragmatism and Environmental Thought in America* (Cambridge, Mass.: MIT Press, 2006).

49. Consider two examples of letters James wrote to Pauline Goldmark during the last year of his life, as the heart problems brought on by his hiking worsened. On June 22, 1909, he urged her to "lose no chance during all these young years to live with nature—it is the eternal normal animal thing in us, overlaid by other more important human destinies, no doubt, but holding the fort in the middle of the security of all the rest." On September 5 of that year he wrote that her letter from the West "gladdened my heart by awakening lively images of the bath in Nature's beauties and wonders which you were about to have. I hope you have *drunk deep,* for that goes to a certain spot in us that nothing else can reach, more 'serious' and 'valuable' though other things profess (and seem) to be." For a rich selection of the letters James wrote to her sister Pauline, see Josephine Goldmark, "An Adirondack Friendship," in *William James Remembered,* ed. Linda Simon (Lincoln: University of Nebraska Press, 1996), pp. 174–98. It was through another Goldmark sister, Alice, who married Louis Brandeis, that James and Brandeis first became acquainted.

2. The Enemies of Pragmatism

. . . .

MARK BAUERLEIN

For those students exposed to pragmatism in the customary way, in survey courses in modern philosophy or American intellectual history, it is easy to overlook one of the functional and diverting aspects of its early development. Apart from Charles Sanders Peirce's programmatic essays from the 1870s, the most common assigned texts date from the first decade of the twentieth century—William James's *Pragmatism* (1907) and *The Meaning of Truth* (1909), essays by John Dewey on knowledge and psychology, Peirce's "What Pragmatism Is" (1905), and, perhaps, a piece by F. C. S. Schiller on "humanism." In these works we find the central themes of meaning, method, reality, and truth expounded at length in various ways and styles, for instance, Peirce's eccentric mix of semiotics and epistemological realism and Schiller's confrontational insistence on the human element in the most reflective inquiries. Philosophy teachers can mine these materials for provocative ideas and formulations, treating James's description of the true as "whatever proves itself to be good in the way of belief" (*P*, 42) as an acute expression of modern thought or as a violation of logical distinctions. Intellectual historians might link Dewey's cognitive psychology to the spread of evolutionary thinking, or James's "cash-value" approach to ideas to Gilded Age mores. Literary theorists can cite Peirce on interpretation as an anticipation of post-structuralist theory.

These are important connections rightly included in the study of pragmatism in its formative phase. But in many prominent statements of the time, especially during the prolific years 1904–1908, the pragmatists addressed more immediate influences, arguments, and adversaries. The texts they responded to included those originating not only many years earlier (*The Origin of Species* was already a half-century old), but just a few months or weeks before. The antagonists included not only famed figures of ancient and modern philosophy, but contemporary professors minor in their own time and forgotten today. And the full context of the pragmatists' expositions comprised not only highlights of meditation through the ages, but also statements in a local, unfolding, and piecemeal setting: the philosophy periodicals circa 1905.

The role of the periodicals in the development of pragmatism was crucial. Of more or less recent creation and open to several schools of thought, they provided James, his allies, and their critics an ongoing forum in which to explain, denounce, analyze, and confute the meaning and implications of the movement. They helped pragmatism consolidate as a movement, as a concerted endeavor emphasizing its own newness and drawing battle lines in the philosophical community. They contained full-length articles, reviews of books and notices of articles in other journals, plus critical discussions in a point/counterpoint mode. They hosted meticulous examinations of minute aspects of the philosophy, sometimes running in successive issues a critique of one element in pragmatism, then a response to the critique, then a response to the response. For five years or so, the journals *Mind*, *The Philosophical Review* (hereafter *PR*), and *The Journal of Philosophy, Psychology, and Scientific Methods* (founded 1904; hereafter *JP*) offered something related to pragmatism in almost every number, a remarkable fact given that *JP* was a biweekly and *PR* a bimonthly (*Mind* was a quarterly). (Several other periodicals weighed in on pragmatism, such as *The Monist* and *Psychological Review*, but with much less frequency.) Some of the most adamant and belittling objections to pragmatism went into their pages. Moreover, some of the most dense and combative rejoinders by the pragmatists appeared there as well, demonstrating that the pragmatists respected the authority of the journals and understood that the criticisms demanded a prompt reply in the same venue.

Furthermore, in this heated forensic climate appeared some important clarifications by the pragmatists, statements that still draw attention today. James is the foremost example. As the lectures that became chapters in *Pragmatism* were taking shape in his mind, he engaged in direct disputes with antagonists in the journals, and his sallies often ended up in later volumes. Chapter 3 in *The Meaning of Truth*, "Humanism and Truth," first materialized in October 1904 in *Mind*. Chapter 4, "The Relation between Knower and Known," came out of an essay from the Sept 29, 1904, *JP*, and chapter 5, "The Essence of Humanism," appeared in *JP* the following year. Of the longer entries in the posthumous volume *Essays in Radical Empiricism*, edited by Ralph Barton Perry (who also commented on pragmatism and its critics in the journals), every one except "La Notion de Conscience" and "The Experience of Activity" originated in *JP* or *Mind*. This is not to mention the shorter pieces in both volumes, such as "A Reply to Mr. Pitkin" and "Professor Pratt on Truth," which originated in the discussion sections of the journals. The opening sentence of "Humanism and Truth" nicely captures the instigating strategies of the editors: "Receiving from the Editor of Mind an advance proof of Mr. Bradley's article on 'Truth and Practice,' I understand this as a hint to me to join in the controversy over 'Pragmatism' which seems to have seriously begun."

Because the contents of the collections had already passed through or, in some cases, were called forth by the editors, contributors, and readers of the journals, by the time of their publication in book form their significance in philosophical circles had already begun to play out. And the nature of those professional circles suggests one reason why James chose to present his ideas in short bursts in the journals and to repeat them in heftier form months and years later in summary collections. A letter from Schiller to James dated February 12, 1906, received many months before James composed his Pragmatism lectures, helps explain the dual publication. "No doubt as you say," Schiller conceded, "if all the different ways in which 'truths' work and concepts are practical, had been presented by us neatly labeled in a magnum opus there w^d have been less misunderstanding . . . but whence w^d you or Dewey or I have got the time to have done such a thing? The ambition w^d have meant years of delay, & meanwhile the people were perishing! As far as I was concerned, publication & aggression were practical necessities" (CWJ, XI, 175). To Schiller, pragmatism had to venture forth in roving skirmishes, perturbing the philosophy establishment in its central organs. Its mature exposition would best emerge after being tried and tested in the professional marketplace.

James preferred a less confrontational approach—he told Schiller that his "whole mental tone against our critics is overstrained" (CWJ, X, 447), and complained to another correspondent about Schiller's "ultra bellicose tone" (CWJ, X, 467)—but not by much. In "The Pragmatist Account of Truth and Its Misunderstanders," first published in PR (January 1908) and later as chapter 8 of The Meaning of Truth, James begins by regretting his critics' "persistent misunderstanding" and the "fantastic character of the current misconceptions" (MT, 99). And a few words later he adds to the charge of obtuseness that of mean-spiritedness: "The critics have boggled at every word they could boggle at," and their "second stage of opposition, which has already begun to express itself in the stock phrase that 'what is new is not true, and what is true not new,' in pragmatism, is insincere." Even when in a more conciliatory mode, James makes the us-versus-them character of the situation plain. In "A Word More about Truth," chapter 6 in The Meaning of Truth but first published in JP July 18, 1907, he opens: "My failure in making converts to the conception of truth which I published in your number for March 14 of this year, seems, if I may judge by what I hear in conversation, almost complete" (MT, 78). In his correspondence he could be harsher, for instance, referring to a critical article in Archive f. Systematische Philosophie penned by "that portentously solemn ass G. E. Moore" (CWJ, X, 412).

Furthermore, James's publication history suggests his overall agreement with Schiller's take on how and where to engage the reigning models of philosophy. To publish first in the experts-only periodicals using a daring rhetoric and an accessible idiom, then to republish selected writings, slightly revised, in book form for a broad reading public, made for a successful two-part strategy. Executed well, it would meet the professors on their own ground and win a larger audience. "There is also, you will admit, a further reason for writing in a lively & interesting way," Schiller wrote to James in February 1904. "It is necessary to recapture the reading public wh[ich] the dull, bad, & obscure writing of the profs has driven away from phil^y. And it is necessary also to persuade the profs to write a little better" (CWJ, X, 380).

This is not to say that the periodical setting actually determined the central ideas and arguments of early pragmatism. Peirce's first formulations of pragmatism were inspired by his own genius and by intellectual influences far from the editorial offices of the journals. And the text that threw pragmatism in the spotlight, James's 1898 lecture at Berkeley, had little bearing upon what *Mind* and *PR* published in the 1890s.

But the periodical setting did direct the pathway of those ideas and arguments once they gained notice. Because of the frequency of their publication, the periodicals intensified and accelerated the debate over pragmatism. More people, and in less time, took the chance to speak their piece. As a result, the course of the new philosophy from introductory presentation to favorable and unfavorable response to defense and elaboration to revised and refined presentation unfolded over just a few years' time.

A survey of the periodical entries on pragmatism during the early years gives a fair idea of the intensity and frequency of the exchanges. Several leading philosophy professors found their way into print, their statements representing, most likely, hundreds more who were excited or put out by the movement. Issues of *The Journal of Philosophy, Psychology,* and *Scientific Methods* released around the time of James's pragmatism lectures are an illustrative case in point. James delivered the lectures in the winter of 1906–1907, and when *Pragmatism: A New Name for Some Old Ways of Thinking* came out later in June 1907, Charles Bakewell noted in his November review in *PR* "the unparalleled success which attended the delivery of these lectures in Boston and in New York."[1]

The live audiences may have been enthusiastic, but the exchanges in *JP* weren't so kind. The interest of *JP* in pragmatism arose in its initial volumes, and disagreements followed quickly. In the first few months of the periodical's existence, nearly three years before James's lectures, several articles appeared that have an expository aim, as if they acknowledge the advent of a fresh angle of thought in need of definition and explanation. Dewey's "Notes upon Logical Topics" was printed in the third number (Feb. 4, 1904), and it contains a straightforward attempt to classify different conceptions of logic. Along the way Dewey touches upon Kant, Aristotle, Mill, Benjamin Peirce (Charles's father, an important mathematician), and Venn. He summarizes, among others, formal logic, empirical logic, and "psychological logic," the latter providing "at once such a novel and such a significant interpretation of the nature of thought in general."[2] Indeed, James's theories of "selective attention" and of the stream-of-consciousness, he estimates, will have far-reaching consequences for "logic proper." Clearly, Dewey recognizes the new thinking as a momentous step in the progress of philosophy, and his article attempts to meet a necessary task in the appreciation of the new: to situate it amongst its forebears.

Six weeks later, on March 17, J. A. Leighton of Hobart College has a discussion piece titled, simply, "Pragmatism." The essay examines the humanism of Schiller and the cognitive psychology of Dewey, surveying major concepts and, putatively, assessing their strengths and weaknesses. Here, already, the contentiousness has commenced. Leighton characterizes Schiller straight off as "the most pugnacious and the most facetious protagonist of pragmatism," and his writings sink into "repeated and often tasteless sallies of wit."[3] Still, he promises, "When the witticisms, jibes and other 'literary' flights are discounted there is left a residuum of philosophical argument and it is with this that I shall deal." Nonetheless, Leighton skips the strengths and singles out the flaws, for instance, Schiller's emphasis on the nullity of "Useless Knowledge." "Must we await," Leighton asks, "the conversion of number-theory into cash-value before admitting its truth, while in the meantime we are absolutely convinced of the soundness of the reasonings of Dedekind, Canto et al?"[4]

In his treatment of Dewey, he isolates the attribution of validity to an idea according to its "instrumental use in effecting the transition from a relatively conflicting experience to a relatively integrated one."[5] Leighton's objection: that truth is more than "a mere instrument of easy transition to peace and harmony." These are not sustained counterarguments, it should be noted. They are quibbles of a first-response kind, and, from our perspective one hundred years on, they are significant precisely for their character as initial reactions of the philosophy profession.

Dewey returns in the next issue of *JP* with "Notes upon Logical Topics: II. The Meanings of the Term Idea." Here we have another brief and general survey of definitions, this time running from Plato to Locke to, again, James. The mode is entirely expository, and only at the end does Dewey pose a critical question, a new version of an old epistemological contest: are ideas "independent psychical entities," or are they simply "methodological device[s] for facilitating and controlling knowledge—that is to say, acquaintance and transactions with objects?"[6]

The very next issue of *JP* picks up on Dewey's work in "psychological logic." A discussion piece by A. K. Rogers of Butler College titled "The Standpoint of Instrumental Logic" (April 14, 1904) follows the general admission that pragmatism in its diverse forms represents something innovative in philosophical study. "The recent Logical Studies from the University of Chicago represent a somewhat notable contribution to American philosophy," it begins.[7] But it is precisely in this break with tradition that Rogers grows suspicious, worrying that if instrumental logic "simply involves throwing out of court as illegitimate most of the questions which have represented difficulties in the past, it may easily appear to be a purely artificial simplification."[8] The closer he looks at it, in fact, the more Rogers runs into a basic incomprehension. The particulars of his disputes are dense, but suffice it to say that Rogers sprinkles admissions of befuddlement throughout: "I must confess, at the risk of appearing unphilosophical, that I cannot understand how anybody";[9] "I for one find it quite impossible to realize";[10] "Just how are we to understand";[11] and "I can not at all understand how the position is to be carried out consistently."[12]

Once again, we have a first-response expression, this time sliding into puzzlement. "This just doesn't sound right," it seems to say. "I don't get it." The same thing happens a few months later, when Simon F. MacLennan of Oberlin College devotes the last pages of an article titled "Two Illustrations of the Methodological Value of Psychology in Metaphysic" (July 21, 1904) to a tentative summary of

Josiah Royce and pragmatism. MacLennan confesses, "I may have failed entirely to understand what the pragmatists are aiming at,"[13] and when he criticizes Royce he inserts qualifications such as "unless I have been thinking entirely beside the mark."[14]

These early expressions and responses are symptomatic of pragmatism's entry into professional philosophy through the periodicals. In both positive and negative assessments, we have a universal recognition of its energy, its compelling vision and fresh approach. But the meaning and implication of pragmatism remain unclear. The pragmatists fudge traditional distinctions and enlarge the functions of thought, that is obvious, and many people find pragmatism's innovations appealing, but how are philosophers to assimilate an upstart school of thought that proposes to revise basic and long-standing concepts such as "truth" and "mind"?

This explains why during the same weeks we have more exercises in exposition published in *JP*. The essay "Utilitarian Epistemology" by G. A. Tawney of Beloit College (June 23) sets out to provide a basic introduction to pragmatic terms and values. The style is didactic, as Tawney strives to make pragmatism as clear and distinctive as possible.

> Conceptions, according to this theory of knowledge, are simply the meanings which groups of things acquire in our feeling-lives, and truth is that conception or system of conceptions which contributes most to the satisfaction of our practical needs. . . . To the grocer, sugar is an article of merchandise, and the success of his business depends upon his adequately conceiving it so. To the housekeeper, sugar is a white, vegetable compound.[15]

Such are the homely illustrations assumed to be needed to elucidate the new thinking. Note, too, that pragmatism is "this theory of knowledge," a categorization designed to identify pragmatism, to delimit it (in this case, opposite to a "representational theory of knowledge"). Along with the examples, Tawney's outline has a simple purpose: "we repeat, only to illustrate the subject of this paper."[16] By implication, then, a fundamental question hovers over the exposition. What is pragmatism?

That question happens to be the title of an essay by H. Heath Bawden of Vassar College in the August 4th number of *JP*. In its casual and flowing paragraphs, Bawden roams and prods his way into an outline of "what, in recent discussions, the word 'pragmatism' seems to be coming to mean."[17] In thus confining his discussion, he stops well short of evaluating the philosophy's truth or rigor. First, Bawden advises, let's determine what it means.

He notes that pragmatism has elements dating back to the ancient Greeks, but "it is only in recent years that this mode of thought has come into prominence as a philosophic method."[18] Its emergence, however, has elicited too much "glib talk" and "vague and obscure" conceptions. Broaching "first prejudices,"[19] pragmatism has evoked strong emotions and humorous retorts, and while the critics have mischaracterized or tendentiously characterized the movement, the pragmatists themselves have offered partial and angular sketches of their theories. This has produced a curious situation in professional philosophy in 1904. Everybody wants to discuss pragmatism, but nobody except the advocates seems to know what it is. At the previous meeting of the American Philosophical Association at Princeton, Bawden observes, pragmatism was a central topic. Professor Leighton, cited above, criticized the pragmatic standpoint, but admitted that "this movement, in late years, had assumed proportions that must be reckoned with."[20] More importantly, the president of the association, Josiah Royce, seized the occasion of his address to deliver a sharp dismantling of the pragmatic point of view. Significantly, in the ensuing colloquies, the defenders of pragmatism didn't refute the details of the attacks, but instead refused the notion of pragmatism on which they were based, the "tendency to conceive pragmatism in too narrow a way."[21]

Bawden documents these confusions but doesn't take sides. Instead, he wisely casts the debates as a substantive event in themselves. In a judgment extraordinary given the little time that has passed since pragmatism's emergence, Bawden announces, "Pragmatism already is beginning to have a history."[22] At this point, from the pragmatists' side, apart from their own writings, that history is a sequence of misconstructions of pragmatic concepts and axioms, and the critics are, in James's label, "misunderstanders." From the critics' side, however, the history is a series of faulty and high-handed articulations by the pragmatists themselves. The idiom that Schiller suggested to James—direct, lively, concrete—along with James's exemplary usage of it, strikes the philosophers as engaging, but loose and hasty, too, a drawback that James partly concedes in the preface to *The Meaning of Truth* when he acknowledges his "unguarded language" (*MT*, 5). Furthermore, the differences among the pragmatists make it difficult to assign a unitary thrust to the philosophy, a situation acknowledged by Dewey in a 1905 essay in *JP* titled "The Postulate of Immediate Empiricism" (July 20, 1905). It begins, "The criticisms made upon that vital but still unformed movement variously termed radical empiricism, pragmatism, humanism, functionalism, according as one or another aspect of it is uppermost."[23] In the rest of the essay, Dewey proceeds to "do my little part in clearing up the confusion" by outlining what experience means within the new thinking, presuming that much of the quarrel stems from people operating with different assumptions.

Still, the critics might reply, what experience signifies there will differ from what it signifies in "Philosophical Conceptions and Practical Results," in Schiller's *Humanism*, and so on. Dewey says this, James says that, Schiller says that, and Peirce says, well, we're not quite sure. (Even in "Notes upon Logical Topics," cited above, when Dewey mentions the work of Peirce, he adds the qualifier "if I interpret him aright.")[24] While the pragmatists refer to one another in their writings as working along the same lines, they rarely delineate the connections in any detail. Philosophers committed to existing schools of thought such as Idealism, and skeptical of new schools, are left with a confounding field of engagement. Pragmatism has its fans, it possesses the cachet and vitality of the new, and, hardest of all to its enemies, it won't stay still long enough to allow a refutation to unfold and take effect. The very label "enemies" is disparaging, but the partisanship is unavoidable.

Hence the frustration suffusing one critical sally after another in the periodicals in the mid-1900s. In an article in *PR* titled "Pragmatism and Its Critics," Addison W. Moore of the University of Chicago mentions the pragmatists' slippery tactics even as he dismantles the absolutists. Noting that the "American reaction" against the pragmatic movement began the year before at the American Philosophical Association meeting in Princeton, Moore observes, "Not only has the pragmatist been thus suddenly flanked, but he finds himself confronted with his own weapons, some of which, at any rate, he fondly supposed his opponents could not wield."[25] And later: "If the pragmatist regards his constructions as strong enough to serve as a base of operations, he must expect them also to become an object of counter attack."

No wonder various pragmatic writings during the same months fall into patterns of explanation and rebuttal at the semantic level, the impatience expressed by the pragmatists in those writings mirroring the annoyance of their critics. In the second half of 1905, for instance, Dewey published four articles in *JP* that directly respond to previous criticisms, and his presentations are straightforward attempts to clarify and refine pragmatic conceptions. "The Realism of Pragmatism" (June 8) rejects the imputation of "radical subjectivism" to pragmatism, which was made in the preceding issue of *JP*. There, Dewey draws a categorical boundary line. "Speaking of the matter only for myself," he writes, "the presuppositions and tendencies of pragmatism are distinctly realistic; not idealistic in any sense in which idealism connotes or is connoted by the theory of knowledge."[26] That first phrase is echoed later in the piece, and it implicitly recognizes potential discrepancies between him and the other pragmatists—"I speak only for myself, but in giving my hearty assent to what Professor James has said about the nature of truth (see this JOURNAL, p. 118, Vol. II.), I venture to express the hope that he also conceives the matter in some such way as I have suggested."[27]

The next month saw the article cited above, "The Postulate of Immediate Empiricism," followed by a response by Dewey's colleague at Columbia Frederick J. E. Woodbridge titled "Of What Sort Is Cognitive Experience?" (Oct. 12). (Dewey had recently moved from Chicago.) Woodbridge begins by thanking Dewey for sharpening his definitions:

> Professor Dewey's recent article in this Journal [the "Postulate" piece] has definitively contributed to a clearer understanding of what the term "real" means to many advocates of immediate empiricism and pragmatism. The real is simply that which is experienced and as it is experienced. . . . The challenge to the pragmatist to tell what he means by reality appears, thus, to have been met successfully.[28]

But having secured, finally, a clear definition of the pragmatist's reality, Woodbridge believes he has caught Dewey in an epistemological muddle. If reality is the content of particular, actual experiences, how do we study it? How do we know it? Presumably, through another experience of which or through which the preceding experience is the object or content. But, Woodbridge argues, that other experience would have to be an experience of a certain kind, a cognitive experience, in order to secure knowledge about the first experience. To understand reality, we must enter into but one kind of experience—"this question must be answered only a cognitive experience"[29]—and if such experiences are successful at imparting the realities of, say, "moral experience" (which Woodbridge mentions as another "sort"), then we must attribute some measure of transcendence to cognitive attitudes. This, however, contradicts Dewey's anti-transcendence, anti-idealist version of pragmatism.

In November Dewey fought back with "The Knowledge Experience and Its Relationships" (Nov. 23). Dewey approvingly summarizes Woodbridge's focus, "how to justify the peculiar claims of knowledge to provide a valid account of other modes of experience,"[30] but finds numerous errors in its application. The most basic one is that Woodbridge assumes that knowledge about things already transcends those things. Dewey writes, "Some degree of distinction is necessary to any experienced thing, and such determinateness in experience one may agree to call knowledge. This sort of thing can hardly be referred to as transcendent—for what does it transcend? Not the things of other experiences, for it is the things of all experiences."[31] Cognitive actions play a part in any experience in which things are intelligible, and so Woodbridge's isolation of "cognitive experience" from other "sorts" fundamentally misconstrues the pragmatic theory of knowledge. Once again, the pragmatist attributes criticisms of the philosophy to assumptions held by the critic that are themselves denied by pragmatism. "I am convinced," Dewey concludes, "that the charges of subjectivism . . . brought against current empiricism are due to the fact that the critic, because he himself retains a belief in the independent existence of a subject, ego, consciousness or whatever, external to the subject-matters, ascribes similar beliefs to the one criticized."[32] The charges are inapplicable, Dewey claims, for the pragmatist believes that the subject, ego, or "whatever" exists not independently but in relation to "functions, contexts or contents in and of the things experienced." The cognitive aspects of experience surface only when we fall into a situation of doubt, for "it is only when a real is ambiguous and discrepant that it needs definition."[33] Again, we return to basic misunderstandings, and the pragmatist having to explain his meaning.

As further proof of the elemental nature of the debate, on the very next page of the November 23 issue of *JP* appears an article by B. H. Bode of the University of Wisconsin titled "Cognitive Experience and Its Object." Bode ranges back and forth between Dewey's and Woodbridge's positions, siding eventually with the latter. He reiterates the distinction between cognitive experiences and other experiences, and regrets the pragmatic inclination to "do violence to the character of transcendence pertaining to the cognitive experience."[34] Dewey replies the next month with "The Knowledge Experience Again" (Dec. 21), stating once more that the criticisms are misdirected. Dewey's own position "differentiates itself from the realism which Bode criticizes,"[35] and the critics' notion of mental contents confines them too much to objects. Dewey also includes "attitudes, adjustments, coordinations of personal activities."[36] Moreover, just as do idealists, he accepts the distinction in cognitive events between what is immediately perceived and what is mediately conceived. The real distinction between Dewey and his antagonists is that he incorporates into cognition "elements which are not, and can not be reduced to, cognitional terms and relations; which connote emotional and volitional values; and to which 'humanism,' 'pragmatism,' 'radical empiricism,' are desirous of assigning their metaphysical weight."[37] The antagonists do not. The question of whether these "leadings," "colorings," and values participate in knowledge is, for Dewey and his allies, a settled one. The central question is how.

More than a year later, in early 1907, it seems that little progress has been made. In "Pragmatism's Conception of Truth," published March 14 in the *Journal of Philosophy, Psychology and Scientific Methods,* James proclaims, "the Schiller-Dewey view of truth has been so ferociously attacked by rationalistic philosophers and so abominably misunderstood, that here, if anywhere, is the point where a clear and simple statement should be made" (*P,* 95). James had finished delivering his pragmatism lectures, but while audiences had applauded and the chapters headed into book production, a steady battery of assaults had continued in the periodicals. The controversy had advanced to more sophisticated reasonings, but in James's eyes it remained a string of misunderstandings, a non-meeting of minds.

In the October 25th issue of *JP,* John E. Russell of Williams College identifies a basic mistake in "The Pragmatist's Meaning of Truth." He opens by asserting that the semantic difficulty has waned: "I think it can be safely assumed that the readers of this Journal by this time know sufficiently well what the pragmatist means by truth, by a true idea."[38] The problem lies in pragmatism's identification of an idea's truth with its usefulness, instead of recognizing the idea's truth as an independent quality that enables it to yield useful effects.

Two numbers later in the same journal, James, in "The Mad Absolute," feels compelled to defend Schiller against a sarcastic critic who imputes "madness" to pragmatists who deny the absolute (*PP,* 149–50). Eleven pages earlier in the same issue, Walter B. Pitkin, another Columbia professor, lashes out at "the radical empiricist" (he never mentions James's name) with a similar bit of mockery, accusing James of presenting in his arguments "a comedy to which we have been invited by alluring bill-boards."[39] He focuses on the now customary topic of experience and reality, or rather, the relation between the two, and makes a serious point, that is, that radical empiricists consider a "known thing" and the "knowing of it" identical. Quickly, though, Pitkin descends with glee into the mocking mode: "the radical empiricist is forced to the pitiful makeshift of pleading that the thing is never known to have that character save when it is known! May the Gods refrain from interrupting us here with bursts of laughter!"[40] Whatever logical point Pitkin scores gets lost in the derisive rhetoric.

This explains why James replies to Pitkin in December's essay "Mr. Pitkin's Refutation of 'Radical Empiricism'" with a mere half-page of remarks, one of which runs, "Radical empiricism and pragmatism have so many misunderstandings to suffer from, that it seems my duty not to let this one go any farther, uncorrected" (*ERE,* 123). The correction amounts to a simple adjustment. In a word, James doesn't deny entities that are not directly experienced, and he is "perfectly willing to admit any number of noumenal beings or events into philosophy if only their pragmatic value can be shown."

The next week's issue of *JP* contains a curious article by R. W. Sellars of the University of Michigan on "The Nature of Experience" (Jan. 3, 1907). Sellars is sympathetic to James and Dewey, but he connects the "instrumentalist" approach to consciousness to basic physical factors. After citing James's essay "Does Consciousness Exist?" and addressing the mind-body problem, introjection, and the stream of consciousness, Sellars draws a simplifying conclusion. "Our consciousness is, then," he announces, "a function of the total stress relations of that node or focus in the universe usually denominated the psychophysical organism. This focus or ganglion and its complexity are the product of evolution and must not be looked upon as either merely psychical or merely physical."[41] Amidst the other entries during these months, Sellars's article looks like an anomaly, an effort to turn the discussion away from disputes with the idealists and rationalists and toward entirely new directions of speculation.

The next number of *JP* returns to the dominant motif. Schiller has an article defending pragmatism against John Russell's critique of pragmatism's truth, but right after it comes Walter Pitkin's "In Reply to Professor James" (Jan. 17, 1907). There, after stating, "It would be unfair of me to ask Professor James to rewrite his philosophy for my own benefit," and also conceding that his difficulties "may lie in my own ignorance of Professor James's terminology," Pitkin borrows upon modern science to pose a new question. Don't the findings of science indicate that many things do, in fact, exist that are experienced "as that which they are not or are only partially."[42]

On February 14 appears an article by W. P. Montague of Columbia University (again!) that proclaims a new framework of contention in the history of European philosophy. Whereas for one hundred years we have witnessed a battle between German idealists and British empiricists, "this good-humoured rivalry has been disturbed, not only by a vigorous revival of realism on the part of Mr. G. E. Moore and Mr. Bertrand Russell, in England, but also and more noticeably by the coming of the pragmatists."[43] While it remains "a matter of some difficulty to define the principles of this new school in a manner acceptable alike to its adherents and its critics," Montague has no trouble pinning down their basic innovation. Pragmatists think that "[e]xistence does not consist primarily either in being perceived or in being conceived, but rather in being felt and willed." Montague writes in a spirit of disinterestedness, and his article cares more about defending realism against idealists than in taking a position for or against pragmatism, but nonetheless, James would certainly consider his characterization of pragmatism a sorry impoverishment of the theory.

Montague's new note of confidence about what pragmatism is continues in "Pragmatism Versus Science," an article by Herbert Nichols of Chestnut Hill, Massachusetts, in the February 28th number. Nichols offers up a host of pragmatic principles that read more like a parody than an exposition, their simplicities unfolding in sophomoric phrasings. A sample: "for pragmatists 'the physical world' is merely the sum of human percepts and concepts of it";[44] they believe that in an individual mind "[a]ll past states cease to exist, absolutely";[45] according to James, "the mind is an indivisible whole or solidarity";[46] "To all mankind, heretofore, truth has meant 'conformity to fact,'" but with pragmatism, "[t]ruth is 'highest satisfaction,' 'highest belief.'"[47] Surrounding these pejorative slogans are swift and enthusiastic affirmations of the progress of modern science, all of them tied together by the thesis that modern science promises the veritable forward-looking perspective and results that pragmatism claims for itself. It is a cranky performance, and one assumes that the editors included it only to maintain the temperature of the pragmatism controversy.

In the subsequent issue, James published "Pragmatism's Conception of Truth," the sixth part of his lecture series and soon to be chapter 6 of *Pragmatism*. It is the central philosophical statement in the volume, and it bears definite traces of the periodical exchanges from the previous two years. James has watched pragmatism enter the philosophy world only to be treated like a rogue and an incompetent, and we have seen that some of the blame belongs to the pragmatists' own provocative manner in the journals. Here James offers a normalizing outlook on the process: "I fully expect to see the pragmatist view of truth run through the classic stages of a theory's career. First, you know, a new theory is attacked as absurd; then it is admitted to be true, but obvious and insignificant; finally it is seen to be so important that its adversaries claim that they themselves discovered it" (*P*, 95). Of course, those very critics, reading James's words, would only grow more annoyed. To be informed that the theory to which you have devoted so many pages of argument defying, you will soon adopt as having been your own the whole time, grates on your integrity. James pours further condescension on the anti-pragmatists at the end of the piece. "Our critics certainly need more imagination of realities," he mutters, and, concerning the rationalist conception, "I have to confess that it still completely baffles me" (*P*, 112). The adversaries remain in a condition of mutual incomprehension.

James hopes at the start of his lecture that it will push the pragmatic theory beyond the first stage of reception ("it is absurd"), but the next number of *JP* contains a two-page notice of a unfriendly essay in *Philosophical Review,* and the notice is generally approving. The essay is by A. K. Rogers, who earlier criticized Dewey's "instrumental logic," and the notice is by B. H. Bode, who earlier criticized Dewey's notion of consciousness.[48] (In the same number of *PR* appears an essay by John E. Russell arguing that solipsism is the logical end point of radical empiricism.) Rogers's essay begins with what now appears a common complaint. "I believe most readers who have followed the recent discussions about Pragmatism would agree that they leave something still to be desired in the way of a determination, clearly defined and consistently held to, of what the precise point at issue really is."[49] Rogers goes so far as to argue that James himself disagrees with basic pragmatic premises, and that he himself isn't a pragmatist at all! Bode lets the point stand. The next month the questions continue as Evander Bradley McGilvary of the University of Wisconsin returns to James's psychology to doubt the viability of its most famous concept, the stream of consciousness.[50] McGilvary has another essay in the May *PR* assessing pragmatism in relation to the practical realism of contemporary science.

The attention endures in May, first with a disinterested summary of James's presidential address before the American Philosophical Association at Columbia the preceding December. (Titled "The Energies of Men," the address appears in the January 1907 number of *PR*.) Then, in the May 23rd number, we have an exchange of letters between James and John E. Russell. James requested that they be printed in *JP*, and the editors ran them under the title "Controversy over Truth" in 1907, vol. 4. In June, James Bissett Pratt of Williams College takes up the argument of "Pragmatism's Conception of Truth" to claim that James has now hedged on his former conception of truth. Whereas, Pratt states in "Truth and Its Verification" (6 Jun), he "had supposed it pretty well settled that pragmatism identified the truth of an idea with its successful working, with its verification," now James adds to it a general condition of "verifiability,"[51] so that not only actual verifications can make an idea true, but potential verifications. Where are we, then? Pratt wonders. "This, indeed, sounds like logomachy."[52] Verification is a process, something that "happens" to an idea, but verifiability is a condition, something an idea has or not apart from what happens. Pratt dispenses with James's imputed revision and returns to the accepted pragmatic conception of truth as an "event" that happens. He ponders, if truth is an event, then it must take place within experience, and so it is liable to all the errors to which experience is liable. That's truth?

James took Pratt's essay seriously enough to answer in the August 15th number of *JP* in the essay "Professor Pratt on Truth" and to reproduce his response as chapter 7 in *The Meaning of Truth*. As for his addition of potential verifiability to actual verification in the definition of truth, James chooses a commonsense example. "Where potentiality counts for actuality in so many other cases, one does not see why it may not so count here," he replies. "We call a man benevolent not only for his kind acts paid in, but for his readiness to perform others. . . . Why should we not equally trust the truth of our ideas? We live on credits everywhere!" (*MT*, 91). There is a cognitive reason as well, James observes a page later. Ideas function as shortcuts, and when we substitute them for things for convenience, "we habitually waive direct verification for each one of them" (*MT*, 92). Let's not lose our grasp of ordinary experience, James implies, in the pursuit of epistemological quibbles.

In the meantime, between Pratt's essay and James's reply, James published "A Word More about Truth" (July 18), which became a chapter of *The Meaning of Truth*, and his Harvard colleague Ralph Barton Perry published "A Review of Pragmatism as a Theory of Knowledge" (July 4). Surprisingly, the latter piece may be the more significant in terms of the evolving controversy. Perry locates the source of disagreement in the term "truth," but he generously attributes the heat not to the present parties, but to the term itself. "At the very outset," he writes, "there is danger of confusion because of the ambiguity of such a term as truth. It is of the very nature of knowledge that at the point where it is true it sustains relations of peculiar intimacy with being."[53] Truth moves in two directions, toward a knower and toward reality, and so examinations of it may waver confusingly back and forth between subject and object poles. Pragmatism is particularly vulnerable to misapprehension because it concentrates on that moment when knower and known are united. Though Perry doesn't mention them, the moment matches the precise conversion of confusion into certainty that Dewey highlighted above, and the "marriage" of disturbing new facts to old opinions that James describes in his pragmatism lectures, and the "fixation of belief" that Peirce outlined thirty years before. Hence we should shift the debate toward another locus, Perry advises, not upon the meaning of truth but the "experience of arriving at belief."[54]

In spite of its attempt to shift the debate, Perry's summary evokes a critical reply three months later. Additionally, James has a brief exchange with a philosopher who claimed in the August 15th number of *JP* a pragmatic value for the absolute. In *JP*'s first number of 1908 appears the first part of A. O. Lovejoy's lengthy outline of "The Thirteen Pragmatisms," and James would print "'Truth' Versus 'Truthfulness'" not long after (reprinted as chapter 10, "The Existence of Julius Caesar," in *The Meaning of Truth*).

Reading through these volumes of *JP*, not to mention *Mind, Philosophical Review*, and many others containing briefs on pragmatism, one wonders how James continued to engage so readily with so many critics. How did he sustain his momentum when so many arguments arose to cut it short, and when the demands of lecturing and his other activities increased every year?

The journals were a motivation, a persistent antagonist goading him into new formulations, sharpening his rhetoric, helping him identify weaknesses and deflect silly reactions. This was their functional role in the development of pragmatism. The editorial offices of the periodicals were nodal points in the philosophical marketplace, and through them the pragmatists and their critics waged verbal combat, isolated points of contention, and sorted out the real stakes. To understand the genesis of pragmatism before it reached its first serious expression, however, requires that one study a host of diverse sources: the undergraduate club at Harvard during Peirce's and James's student days, Hume's analysis of induction, the progress of nineteenth-century science, and so on. To understand the evolution of pragmatism in subsequent expressions requires that one pore over the periodicals number by number. In these distant volumes, so different from the glossy new copies of *Pragmatism* and *The Essential Peirce* that get assigned in classes, ideas and arguments were contested sometimes brilliantly and scrupulously, and sometimes casually and obtusely, but always, in some way, revealingly. The content of the essays turned on intellectual points, but other factors seeped into the rhetoric and played a consequential role in James's and Dewey's mature articulation of pragmatism. We witness them in the competition of rival schools of thought, in institutional politics (colleagues in the same department attacking one another, or joining together to attack an outsider), and in editors looking to spark controversy. Without the context of the day's periodicals, the advent of pragmatism looks a bit one-sided, speedy, and uncomplicated, a version serviceable to survey-course narratives of modern thought, but unworthy of the intellectual and institutional struggles Dewey and James underwent to prosecute their thinking. In bringing the periodical exchanges more fully into our remembrance of pragmatism, we appreciate better the dogged labors and convictions necessary for Dewey and James to change the habits of academic thinking. We also impart more accurately one of the most interesting and fruitful half-decades in the history of American philosophy.

NOTES

1. Charles Bakewell, Review of *Pragmatism: A New Name for Some Old Ways of Thinking*, in *Philosophical Review* 16 (1907): 623–34, at 625.

2. John Dewey, "Notes upon Logical Topics," *Journal of Philosophy, Psychology, and Scientific Methods* 1 (1904): 57–62, at 60.

3. J. A. Leighton, "Pragmatism," *Journal of Philosophy, Psychology, and Scientific Methods* 1 (1904): 148–56, at 148, 149.

4. Ibid., p. 150.

5. Ibid., pp. 154–55.

6. John Dewey, "Notes upon Logical Topics: II. The Meanings of the Term Idea," *Journal of Philosophy, Psychology, and Scientific Methods* 1 (1904): 175–78, at 178.

7. A. K. Rogers, "The Standpoint of Instrumental Logic," *Journal of Philosophy, Psychology, and Scientific Methods* 1 (1904): 207–12, at 207.

8. Ibid., p. 208.

9. Ibid., p. 209.

10. Ibid.

11. Ibid., p. 210.

12. Ibid., p. 211.

13. Simon F. MacLennan, "Two Illustrations of the Methodological Value of Psychology in Metaphysic," *Journal of Philosophy, Psychology, and Scientific Methods* 1 (1904): 403–411, at 409

14. Ibid., p. 410.

15. G. A. Tawney, "Utilitarian Epistemology," *Journal of Philosophy, Psychology, and Scientific Methods* 1 (1904): 337–44, at 337.

16. Ibid., p. 339.

17. H. Heath Bawden, "What Is Pragmatism?" *Journal of Philosophy, Psychology, and Scientific Methods* 1 (1904): 421–27, at 421.

18. Ibid., p. 422.

19. Ibid., p. 421.

20. Ibid., p. 426.

21. Ibid., p. 427.

22. Ibid., p. 422.

23. John Dewey, "The Postulate of Immediate Empiricism," *Journal of Philosophy, Psychology, and Scientific Methods* 2 (1905): 393–99, at 393.

24. Dewey, "Notes upon Logical Topics," p. 60.

25. Addison W. Moore, "Pragmatism and Its Critics," *Philosophical Review* 14 (1905): 322–43, at 323.

26. John Dewey, "The Realism of Pragmatism," *Journal of Philosophy, Psychology, and Scientific Methods* 2 (1905): 324–27, at 324.

27. Ibid., p. 326.

28. Frederick J. E. Woodbridge, "Of What Sort Is Cognitive Experience?" *Journal of Philosophy, Psychology, and Scientific Methods* 2 (1905): 573–76, at 573.

29. Ibid., p. 575.

30. John Dewey, "The Knowledge Experience and Its Relationships," *Journal of Phi-

losophy, Psychology, and Scientific Methods 2 (1905): 652–57, at 653.

31. Ibid., p. 654.

32. Ibid., p. 656.

33. Ibid., p. 657.

34. "Cognitive Experience and Its Object," *Journal of Philosophy, Psychology, and Scientific Methods* 2 (1905): 658–63, at 663.

35. John Dewey, "The Knowledge Experience Again," *Journal of Philosophy, Psychology, and Scientific Methods* 2 (1905): 707–11, at 708.

36. Ibid., p. 708.

37. Ibid., p. 711.

38. John E. Russell, "The Pragmatist's Meaning of Truth," *Journal of Philosophy, Psychology, and Scientific Methods* 3 (1906): 599–601, at 599.

39. Walter B. Pitkin, "A Problem of Evidence in Radical Empiricism," *Journal of Philosophy, Psychology, and Scientific Methods* 3 (1906): 645–50, at 650.

40. Ibid., p. 649.

41. R. W. Sellars, "The Nature of Experience," *Journal of Philosophy, Psychology, and Scientific Methods* 4 (1907): 14–18, at 18.

42. Walter Pitkin, "In Reply to Professor James," *Journal of Philosophy, Psychology, and Scientific Methods* 4 (1907): 44–45.

43. W. P. Montague, "Current Misconceptions of Realism," *Journal of Philosophy, Psychology, and Scientific Methods* 4 (1907): 100–105, at 100.

44. Herbert Nichols, "Pragmatism Versus Science," *Journal of Philosophy, Psychology, and Scientific Methods* 4 (1907): 122–31, at 123.

45. Ibid.

46. Ibid., p. 126.

47. Ibid., p. 129.

48. Published respectively as Rogers, "Professor James's Theory of Knowledge," *Philosophical Review* 15 (1906): 577–96, and Bode, Review of "Professor James's Theory of Knowledge," *Journal of Philosophy, Psychology, and Scientific Methods* 4 (1907): 192–94.

49. Rogers, "Professor James's Theory of Knowledge," p. 577.

50. Evander Bradley McGilvary, "The Stream of Consciousness," *Journal of Philosophy, Psychology, and Scientific Methods* 4 (1906): 225–35.

51. James Bissett Pratt, "Truth and Its Verification," *Journal of Philosophy* 4 (1907): 320.

52. Ibid., p. 321.

53. Ralph Barton Perry, "A Review of Pragmatism as a Theory of Knowledge," *Journal of Philosophy, Psychology, and Scientific Methods* 4 (1907): 365–74, at 366.

54. Ibid.

3. The Earth Must Resume Its Rights: A Jamesian Genealogy of Immaturity

Ross Posnock

I.

For Kant, famously, maturity was the short answer to his momentous question of 1784, "what is Enlightenment?" "Have the courage to use your own understanding!" he insists, for only by thinking for himself does man emerge from his "self-incurred immaturity." "It is so easy to be immature," remarks Kant; all one need do is rely on the panoply of authorities that surround one—starting with the books one reads. But maturity requires, says Kant, that one always "look within oneself . . . for the supreme touchstone of truth."[1] More than two centuries after Kant, maturity and immaturity retain currency as terms of debate in characterizing one's relation to Enlightenment. In the lively collection of papers and responses gathered together as *Rorty and His Critics* (2000), accusations of "juvenile arrogance," "infantilism," and other modes of immaturity fly fast and furious. At one point, Rorty, one of the most famous pragmatists, finds a lack of "seriousness, decency, and trustworthiness"—immaturity in short—in the "cultural chauvinism" of "scientism" that he sees animating analytical philosophy's scorn for postmodern relativists. "The religious chauvinism we loathe when it appears in national politics should not be mimicked by a scientistic chauvinism in academic politics"—the belief that analytic philosophy and natural science "have a special relation to 'Truth' (valuing it more, for example, or having more faith in it) that their more 'literary' colleagues lack."[2] Analytic philosophy, Rorty warns, "will never become mature enough to make a contribution to the conversation of the intellectuals" until it gets over its "jejune self-image as 'more scientific,' and therefore more morally virtuous, than non-analytic philosophy." In this clever reversal, Rorty saddles scientistic chauvinists with the "arrogant frivolity" that they decry in postmodernists.

The implied correlation Rorty makes between the immature "chauvinism" of religion and science is elaborated by John McDowell later in the volume. He cites

John Dewey's "narrative of Western culture's coming to maturity," a narrative rooted in Dewey's personal struggle to shake off the sense of sin inculcated in him by his God-fearing mother. "A religion of abasement before the divine Other" demands a posture "infantile in its submissiveness" before a non-human authority. But a humanism that would abolish this "humanly immature conception of the divine" is incomplete if it does not include a "counterpart secular emancipation as well," a liberation from scientism's sanctification of objective truth. As Rorty sees things, this non-human idol replaced God, a "secular analog to a religion of abasement." McDowell describes Rorty's logic: "[P]articipating in the discourse of objectivity merely prolongs a cultural and intellectual infantilism, and persuading people to renounce the vocabulary of objectivity should facilitate the achievement of full human maturity." Replacing objectivity with human solidarity would banish trans-human authority and contribute "to world history that is, perhaps surprisingly, within the power of mere intellectuals."[3] McDowell is unpersuaded that the "vocabulary of objectivity reflects an intellectual and cultural immaturity," and concludes that "the boot is on the other foot. If there is a metaphysical counterpart to infantilism anywhere in this vicinity, it is Rorty's phobia of objectivity. . . . Acknowledging a non-human external authority over our thinking, so far from being a betrayal of our humanity, is merely a condition of growing up."[4] In response, Rorty confesses that he is "chastened" by the reminder that "the charge of infantilism is a two-edged sword."[5]

The persistence of maturity and immaturity to describe and assess the contemporary pragmatist's relation to Enlightenment is notable in itself but takes on new significance when the example of William James is invoked. For he disrupts the binary configuration that organizes these terms into stable meaning—maturity equals achieved self-authorization, immaturity equals a worship of false gods—by denying the exclusively intellectual or "metaphysical" tenor of the terms. Instead, James turns them into modes of being redolent of the visceral "personal flavor" that in *Pragmatism* he will call "temperament" (*P*, 24). Indeed, flight from the visceral, the messily human, is the very meaning of "refinement," a quality at once the signature of temperamental maturity, and its philosophic equivalent, rationalism, and also the marker of genteel social prestige. These modes of maturity—of temper and thought and cultural distinction—comprise three of James's basic targets. Hence Rorty's commitment to "the achievement of full human maturity" sounds closer to the transcendence of what James stresses—vulnerable, plunging creatures who "like fishes swimming in the sea of sense" live immersed in the "water" of "sensible facts" while "bounded above by the superior element"—abstract ideas—"but unable to breathe it pure or penetrate it" (*P*, 64). In James's late thinking, especially *Pragmatism* and *A Pluralistic Universe*, the human and the non-human, adult and child, maturity and immaturity, philosophy and life, are in ferment, no longer mutually exclusive but opened up to their (alleged) opposites. In the spirit of that ferment, the present essay examines a surprising web of connections, looking backward and forward, that James's assault on maturity engenders.

From the start of *Pragmatism* James seizes the low ground: whereas "absolutistic philosophers"—proponents of intellectualism and rationalism—"dwell on so high a level of abstraction that they never even try to come down," preferring the "purity and dignity" of the "sanctuary" of the classroom, the pragmatist takes to the "street," to the "concrete personal experiences" that occur there, and delights in finding it "multitudinous beyond imagination, tangled, muddy, painful and perplexed" (*P*, 16–18). By his next book, *A Pluralistic Universe* (1909), James has in effect burrowed into the street, so strenuously opposing intellectualism (belief in "the divine right of concepts to rule our minds") that he dives into "the middle of experience, in the very thick of its sand and gravel," looking "downward and not up" (*APU*, 125). Getting down and dirty might help us break free of the insulating idealism imbibed from Plato, the assumption that "what a thing really is, is told us by its definition . . . that reality consists of essences, not of appearances." We can shake this habit of "vicious intellectualism" only if we put off "our proud maturity of mind" and become "again as foolish little children in the eyes of reason" (*APU*, 99, 121). Anticipating his audience's unease, James notes: "Philosophy, you will say, doesn't lie flat on its belly in the middle of experience, in the very thick of its sand and gravel. . . . Philosophy is essentially the vision of things from above" (*APU*, 125).

Fittingly, James's effort of realignment takes inspiration from Whitman, still America's most flagrant cultural revolutionary, the poet of "barbarism" (as Santayana called him), who "wallowed in the stream of his own sensibility":[6] "Not only Walt Whitman," notes James, "could write 'who touches this book touches a man.' The books of all the great philosophers are like so many men" (*P*, 24). James here cites Whitman as precedent for his effort to puncture the pretense of pure impersonal reason as the basic motor of philosophy. Given the logic of James's "undignified" insistence on "temperament," the decision to reject rationalism and adopt pragmatism's embrace of a "loose" universe of "mere mess" and "confusion" is always more than a philosophical choice; it is to grasp, as did Whitman, the virtues in loosening up maturity, turning immaturity into a mode of living no longer willing to abide the anal deformities that constitute refinement in late nineteenth-century America (*P*, 11, 62).

James should be seen as continuing the interrogative pressure from those of the previous generation who refuse to take for granted that "full human maturity" is a known quantity. Recall Thoreau, who at the end of Walden remarks: "there is not one of my readers who has yet lived a whole human life."[7] Recall Whitman, who asks in "Song of Myself," "What is a man anyhow? / What am I? What are you?"[8] Like James, they open questions most had assumed settled, as they ponder a quandary about American life that also absorbed their mentor Emerson—the prevalence of socially imposed psychic impoverishment amid material prosperity. They wish, to borrow from the opening of Thoreau's "Walking," to "speak a word for absolute freedom and wildness," "to make an extreme statement . . . for there are enough champions of civilization: the minister and the school committee."[9]

The transvaluation of values that Thoreau so matter-of-factly proposes here tallies with a remarkable moment in *Pragmatism* when James declares that "the centre of gravity of philosophy must . . . alter its place. The earth of things . . . must resume its rights" (*P*, 62). With this axial shift from vertical to horizontal James repositions his philosophic alliances and soon declares allegiance to the earthiest, most radically immature, of ancient philosophers—the Cynic Diogenes, whom James inserts in *Pragmatism* as a model of the "anarchistic" and game "radical pragmatist" (*P*, 124). Whitman too admired Diogenes and took him as a model. The poet, like James and Thoreau, who was himself dubbed "the Yankee Diogenes" in 1854, is drawn to the Cynic's rude questioning of what conventionally counts as human. Diogenes went out in the noonday sun with his lantern ablaze looking for free human beings, evidently regarding Athenians as having betrayed that status by existing as merely passive conformists to social dictates.

James's descendental move down to earth is steeped in suggestiveness for Western intellectual history and merits being read as an icon of unsettlement that belongs to an international cultural genealogy. In attempting, within limited space, to show the unabated vitality of *Pragmatism* for world culture, I will offer only a selection of figures from what surely could be a larger group. The genealogy commences with Diogenes and includes predecessors who were important to James—Montaigne, Whitman, and Thoreau—but then leaps into modernist currents of the 1930s, when self-conscious theorists of immaturity emerged such as the Polish writers Witold Gombrowicz and Bruno Schulz and the Frenchman Georges Bataille. Later American figures of scandal Jackson Pollock and Philip Roth also deftly upend the appropriate. Here I will sketch these affiliations before returning to James and, eventually, to focusing on how his toppling of vertical for horizontal intersects perhaps most tellingly with the later work of his fellow anti-philosopher and admirer Wittgenstein. *Philosophical Investigations* urges a similar shift, and *On Certainty* shows how intellectualism cannot describe "man as an animal . . . a creature in a primitive state," that is, in a state of certainty.

In interwar Poland, the cultural theory and literary practice of immaturity were vigorously enacted, respectively, by Schulz and Gombrowicz. In 1930s Warsaw, Gombrowicz will argue that dirt—"hidden, intimate immaturity"—conditions the genesis of reason, and the interpenetration of seeming opposites is a fascination he shares with his friend and fellow fantasist the great Polish-Jewish writer Schulz. Four years before his death, in a 1938 essay on Gombrowicz, Schulz calls the "sewer drain of immaturity" the "primeval womb" of culture.[10] From the standpoint of culture, Schulz writes, immaturity manifests itself as the "waste products of the cultural processes, a zone of subcultural contents, misshapen and crude, a gigantic scrapheap littering the periphery of culture. Yet this world of sewers and gutters, this monstrous drain . . . forms a basic substance, a compost, a lifegiving pap out of which every value and every culture grows." Gombrowicz's attention in his surrealist novel of 1938, *Ferdydurke*, to this subcultural realm of the immature is, says Schulz, a "profound diagnosis of the very essence of culture."[11] "Until now a man looked at himself . . . exclusively from the official side of things," perceived himself "through the prism of finished and completed form," and acted out "an official plot, mature and acceptable."[12]

The dirt and filth that Schulz and Gombrowicz both wish to make conspicuous—the "lower forms" that mock our pious "homage to more elevated and refined values"—is a project that strikingly complements one that Georges Bataille had been adumbrating just a few years before in Paris.[13] In 1929 and 1930 Bataille began discussing "base materialism" and its most important manifestation, the *informe*—the formless. The formless, writes Bataille, is a "term that serves to bring things down in the world. . . . Whatever it designates has no rights in any sense, and gets itself squashed everywhere, like a spider or an earthworm."[14] Of the imperative derived from base materialism, Bataille says, it is a "question above all of not submitting oneself, and with oneself one's reason, to whatever is more elevated, to whatever can give a borrowed authority to the being that I am, and to the reason that arms this being. This being and its reason can in fact only submit to what is lower, to what can never serve in any case to ape a given authority."[15]

Flamboyant turns to the horizontal are abundant in postwar American culture, but none is more notorious than Jackson Pollock's. Outrage ensued when he began to throw, fling, pour, and drip paint over a canvas not set on the vertical plane of the easel but nailed down to the floor. He crouched over and walked upon it, making his random markings, leaving the canvas unprotected from whatever detritus—buttons, cigarette stubs, coins, glass, and the like—found its way in. The alarm directed at Pollock's kinetic act of horizontal art making, where accident seemed messily to mingle with purpose, was not confined to philistine cries that children with finger paints or dogs or cats could do better. Fellow artists accused Pollock of making his drip paintings by urinating on the grounded canvas. Influenced by the automatic writing favored by the Surrealists in their effort to release the uncensored impulses of the unconscious, Pollock "in the name of the unconscious wished to strike against form"—aligned, by gestalt psychology, with the "viewer's upright body"—and "thus against the [vertical] axis of the human body. But equally in the name of the unconscious, Pollock needed to strike against culture," as Rosalind Krauss remarks. Pollock undermined the two together by attacking the "verticality of the axis the body shares with culture."[16] In refusing the vertical, Pollock refused the very move, according to Freud, that reorients man "away from the animal senses of sniffing and pawing," away from the ground where touching and seeing are linked, and toward the purified, distanced activities of the erect being—sublimation and domination—supervised by the reign of the visual and the optical, "the look."[17]

A successor to Pollock's postwar body art was Roth's late-sixties performance art, the torrential monologue *Portnoy's Complaint,* that epochal and reviled eruption of the "sewer drain of immaturity, a region of disgrace and shame" (Schulz) that would leave an indelible human stain upon the official plot of sublimation that organizes bourgeois American family life, especially its Jewish version. Setting on their heads idealizing myths of the Jew as pure mind and moral virtue, Roth has Portnoy by the end of his complaint throw in the towel and go to the dogs: "Maybe the wisest solution for me is to live on all fours! . . . and leave the rightings of wrongs and the fathering of families to the upright creatures!"[18] Three decades later Mickey Sabbath of *Sabbath's Theater,* that unregenerate man of filth, a failed puppeteer in his late sixties whose insatiable sexual appetite remains undiminished, becomes Roth's apotheosis of lowness, of abandonment to creaturely life. Sabbath is a Whitmanic figure (like the poet he wends his way along the Jersey shore) and a descendant of Diogenes (he urinates and masturbates in public) who pushes at the bounds of "normal" definitions of the human. "It's never been easy to say what you really are, Mickey," says an old friend. "'Oh, failure will do.' 'But at what?' 'Failure at failing, for one.' 'You always fought being a human being, right from the beginning,' replies his friend. 'To the contrary,' said Sabbath. 'To being a human being I've always said, Let it come.'"[19] Later feeling "uncontrollable tenderness for his own shit-filled life," Mickey remarks to himself: "say what you will about me, it's been a real human life!"[20] As often in Roth, what counts as human being and human life remain open questions, and Sabbath insists on keeping them open, as he does everything else.

The protagonist of *Sabbath's Theater* might have appealed to James. After all, Sabbath's downward spiral moves in the direction James recommends to relieve bourgeois spiritual desiccation (due to being "stuffed with abstract conceptions, and glib with verbalities and verbosities"). In "On a Certain Blindness" (1899), he urged that we "descend to a more profound and primitive level" where "seeing, smelling, tasting, sleeping, and daring and doing with one's body, grows and grows" (*TT*, 146). In *Pragmatism*, James's liberation from the rationalist's "doctrinaire and authoritative . . . 'must be'" inspires a passion for shoving the "real world of sweat and dirt" under the upturned noses of those of "rationalistic temper" (*P*, 40). From the opening of *Pragmatism*, James's calculated strategy and psychic need is to *épater le bourgeois,* particularly those who practice Philosophy with a capital P.

As we saw at the start, Rorty's more recent dissent from Philosophy has its own style of biting insouciance, dismissing, for example, analytical philosophy's attachment to objectivity. But his mockery is confined to achieving intellectual maturity, whereas James flaunts a self-abasing immaturity as the "personal flavor" of his pragmatist "temperament" (*P*, 24). The difference is worth probing because it is symptomatic of Rorty's distaste for the Jamesian sense of experience as, potentially, an ambush or undergoing, a suffering, that can be prior to or escape language. What some (Martin Jay, F. R. Ankersmit) have called Rorty's "linguistic transcendentalism" (the belief that language goes all the way down and that human beings are simply the vocabularies they possess) has no place for preverbal experience of the world (save for pain), ironically making Rorty's pragmatism vulnerable to the charge of intellectualism—the proposition that all experience is a mode of knowing.[21] This intellectualist assumption, says Dewey, "goes contrary to the facts of what is primarily experienced. For things are objects to be treated, used, acted upon and with, enjoyed and endured, even more than things to be known. They are things had before they are things cognized."[22] For Wittgenstein, certainty of belief is had before cognized, and he proves more rigorous than James in grasping this, thus edging him out for the title: "the greatest anti-intellectual intellectual of the twentieth-century."[23]

To regard experience as encompassing the noncognitive, prominent in both Dewey and James, is to insist on what most philosophers repress by imposing an "unreasonable ideal of reasonableness," to borrow James Conant's phrase.[24] He is glossing some ideas of Hilary Putnam, who, not coincidentally, admires James's stress on temperament and the cultivation of sensibility as a challenge to the "prevailing philosophical ideal of rationality" that "distrusts any form of conviction that is not based on argument."[25] For Putnam, writing in a Jamesian spirit, "reasoning in the full sense of the word involves not just our logical faculties, in the narrow sense, but our full capacity to imagine and feel, in short, our full sensibility."[26] Putnam is also in tune with Stanley Cavell's longstanding project to put "the human animal" back into philosophy.[27] Wittgenstein's *Philosophical Investigations* accomplishes this goal, says Cavell, for it shows us how to live with skepticism's contempt for merely human finitude. In words that might have been uttered by James, Cavell says: "[T]here is inherent in philosophy a certain drive to the inhuman, to a certain inhuman idea of intellectuality, or of completion, or of the systematic"[28]

James seeks to arrest this drive by disturbing the ossified assumptions and habits congealed in the concept of maturity—as it pertains to adulthood or to Philosophy.

Since the second paragraph of *Pragmatism* (where we are told that "the philosophy which is so important in each of us is not a technical matter; it is our more or less dumb sense of what life honestly and deeply means . . . our individual way of just seeing and feeling the total push and pressure of the cosmos"), James has been bent on decomposing the rationalist definition by in effect practicing the critique of identity logic that he will explicitly preach in *A Pluralistic Universe*—the logic that compels us "when we conceptualize" to "cut out and fix, and exclude everything but what we have fixed" (*P*, 9; *APU*, 113). The excluded, what James also calls the "remainder, "the more," possess a density instantiated in the "tangled" and "muddy," qualities that James sponsors as one way to resist a main current in Philosophy—the idealist and rationalist tradition (Plato and Descartes, for instance), whose abstractions, dualisms, and intellectualism drain human experience of color and vitality.[29]

James's late work attempts a massive recovery of experience as synonymous with live possibility and risk, with recalcitrant excess or overflow that eludes efforts to capture it in concepts and language. The urge to capture the unassimilable is what drives the reigning academic orthodoxies of intellectualism and rationalism with their closed systems grounded in belief in a fixed and finished universe. In defiant contrast, James's universe is in process, comprised solely of "finite experience" and "as such is homeless." With pride he declares: "Such a world would not be respectable philosophically. It is a . . . dog without a collar, in the eyes of most professors," and to preside over it he invokes the audaciously immature

Diogenes the Cynic (the latter word derives from *kunikos,* meaning dog-like, and describes Diogenes' immunity to embarrassment). Of the "radical pragmatist," James says: "[I]f he had to live in a tub like Diogenes he wouldn't mind at all if the hoops were loose and the staves let in the sun" (*P,* 124).

This identification, though made in passing and not repeated, is a pregnant passage in *Pragmatism,* one that "overflows its own definition," to borrow what James says of "every state of consciousness, concretely taken" (*APU,* 129). By overflow I want to suggest that James here speaks perhaps more than he intends. Or, rather, he is at once confessing and deflecting (by domesticating) a scandalous kinship that emits a brief glimpse of the depth of his cultural iconoclasm and alienation.[30] Living in a tub may have been the best-known but the least shocking thing for which Diogenes was infamous. Notorious in Athens as a perpetual wanderer and mocker of the respectable, who masturbated, urinated, and defecated in public, Diogenes let his body, rather than any doctrine, enact his cultural critique; he left no writing behind, and all we have are anecdotes. This triumph over abstraction would have deep appeal to James, who at one point in *A Pluralistic Universe* reaches the end of his patience with concepts and turns to his audience: "I am tiring myself and you, I know, by vainly seeking to describe by concepts and words what I say at the same time exceeds either conceptualization or verbalization. As long as one continues talking, intellectualism remains in undisturbed possession of the field. The return to life can't come about by talking. It is an act; to make you return to life, I must set an example for your imitation. . . . I say no more: I must leave life to teach the lesson" (*APU,* 131–32). Later, I will remark a certain pathos and impasse here.

But there is also a liberatory note. For James (who, alas, was being metaphorical, for he was only partly through his lecture) in effect imagines leaving capital-P Philosophy to join hands with the Ancients, for whom philosophy was above all a spiritual exercise, a way of life. As a "mode of existing-in-the-world," philosophy sought, says Pierre Hadot, "wisdom itself. For real wisdom does not merely cause us to know: it makes us 'be' in a different way."[31] As Hadot has noted, "in antiquity one historian wondered whether Cynicism could be called a philosophical school—whether it mightn't be instead, only a way of life." Cynic philosophy, remarks Hadot, "was exclusively a choice of life: it was the choice of freedom—complete independence from useless needs—and the refusal of luxury and vanity." They chose a way of life because they "believed that the state of nature, as seen in the behavior of animals or children, was superior to the conventions of civilization. Diogenes threw away his bowl and his cup when he saw children do without such utensils" and felt affirmed when he "saw a mouse eat a few crumbs in the dark."[32] He shocked Athenians out of their complacencies by making his life embody freedom as found in obedience to nature rather than to society. With all his worldly possessions kept in a knapsack, Diogenes practiced an ascetic refusal of comfort and routine, content to call himself a citizen of the world. Shameless and self-reliant, he presides over a "tramp and vagrant world," to borrow James's words, a supreme emblem of the philosopher as unassimilable. Given the crucial status of this notion in James's late thought, it may be only small exaggeration to say that Diogenes presides over it as a tutelary deity, present by name at a single telling point but casting a larger influence.

In his late works, *Pragmatism* and *A Pluralistic Universe*, James instigates a return of the repressed, subjecting the covering concepts of Philosopher and Philosophy to the refractory indignities of experience, exposing the history of Philosophy as "the clash of human temperaments with their cravings" (an emphasis "undignified" to many of his colleagues), immersing immaculate rationalist views of a monistic Universe in the mess of animal immediacy prior to language (our "dumb sense" of "just seeing and feeling"); in sum, he insists on reality's "waywardness" that unravels any pretension to the aloofness of absolute authority (*MT*, 47). James's reinstatement of dynamism, incorrigibility, and the "personal flavor" of subjective bias reflects pragmatism's distrust of whatever is "august and exalted above facts" and preference for the telluric. He evokes this in the dramatic image that ends his third lecture: pragmatism requires rotating the axis of philosophy from the vertical to horizontal, as it "shifts the emphasis" from exalted first principles, abstractions such as God and Free Will. This shift means that "the centre of gravity of philosophy must therefore alter its place. The earth of things, long thrown into shadow by the glories of the upper ether, must resume its rights. . . . It will be an alteration in the 'seat of authority' that reminds one almost of the protestant reformation" (*P*, 62).

James's axial shift downward crystallizes his campaign against "refinement" ("what characterizes our intellectualist philosophies" in their craving for a "refined object of contemplation") that he has been conducting since the opening lecture. Upending verticality and stripping homo erectus of the privileged stance of "admiring contemplation" (*P*, 18, 63), James shows his willingness to descend into "the dust of our human trials" (*P*, 40). This bespeaks an insouciance about his own dignity that is at odds with his decorous idealizing of pragmatism at the end of the second lecture as a "completely genial" woman without prejudice (*P*, 44). This graceful figure of "democratic" flexibility and resourcefulness brokers a "solution" to the conflict between (rationalist) principles and (empiricist) facts—namely pragmatism's pluralism that combines "scientific loyalty to facts" with respect for religious spontaneity (*P*, 17).

To persuade readers of the well-balanced, sensible efficacy of pragmatism as an efficient mediating instrument between the tough and the tender-minded is of course the burden of James's book. But something else leaks out (here and in *A Pluralistic Universe*): the "revelation of how intensely odd the personal flavor of some fellow creature is" (*P*, 24), a revelation that in this case traffics not with the balanced and graceful but with the dirt. James's affinity for the low is one way he scrambles conventional notions of authority: depriving it of anchorage, he redescribes it as the flexibility to flourish in a world where "nothing outside of the flux" affords security (*P*, 125). In this "homeless" and "loose universe," masterful maturity, seemingly second nature of the "doctrinaire and authoritative" rationalist, struggles to gets its footing only to step into a void, its usually confident "'must be'" sounding increasingly desperate. Instead of the rationalist's flailings, James commends the relaxed "happy-go-lucky" stance of the pragmatist as a tramping Diogenes. The Cynic in effect is invited to occupy the now ungrounded "'seat of authority'" in a world "adrift in space," unsupported by "Reality with the big R" (the lodestar of all rationalists).

To rationalists, according to James, his reinstatement of unredeemed, obdurate earth and its earthiness will seem "a mere mess of anarchy and confusion . . . so much sheer trash, philosophically" (*P*, 62). For rationalists have elevated Philosophy, hermetically sealing it in a system and in the pristine shelter of the classroom, taught by professors whose thought and bearing exude the complacency of genteel refinement. Against this scene of smugness, and to expose the shallow optimism of rationalist philosophies, James juxtaposes newspaper accounts (culled from anarchist Morrison Swift's pamphlets) of wretched, suicide-inciting poverty in the American Midwest. Here the "excluded" remainder acquires socioeconomic reality. James was not (emotionally) exempt from the class discrepancies he is opening up here. The beneficiary, with his four siblings, of a large family fortune made by his Irish immigrant grandfather, James nevertheless felt out of place in relation to Harvard and its philosophy department. He was a "sort of Irishman among the Brahmins," as his sardonic former colleague Santayana remarked in a famous portrait of James's professorial unease. He was adored, but "even his pupils felt some doubts about the profundity of one who was so very natural." They "laughed at his erratic views and undisguised limitations. . . . The precise theologians and panoplied idealists . . . shook their heads. What sound philosophy, said they to themselves, could be expected from an irresponsible doctor, who was not even a college graduate, a crude empiricist, and vivisector of frogs? . . . [T]hey could not quite swallow a private gentleman who dabbled in hypnotism, frequented mediums, didn't talk like a book, and didn't write like a book, except like one of his own."[33] Philosophy to James, says Santayana, was a "maze," and he was looking for "a way out."[34]

Santayana is one of the few (John Jay Chapman another) to catch the note of despair in James's academic life. Philosophy was not a "consolation and a sanctuary" to him, and "in the presence of theories of any sort" he was "as a child lives among grown-up people; what a relief to turn from those stolid giants . . . to another real child or a nice animal!"[35] When set against the outrageous antics of the anti-theorist Diogenes, who, as noted above, also took children and animals as inspiring models of behavior, the James who emerges in Santayana's affectionate condescension is a diminished thing, a late Victorian Cynic in uneasy proximity to poignant puerility and defeat. Nevertheless, within the constraints of his mugwump world, James insisted on his intellectual and personal idiosyncrasy, no small achievement, as John Stuart Mill, to whom *Pragmatism* is dedicated, would have recognized. "That so few now dare to be eccentric marks the chief danger of the time," avers Mill in *On Liberty* (1869). It is crucial "to give the freest scope possible to uncustomary things."[36]

If eccentric by Brahmin standards, James was also of course a man of the Enlightenment, a scientist who insisted that pragmatism be on intimate terms with facts. At the same time, his relish of philosophic "anarchy" and his temperamental distaste for the Brahmin class code of "refinement" registers his romantic dissent. For Enlightenment or Cartesian rationalism narrowly construes reason as abstraction, severs body from mind, and conceives childhood as something only to be overcome. These deadly attenuations taboo impulse and risk while flattening out experience on a static dualistic grid that reduces man to spectator—a purified, solitary subject—a deformation that Dewey will later deplore. In assessing its tangled relation to Enlightenment, the philosopher Robert Brandom calls pragmatism a "second enlightenment" that also "echoes themes introduced and pursued by earlier romantic critics of the first enlightenment." But he warns that pragmatism "is not a kind of romanticism. Though the two movements of thought share antipathy to Enlightenment intellectualism, pragmatism "does not recoil into the rejection of reason, into the privileging of feeling over thought, intuition over experience, or of art over science." The pragmatists "thought of themselves as continuing the Enlightenment philosophical tradition of Descartes, Locke, Hume and Kant—all of whom thought that being a philosopher meant being a philosopher of science." While claiming that "romanticism had almost no direct influence on American pragmatism," Brandom also grants that Emerson is a "conduit for idiosyncratically filtered and transfigured romantic ideas" that "clearly affected" the thought of James and others "in complex ways."[37] James's attraction to the health of immaturity and eccentricity is one American romantic, specifically Emersonian, inheritance and one seldom discussed.

Perhaps one reason for the neglect is that Emerson has been "mummified as a late-Victorian gray eminence," the soul of New England gentility.[38] But Emerson in fact has a belligerence that emerges in his praise of whim and rudeness—"let us affront and reprimand the smooth mediocrity and squalid contentment of the times," he avers. "This is to be done in our smooth times by speaking the truth. Check this lying hospitality and lying affection. Live no longer to the expectation of those deceived and deceiving people with whom we converse."[39] This pugnacity informs the spirit of James's own satirical jabs in *Pragmatism*. The Greeks called such frank talk and blunt truth-telling *parrhesia*, and the Cynics, especially Diogenes, were notorious for it.[40] In mid-nineteenth-century America, two of Emerson's disciples surpass his impatience with bourgeois politeness, and both are legatees of different aspects of the ancient Cynic. Whitman reanimates Diogenes' tramping, sexually wayward impulses. In lines redolent of the Cynical spirit, the poet, a professed admirer of Diogenes, declares: "Let faces and theories be turned inside out! Let meanings be freely criminal, as well as results! . . . Let nothing remain upon the earth except the ashes of teachers, artists, moralists, lawyers and learned and polite persons!" "Let none but infidels be countenanced."[41] Thoreau embodies Diogenes' ascetic discipline; that later apostle of minimalism, both material and ontological, declared in the lecture "Misspent Lives": "Don't be afraid to have nothing. Don't hesitate to be a nobody." Contemporary newspaper accounts of that talk dubbed Thoreau the "Yankee Diogenes" and a "sort of Diogenes, to whom everything but nature appears to be just what it should not be."[42]

As a fertile homegrown resistance to the renunciations required by adulthood, immaturity began to emerge as such in the American renaissance of the mid-nineteenth century as part of Romanticism's celebration of the child and of spontaneity. This open, unguarded sensibility, earlier discounted by Enlightenment scientism and rationalism, is in touch with Renaissance humanism, witness Emerson's esteem for Montaigne. A contemporary of Rabelais, Montaigne describes his essays as "some excrements of an aged mind, now hard, now loose, and always undigested."[43] Unconstrained by canons of respectability, Montaigne, like Diogenes, offers bodily processes as a model of the volatility of thinking that makes the prospect of definitive knowledge antithetical to human being. "Human ignorance" is "the most certain fact."[44] Body and mind are so fused in Montaigne's work that no book, Emerson says of *The Essays*, seems "less written": "Cut these words, and they would bleed; they are vascular and alive."[45]

Fifty years after Montaigne and his bawdy essaying of things, "without a plan and without a promise,"[46] the Cartesian "quest for certainty," to recall Dewey's famous phrase, supplanted humanism. Cartesianism wiped the slate clean, emphasizing decontextualized abstraction to establish permanent, timeless truths of natural science and Philosophy; thus the operations of reason were purified of the swarm of particulars that comprise our embeddedness in nature. One consequence was that "skeptical acceptance of ambiguity and a readiness to live with uncertainty" were no longer viable intellectual options.[47] Human maturity in effect was redefined as the capacity for (abstract) rational thought and action. Left behind was Montaigne's modest approach to philosophy:

> Of the opinions of philosophy I most gladly embrace those that are most solid, that is to say, most human and most our own: my opinions, in conformity with my conduct, are low and humble. Philosophy is very childish, to my mind, when she gets up on her hind legs and preaches to us that it is a barbarous alliance to marry the divine with the earthly, the reasonable with the unreasonable, the severe with the indulgent, the honorable with the dishonorable; that sensual pleasure is a brutish thing unworthy of being enjoyed by the wise man.[48]

Here Montaigne anticipates later thinking by implicitly disrupting conventional meanings of maturity and immaturity, refusing to simplify them as mere opposites. That is, in Montaigne's act of transvaluation, philosophy is "childish" precisely when it acts as the mature adult and rises on its hind legs to establish a presumptive superiority to what is below. The view from above, which imagines it perceives firm, discrete boundaries (earthly and divine, body and mind), turns out to be childish because it keeps itself aloof from experience, busy preaching instead of plunging into excess and flux, where purity dissolves and alleged opposites mix. Unchildish philosophy, actual maturity, from Montaigne's perspective, embraces what seems childish—being on all fours.

William James would have concurred. Called a philosophic descendant of the Frenchman, James in effect renews Montaigne's project in the late nineteenth century when he announces that philosophy's "centre of gravity" must shift downward. But more immediately at hand for James than Montaigne's descendental perspective is Whitman's, for the poet had accomplished his own gravitational shift in 1855, occupying the horizontal in the opening lines of "Song of Myself": "I loafe and invite my soul, / I lean and loafe at my ease observing a spear of summer grass." And soon a child approaches to ask, "What is the grass? Fetching it to me with full hands, / How could I answer the child? I do not know anymore than he."[49] Leaning and loafing down on the ground, refusing upright authority, Whitman has altered poetry's center of gravity by abolishing the poet's role of sovereign knower and teacher for the stance of perpetual learner. His horizontality is a democratic dispersion of authority that makes him at one with the questioning child.[50]

For Whitman, the bodily posture of leaning and loafing had a philosophical pedigree. In 1840 the poet had declared: "of all human beings, none equals your genuine" loafer, by which he meant not just the casually lazy but a "calm, steady, philosophick [sic] son of indolence," and salutes Diogenes: "he lived in a tub, and demeaned himself like a true child of the great loafer family."[51] Diogenes' most notorious moment of loafing occurred as he was lazily sunning himself on his back when the young Alexander of Macedonia (the future Alexander the Great), intrigued by Diogenes' fame, came to ask the philosopher what wish he might grant him. "Stop blocking my sun!" was Diogenes' reply. This is "perhaps the most well known philosophical anecdote from Greek antiquity, and not without justice," notes Peter Sloterdijk, whose *Critique of Cynical Reason* marks the postmodern appropriation of Diogenes as an apostle of "physiognomic thought" or "somatic anarchism."[52] Regarding Diogenes' impudent response, Sloterdijk remarks: "It demonstrates in one stroke what antiquity understands by philosophical wisdom—not so much a theoretical knowledge but rather an unerring sovereign spirit. . . . [T]he wise man . . . turns his back on the subjective principle of power, ambition, and the urge to be recognized. He is the first one who is uninhibited enough to say the truth to the prince. Diogenes' answer negates not only the desire for power, but the power of desire as such."[53]

Diogenes' rude riposte to Alexander no doubt delighted William James, not least because it speaks directly to what in *The Varieties of Religious Experience* he calls "the value of saintliness." He associates the freedom from desire and power with a saintly virtue that he seeks to "rehabilitate" as a live moral option in contemporary life. Asceticism, James urges, should become synonymous with the "strenuous life" reconceived as an embrace of poverty rather than "wealth-getting." "We have grown literally afraid to be poor. We despise anyone who elects to be poor in order to simplify and save his inner life. . . . We have lost the power even of imagining what the ancient idealization of poverty could have meant," he says, and then goes on to enumerate its meanings as if he is describing Diogenes: "the liberation from material attachments, the unbribed soul, the manlier indifference, the paying our way by what we are or do and not by what we have, the right to fling away our life at any moment irresponsibly" (*VRE*, 289, 293).

One enthusiastic reader of *Varieties* seemed to take James's words to heart, for in 1919 he disinherited himself from his share of a large family fortune and for the rest of his life lived as an ascetic. In 1912 Ludwig Wittgenstein had written to Bertrand Russell about *Varieties*: "[T]his book does me a lot of good. I don't mean to say that I will be a saint soon, but I am not sure that it does not improve me a little in a way in which I would like to improve very much."[54] Saintliness fascinated Wittgenstein, and on at least one occasion he admitted that he sought moral perfection.[55] He was devoted to rigorous self-examination and confession, and at times in his life he thought of joining a monastery and becoming a monk. Unsparing personal self-scrutiny—what he called "the terribly hard work" of dismantling "the edifice of your pride"—is required for both personal and philosophical honesty: "if anyone is unwilling to descend into himself, because this is too painful, he will remain superficial in his writing."[56]

One reason he may have been so taken with *The Varieties of Religious Experience* is the intimacy and compassion of James's portrait of "the sick soul," an empathy that derives from his own torment, decades earlier, from morbid indifference. This experience left James with an acute sense of the precariousness of any absolute claim to health: "[T]he sanest and best of us are of one clay with lunatic and prison inmates"; and later he remarks that "the normal process of life contains moments as bad as any of those which insane melancholy is filled with" (*VRE*, 46, 136). What makes William James a good philosopher, Wittgenstein remarked to a friend, is that "he was a real human being,"[57] as if acknowledging the efficacy of James's descent into self, and as if endorsing James's belief that each philosopher reveals his own "personal flavor."[58] Particularly after the First World War (in which he served at the front) and until his death in 1951, Wittgenstein, like James, was on uneasy, indeed tormented, terms with his professional vocation, particularly the prestige of scientism with its fetish of abstraction and theory that evacuates the ordinary.[59] In contrast, he insisted on connecting philosophy and life. And the entanglement was scarred by history, for twentieth-century life was a century of slaughter. In the preface to *Philosophical Investigations* (published posthumously) he glumly remarks: "It is not impossible that it should fall to the lot of this work, in its poverty and in the darkness of the time, to bring light into one brain or another—but, of course it is unlikely."[60] Out of historical bleakness and Wittgenstein's own deliberate impoverishment of capital-P Philosophy, a glint of optimism remained as a reminder of why philosophize at all: "[W]hat is the good of philosophy if it does not make me a better human being?"[61]

To make a "better human being" requires philosophy to be better. To start, one must "imperturbably bear witness to the spirit" of poverty, to borrow James's words (*VRE*, 293), a fidelity that requires dismantling not only personal but philosophic pride. Philosophic pretensions, often the result of aping positivist science, need to be stripped away; to replace confusion with clarity is to banish the "craving for generality" that animates the Platonic and Cartesian grand search for epistemological foundations. This search, in turn, produces doctrine and theories—the whole pursuit a testimony to what Wittgenstein calls our "subliming" or elevating "of logic."[62] He pointedly poses to himself the question: "In what sense is logic something sublime?" We assume that logic by its nature possesses a "peculiar depth. . . . Logic, lay it seemed, at the bottom of all the sciences. For logical investigation explores the nature of all things. It seeks to see to the bottom of things and is not meant to concern itself whether what actually happens is this or that.—It takes its rise, not from an interest in the facts of nature . . . but from an urge to understand the basis, or essence, of everything empirical."[63] The desire such a depth model produces is the desire to "penetrate phenomena . . . something that lies beneath the surface."[64] But in fact we are "in pursuit of chimeras"; we have surrounded thought with a "halo" of logic that is of "purest crystal," for it is imagined to exist as the "a priori order of the world. . . . [I]t is prior to all experience, must run through all experience; no empirical cloudiness or uncertainty can be allowed to affect it."[65]

True to his devotion to poverty, Wittgenstein is determined to deny philosophy its halo of purity, its nimbus of Olympian scientific objectivity.[66] Not only does this determination to deflate recall James's relation to rationalism, but Wittgenstein's image announcing his reorienting of philosophy is strikingly Jamesian. "The preconceived idea of crystalline purity can only be removed by turning our whole examination around. (One might say: the axis of reference of our examination must be rotated, but about the fixed point of our real need.)"[67] The rotation insists on recovering the horizontal surface of the earth. Only then will we be free of our (misguided) assumptions that logic involves the extraction of essences from below or is hidden beneath the empirical or phenomenal. In rotating our axis to the horizontal we "attend the logic of language as that is manifest in the empirical contexts within which our life with words is lived." In contrast, to remain on a vertical axis is to "sublime" or to "purify" our logic, which suggests another sense of refinement, as in a chemical process of extraction that, says Stephen Mulhall, distills "crystalline" form from the messiness of everyday experience.[68]

To paraphrase James, Wittgenstein's axial shift announces that the surface of the earth must resume its rights. Devotion to logic's alleged "crystalline purity" has led us astray, led us, in Wittgenstein's image, "on to slippery ice where there is no friction and so in a certain sense the conditions are ideal, but also, just because of that, we are unable to walk. We want to walk: so we need friction. Back to the rough ground!"[69] With this famous directive (which recalls the opening pages of "Experience" by Emerson, an author Wittgenstein read, with its imagery of "slippery sliding surfaces" and "no rough rasping friction"),[70] Wittgenstein simply returns to what is "already in plain view"—"nothing out of the ordinary is involved"—but precisely what has been occluded by the subliming of logic with its essentialist reflex of unearthing the hidden.[71] Our energy will be devoted to describing our everyday use of language by reminding us of our taken-for-granted presuppositions—rules, conventions, norms, all comprising what he calls the grammar that governs a "language game"—rather than attempting to grasp "incomparable essence": "when philosophers use a word . . . and try to grasp the essence of the thing, one must always ask oneself: is the word ever actually used in this way in the language-game which is its original home?—What we do is bring words back from their metaphysical to their everyday use."[72] "And we may not advance any kind of theory. There must not be anything hypothetical in our considerations. We must do away with all explanation, and description alone must take its place."[73] What we describe are "forms of life" (or language games) made of the transpersonal but humanly fashioned integuments by which cultural practices cohere and together comprise a community's "inherited background" against which we make sense of our experience.

Explanations traffic in reasons and reasons demand giving grounds, in penetrating into them; but Wittgenstein's axial shift leaves grounds intact, their surfaces preserved as what we walk on; philosophy, now confined to description, "leaves everything as it is."[74] "Since everything lies open to view, there is nothing to explain. For what is hidden . . . is of no interest to us."[75] Clarity, in Wittgenstein's understanding, makes philosophical problems "completely disappear"; and this discovery that he is able to "stop doing philosophy" when he wants furnishes philosophy with "peace, so that it is no longer tormented by questions which bring itself in question."[76]

In attaining peace, what Wittgenstein calls the therapeutic motive of his work, he leaves unsaid the specific philosophical problems now rendered null and void. The dominant problem would be that prime product of intellectualism— the doubt of the skeptic, doubt fed by hunger for certainty, beyond what humans can provide, of the external world or other minds. The skeptic, if obsessed, is insatiable for reasons, for he is infected with *Grubelsucht*, the wonder sickness or questioning mania that William James discusses in *The Principles of Psychology*. It "consists in the inability to rest in any conception, and the need of having it confirmed and explained. 'Why do I stand here where I stand?' 'Why is a glass a glass, a chair a chair?'" (*PP*, II, 914).[77] In *The Meaning of Truth*, written to answer critics of *Pragmatism*, James describes skepticism as immune to logical refutation: "General skepticism is the live mental attitude of refusing to conclude. It is a permanent torpor of the will" (*MT*, 107).

As a young man James himself suffered the torpor of a collapsed will (acedia), and his pragmatism implicitly can be (and has been) understood therapeutically, as his attempt at an antidote to skepticism's threat to disable the springs of action. Like Wittgenstein, he too seeks philosophic and spiritual "peace." The pragmatic method (which asks what "practical difference" would it make to hold one notion as opposed to another) "is primarily a method of settling metaphysical disputes that otherwise might be interminable" (*P*, 28).[78] Hence his stress that "true thoughts mean everywhere invaluable instruments of action" and that "unverified truths" are "overwhelmingly" the majority of the truths we live by ("just as we here assume Japan to exist without ever having been there, because it works to do so," so we assume the object on the wall is a clock—"altho no one of us has seen the hidden works that make it one"—and "use it as a clock") (*P*, 97, 99). "Our experience is all shot through with regularities" (*P*, 99) and thus is supple enough to accommodate "new truth" not as disruption but as a "smoother-over of transitions," marrying "old opinion to new fact" (*P*, 35). In James's famous words, "truth lives, in fact, for the most part on a credit system. Our thoughts and beliefs 'pass,' so long as nothing challenges them, just as bank-notes pass so long as nobody refuses them. But this all points to face-to-face verifications somewhere, without which the fabric of truth collapses like a financial system with no cash-basis whatever" (*P*, 100).

James's anxious last claim is that hard currency ("cash-basis") ultimately must ground verification (a worry that weirdly refracts the gold and silver currency debates of the late nineteenth century, with their demand that the proliferation of paper be backed by metal) and exposes the empirical and positivist residue in James's pragmatist conception of truth. Empirical verifications function as the unspoken "posts of the whole superstructure" (*P*, 100); whereas for Wittgenstein certainty has no grounding but instinct, "something animal."[79] Yet James's emphasis that, practically speaking, unverified belief works has general affinities with Wittgenstein's answer to the skeptic's question of how to live in the face of doubt. That affinity is based on a shared premise: to bring "words back from their metaphysical to their everyday use."[80] Far from expressing any direct sense of kinship with pragmatism, "Wittgenstein does not show anywhere a positive attitude toward" it.[81] Yet his distaste, as he gnomically suggests, is directed at the pragmatist *Weltanschauung*—presumably its trust in science and progress—about which Wittgenstein feels "thwarted"; at the very same time he admits: "I am trying to say something that sounds like pragmatism."[82]

Wittgenstein shuts down *Grubelsucht* in a pragmatist-sounding way: "Why do I not satisfy myself that I have two feet when I want to get up from a chair? There is no why. I simply don't. This is how I act."[83] The "why" of explanation doesn't arise under normal conditions because our lives are already embedded in the web of conventions, the "inherited background"[84] we have imbibed through the "seamless, unhesitating assimilation of the resources" of one's mother tongue, including the taken-for-granted following of its rules and practices that comprise a "language game."[85] Indeed, "absence of doubt belongs to the essence of the language-game" which is threatened with dissolution by the question "How do I know."[86] The burden of Wittgenstein's final work, the posthumously published *On Certainty*, is to understand certainty as a doing not a knowing, more a matter of body than mind, of animal instinct than ratiocination, of horizontal than vertical.

"'Knowledge' and 'certainty' belong to two different categories"; the ungrounded ground called certainty is what stands fast for us without evidence, without explanation.[87] *On Certainty* shows how minimal is mental activity—knowledge and interpretation—and how crucial is pre-reflective behavior—obeying, following, absorbing—in the way a child learns or, more precisely, is initiated into, the rules of the relevant language-games. A child first learns to react "and in so reacting it doesn't so far know anything. Knowing only begins at a later level." Children "do not learn that books exist, that armchairs exist, etc. etc.,—they learn to fetch books, sit in armchairs, etc."[88] "We teach a child 'that is your hand,' not 'that is perhaps [or 'probably'] your hand.' That is how a child learns the innumerable language-games that are concerned with his hand. An investigation or question, 'whether this is really a hand' never occurs to him."[89] So the skeptic has not understood the rules of the language-game, that doubting is not infinite but must come to an end.

Giving grounds comes to an end, says Wittgenstein, but not when one receives an epiphanic bolt of knowledge; instead, there comes a point when our explanations are superfluous and give way to "our acting, which lies at the bottom of the language-game."[90] And this acting, because embedded in the habit of unexamined certainty, has "something animal" about it: it "lies beyond being justified or unjustified."[91] This animal quality had been implied in *Philosophical Investigations:* "When I obey a rule, I do not choose. I obey the rule blindly." And also in his serene response to the skeptic's doubt—"'But if you are certain, isn't it that you are shutting your eyes in face of doubt?'" "They are shut."[92]

This response—"they are shut"—is the "voice of human conscience," of "human finitude," says Cavell, and it says that one can "live in the face of doubt."[93] Now vanquished is the "quest for the inhuman," which for Cavell "is an essential part of the motivation to skepticism."[94] But we can add that the trumping of skepticism in effect makes maturity fugitive—the prehuman, the pre-reflective animal in man, defeats the skeptic's pursuit of inhuman certainty. If the cause of skepticism, according to Cavell, is the "attempt to convert the human condition, the condition of humanity, into an intellectual difficulty," the antidote seems to be the banishing of man's intellectual capacities for his animal ones.[95] *On Certainty* is emphatic: "I want to regard man here as an animal; as a primitive being to which one grants instinct but not ratiocination. As a creature in a primitive state. . . . Language did not emerge from some kind of ratiocination."[96] He brings back the human into philosophy by showing the remarkable degree to which ordinary behavior depends on internalizing rules ("to think one is obeying a rule is not to obey a rule"). Wittgenstein's stress on the primitive mocks not only traditional philosophy's investment in the grandeur of man's mental powers but also professional philosophy's presumptive superiority to the everyday, be it to commonsense or to ordinary language. Humbled as well is the status of "experience"—pragmatism's pride, its locus of value as the realm of peril that prompts experiment. Blindly following a rule makes for certainty and releases ease of movement, but not experience. After Wittgenstein, as after Freud, man is no longer master in his own house.

Wittgenstein's insistence on an animal perspective—what one might call his version of immaturity—in understanding human certainty is part of what comprises his axial shift from logic's "crystalline purity"—the vertical—to the "rough ground" of the noncognitive—the horizontal. "Don't think, but look!" is his pithiest expression of this shift.[97] The move's downward arc is comparable to William James's earlier altering of philosophy's "center of gravity" from high to low. But, as we have seen, when their accounts of belief are compared Wittgenstein reveals a more rigorous commitment to the low, locating the springs of certainty, to borrow James's words, in the "more or less dumb sense" of our "just seeing and feeling," whereas James makes empirical verification, presumably conducted by science, the ultimate court of approval (*P*, 9). Thus there is credence in Russell Goodman's claim that Wittgenstein shows that "the James of *Pragmatism* overintellectualizes the story of how we arrive at our 'commonsense beliefs.'"[98]

If James, for all his mockery of rationalism, remains in *Pragmatism* (in his account of belief) within the confines of intellectualism, he bursts its bonds in *A Pluralistic Universe*. Yet the liberating result seems shadowed by regression. As Wittgenstein will simply shut his eyes in the face of doubt, James deafens himself and us to talk: "I saw that philosophy had been on a false scent ever since the days of Socrates and Plato" and "that an intellectual answer to the intellectual-ist's difficulties will never come, and that the real way out of them . . . consists in simply closing one's ears to the question" (*APU*, 131). Now deaf, he also elects dumbness: "I say no more. . . . The return to life can't come about by talking. It is an act" (*APU*, 131–32).[99] James here is close literally to enacting a belief basic to Wittgenstein: "Language—I want to say—is a refinement, 'in the beginning was the deed.'"[100] The quotation, from Goethe's *Faust,* was one that Wittgenstein regarded as a motto of his later thought. At war with refinement from the start of *Pragmatism,* James embraces the deed and the beginning, willing, as he says in *A Pluralistic Universe,* to "fall back on raw unverbalized life" and to put off his "proud maturity of mind" and become "again as a foolish little" child "in the eyes of reason." Even though "philosophy, you will say, doesn't lie flat on its belly in the middle of experience" but is "essentially the vision of things from above" (*APU*, 121, 125).

Wittgenstein would have found congenial the (downward) drift of James's thinking here, as it immerses itself in the ordinary and looks for the exit sign from Philosophy. Congenial but also alarming: for whereas James puts philoso-phy "flat on its belly" and leaves us helpless infants, Wittgenstein wants "to walk" on the "rough ground." Hence he will "regard man here as an animal," that is, one who moves confidently and spontaneously at home in the world, imbued with a "peace" unafflicted by doubt about what is certain. In sum: in *A Pluralistic Uni-verse,* James's long-term investment in immaturity seems to reach an impasse of immobility, as he concludes plaintively that he must let "life" teach the lesson. Wittgenstein in effect supplies the teaching: "my life shows" that I am certain, as he sets his own version of immaturity to philosophic work against skepticism's pernicious intellectualism.[101]

At the same time, in shedding his "proud maturity," James is also setting a scene, dramatizing an interrogation of authority analogous to Whitman's refusal to answer the child's question ("How could I answer the child? I do not know anymore than he") and Diogenes' impudent retort to Alexander. All three could be said to take the occasion to throw themselves back upon their culture and, to borrow Cavell's words (themselves summoned in response to a child's insistent questions that make his answers seem "thin" and "merely conventional"), "ask why we do what we do, judge as we judge, how we have arrived at these cross-roads." "What I require," continues Cavell, "is a convening of my culture's crite-ria, in order to confront them with my words and life as I pursue them and as I may imagine them; and at the same time to confront my words and life as I pursue them with the life my culture's words may imagine for me: to confront the culture with itself, along the lines in which it meets in me."[102]

This task "warrants the name of philosophy" and also describes, says Cavell, "something we might call education." Both activities, because they require the posing and entertaining of questions, make us teachers and pupils, adults and children. Philosophy is the task of living with this double role; and while "each of us struggles with the twin perils of becoming either a precocious child or a dismissive adult—either a dogmatist or a nihilist," we may resolve the conflict by accepting the "presence of a confused and inquisitive child within each of us" as a "constitutive feature of our being human."[103]

James calls his 1907 axial shift from vertical to horizontal an "alteration in the seat of authority" that reclaims "the earth" while also reclaiming "minds of a less abstractionist type than heretofore," minds "more scientific and individualistic in their tone"; evidently they look "forward into facts" but with the uncensored gaze of the questioning child until now kept insulated by or obedient to religious and philosophic abstractions (P, 62). Opening maturity and immaturity to each other, James's realignment announces a shift of perspective that, when read as a (recurring) figure in intellectual history, is best understood as a convening and confrontation. Writers and artists at exorbitant odds with their culture's conventions and criteria—above all those that define mature human being in a variety of domains—insist on confronting the culture with itself as it meets in each of them. Inevitably, the face-off has elicited shock and mockery and confusion, not inappropriate responses considering that at stake is a matter—"full human maturity"—assumed settled by Enlightenment, by Kant in 1784, but suddenly turned into a question: "What is a man anyhow?" (Whitman's query is implicitly posed by all of my figures). The periodic eruption of this question warrants a culture's claim to vitality, for its asking exemplifies a capacity for self-interrogation. And to preserve uncertainty about one's own standards, as Leszek Kolakowski has noted, is a culture's bulwark against barbarism, whose many shapes bear at least one common feature: absolute certitude.[104]

NOTES

1. Immanuel Kant, "An Answer to the Question: What Is Enlightenment?" rpt. in *What Is Enlightenment? Eighteenth-Century Answers and Twentieth-Century Questions,* ed. James Schmidt (Berkeley and Los Angeles: University of California Press, 1996), pp. 58, 17.

2. Richard Rorty, "Response to Dennett," in *Rorty and His Critics,* ed. Robert Brandom (Malden, Mass.: Blackwell, 2000), p. 107.

3. John McDowell, "Toward Rehabilitating Objectivity," in *Rorty and His Critics,* p. 110.

4. Ibid., p. 120.

5. Ibid., p. 125. Later in the volume, in a stunning critique of Rorty's reading of George Orwell, James Conant, in "Freedom, Cruelty, and Truth: Rorty vs. Orwell," traverses the same ground—the "post-Enlightenment project of attaining to full intellectual maturity" (286)—and reaches conclusions about Rorty's "immaturity" that are similar to McDowell's.

6. George Santayana, *Selected Critical Writings,* vol. 1 (London: Cambridge University Press, 1968), p. 92.

7. Henry David Thoreau, *Walden and Resistance to Civil Government* (New York: W. W. Norton, 1992), p. 222.

8. Walt Whitman, *Poetry and Prose* (New York: Library of America, 1996), p. 206.

9. Henry David Thoreau, *Collected Essays and Poems* (New York: Library of America, 2001), p. 225.

10. Bruno Schulz, *Letters and Drawings,* trans. Walter Arndt (New York: Harper and Row, 1988), p. 161.

11. Ibid., pp. 159–61.

12. Ibid., p. 158.

13. Ibid., pp. 159, 162.

14. Bataille's definition is quoted as the frontispiece to Yves-Alain Bois and Rosalind Krauss, *Formless: A User's Guide* (New York: Zone Books, 1987). My discussion is based on pp. 24–25, 79.

15. Georges Bataille, "Base Materialism and Gnosticism," *The Bataille Reader,* ed. F. Botting and S.Wilson (Oxford: Blackwell, 1997), p. 163. I borrow the material on Gombrowicz, Schulz, Bataille, Pollock, and Roth from my *Philip Roth's Rude Truth: The Art of Immaturity* (Princeton, N.J.: Princeton University Press, 2006). Czeslaw Milosz, the younger contemporary of the Polish authors I discuss, read *Varieties of Religious Experience* in early 1940s Warsaw and was entranced by its esteem for what escapes the "intellect's casuistry" ("beyond the ranks of words, there existed something alive and powerful") but drew back to cling to "disinterested, eternal truth." Milosz, *Legends of Modernity* (New York: Farrar, Straus and Giroux, 2005), pp. 65, 73.

16. Bois and Krauss, *Formless,* pp. 94–95.

17. Rosalind Krauss, "Greenberg on Pollock," *Pollock and After,* ed. Francis Frascina (New York: Routledge, 2000), pp. 363–64.

18. Philip Roth, *Portnoy's Complaint* (New York: Random House, 1970), p. 305.

19. Philip Roth, *Sabbath's Theater* (Boston: Houghton Mifflin, 1995), p. 152.

20. Ibid., p. 247.

21. "One of the most hotly contested issues in the [contemporary] revival of pragmatism . . . was the centrality of 'experience' to the tradition," notes Martin Jay. "Rorty was bluntly outspoken in denying its importance" for, in his view, it functioned as a "kind of crypto-foundationalism for thinkers who lacked the courage to live without one"; *Songs of Experience* (Berkeley and Los Angeles: University of California Press, 2005), p. 302. Here again is Rorty's scenario of failed maturity noted earlier: Enlightenment kicks away the crutch of religion, only to have scientism replace it with objectivity, and (immature) pragmatists replace objectivity with experience. The crutch of immaturity remains. Ankersmit's critique of Rorty's linguisticism is "Between Language and History: Rorty's Promised Land," *Common Knowledge* 6, no. 1 (Spring 1997): 44–79.

22. John Dewey, *Experience and Nature* (New York: W. W. Norton, 1929), p. 21.

23. This is how Louis Sass describes Wittgenstein in "Deep Disquietudes: Reflections on Wittgenstein as Anti-Philosopher" in *Wittgenstein: Biography and Philosophy,* ed. J. Klagge (Cambridge: Cambridge University Press, 2001), p. 102. But this caveat, from H. J. Glock, is useful: "Wittgenstein's anti-intellectualism should not be equated with irrationalism; it denies that reason and the intellect have the exalted place traditionally accorded them, but it often does so by rational argument." This applies to William James with equal validity. H. J. Glocke, "Wittgenstein and Reason," in Klagge, p. 197.

24. James Conant, "Introduction," in Hilary Putnam, *Realism with a Human Face* (Cambridge, Mass.: Harvard University Press, 1990), pp. lxxiii, lxiii.

25. Ibid., p. lxiii.

26. Ibid., p. lxii.

27. Stanley Cavell, *The Claim of Reason* (New York: Oxford University Press, 1999), p. 207.

28. Stanley Cavell, "Interview," *Bucknell Review* 32, no. 1 (1989): 50; hereafter "Interview." For Cavell, Wittgenstein restores the human animal by making the ordinary

primary and scrutinizing the ordinary's instantiation in the "language games" (Wittgenstein) we play in our everyday transactions with each other. Later in this essay, I will show some intersections between Wittgenstein and James.

29. James's sponsorship of the excluded remainder had a social, cultural reference; he influenced the African American Harvard students W. E. B. Du Bois and Alain Locke, both fervent admirers of James, and also the novelist Pauline Hopkins. I discuss these affiliations in *Color and Culture: Black Writers and the Making of the Modern Intellectual* (Cambridge, Mass.: Harvard University Press, 1998).

30. An analogous double move—to at once reveal and domesticate affiliation— informs James's relation to the American poetic heir of Diogenes, Whitman. The poet's androgyny and homosexuality were never discussed by James, for evidently it discomfited his own carefully tended virility.

31. Pierre Hadot, *Philosophy as a Way of Life* (Cambridge, Mass.: Blackwell, 1995), p. 265.

32. Pierre Hadot, *What Is Ancient Philosophy* (Cambridge, Mass.: Belknap Press of Harvard University Press, 2002), pp. 109–10.

33. Santayana, *Selected Critical Writings*, p. 304.

34. Ibid., p. 303.

35. Ibid., p. 303.

36. J. S. Mill, *On Liberty* (Indianapolis, Ind.: Hackett Publishing, 1978 [1869]), p. 64.

37. Brandom's account, with its tension between "almost no direct influence" and his admission "clearly affected," leaves fuzzy the relation between pragmatism and romanticism. Robert Brandom, "When Philosophy Paints Its Blue on Gray: Irony and the Pragmatist Enlightenment," *boundary 2* 29, no. 2 (2002): 1–28, at 6–8.

38. Lawrence Buell, *Emerson* (Cambridge, Mass.: Belknap Press of Harvard University Press, 2003), p. 241.

39. Ralph Waldo Emerson, *Essays and Lectures* (New York: Literary Classics of the United States, 1983), pp. 267, 273.

40. Foucault, in his last lectures at the Collège de France, focuses on the *parrhesiast,* the Cynic whose commitment is not to theorize scandal but to live "life as the scandal of truth." The Cynics lived their own version of the "true life" as a mockery of the Platonic model, which construes the phrase as exemplifying a pure life of sincere conduct and rectitude "lived in accord with norms and rules." Thomas Flynn, "Foucault as Parrhesiast: His Last Course at the College de France," *Philosophy and Social Criticism* 12, nos. 2–3 (1987): 213–76, at 221.

41. Whitman, *Poetry and Prose*, p. 679.

42. Walter Harding, "Thoreau at the Boston Music Hall," *Thoreau Society Bulletin* 105 (Fall 1968): 7.

43. Michel de Montaigne, *The Complete Works*, trans. Donald Frame (New York: Everyman's Library, 2003), p. 876.

44. Ibid., p. 1004.

45. Emerson, *Essays and Lectures*, p. 700.

46. Montaigne, *The Complete Works*, p. 266.

47. Stephen Toulmin, *Cosmopolis: The Hidden Agenda of Modernity* (Chicago: University of Chicago Press, 1990), p. 44.

48. Montaigne, *The Complete Works*, p. 1042.

49. Whitman, *Poetry and Prose*, p. 192.

50. And when Whitman gets off the grass—"It is time to explain myself—let us stand up"—it is only to banish explanation and insist on mystery and motion: "What is known I strip away, / I launch all men and women forward with me into the Unknown" (*Poetry and Prose*, p. 238). Whitman standing is rarely standing still: "I tramp a perpetual journey. . . . I have no chair, no church, no philosophy"; instead he effaces himself into a veritable hinge or gateway, launching, leading, pointing each man and each

woman, all of whom, he notes, "are asking me questions and I hear you, / I answer that I cannot answer, you must find out for yourself" (*Poetry and Prose*, p. 242).

51. Walt Whitman, *Uncollected Poetry and Prose*, ed. E. Holloway (New York, 1921), p. 44. The quotation is from "Sun-Down Papers" no. 9.

52. Peter Sloterdijk, *Critique of Cynical Reason*, trans. M. Eldred (Minneapolis: University of Minnesota Press, 1987), p. xvii (from Andreas Huyssen's foreword).

53. Ibid., p. 161.

54. Quoted in Russell Goodman, *Wittgenstein and William James* (Cambridge: Cambridge University Press, 2002), p. 41.

55. Ray Monk, *Ludwig Wittgenstein* (New York: Free Press, Maxwell Macmillan International, 1990), p. 369.

56. Quoted in ibid., p. 366.

57. Quoted in Goodman, *Wittgenstein and William James*, p. 37.

58. Wittgenstein, without mentioning James, once remarked that "it is sometimes said that a man's philosophy is a matter of temperament, and there is something in this." Ludwig Wittgenstein, *Culture and Value*, trans. P. Winch (Chicago: University of Chicago Press, 1984), p. 20.

59. James the scientist revered, like Peirce and Dewey, the scientific ideal of experimentation and empirical engagement but decried the prestige of *positivist* science for diminishing man's importance. Pragmatism was meant to mediate between the "tough-minded" positivist materialist and the "tender-minded" religious believer (*P*, 15). Wittgenstein, a trained engineer and inventor and a philosopher of mathematics, had when young imbibed a heavy dose of Spenglerian world pessimism that encouraged him to equate science and its ideal of progress with the pursuit of mass destruction, a pessimism encouraged as well by the experience of enduring two world wars (in the first of which he served at the front).

60. Ludwig Wittgenstein, *Philosophical Investigations*, trans. G. E. M. Anscombe (Oxford: Basil Blackwell, 1968), p. vi.

61. Quoted by James Conant in "Throwing Away the Top of the Ladder," *Yale Review* 79, no. 3 (1994): 328. Cavell discusses poverty in relation to Wittgenstein and Emerson and others but leaves William James unmentioned. See *This New Yet Unapproachable America* (Albuquerque, N.M.: Living Batch Press, 1989), pp. 69–73.

62. Wittgenstein, *Philosophical Investigations*, § 94.

63. Ibid., § 89.

64. Ibid., §§ 90, 92.

65. Ibid., § 97.

66. In 1930 he in fact announced that "the nimbus of philosophy has been lost." Quoted in Monk, *Ludwig Wittgenstein*, p. 298.

67. Wittgenstein, *Philosophical Investigations*, § 108.

68. Stephen Mulhall, *Inheritance and Originality* (Oxford: Oxford University Press, 2001), pp. 92, 88.

69. Wittgenstein, *Philosophical Investigations*, § 107.

70. Emerson, *Essays and Lectures*, p. 472.

71. Wittgenstein, *Philosophical Investigations*, §§ 89, 94.

72. Ibid., § 116.

73. Ibid., § 109.

74. Ibid., § 124.

75. Ibid., § 126.

76. Ibid., § 133.

77. Cavell has noted that skepticism often raises the question of sanity. "It is fundamental to skepticism with respect to material objects that a firm distinction be drawn between a lunatic and a reasonable doubt of the existence of things. It is equally fundamental that this distinction cannot be firm enough" (*Claim of Reason*, p. 447).

78. In reading James's pragmatism as entangled in answering the threat of skepticism, I diverge from Cavell, who says that James treats skepticism as the malady of a "particular temperament, not something coincident with the human as such." "What's the Use of Calling Emerson a Pragmatist," in Cavell, *Emerson's Transcendental Etudes* (Stanford, Calif.: Stanford University Press, 2003), p. 221. And Russell Goodman claims that for pragmatists, including James, "skepticism is not deeply worrying or important," and they tend to "sidestep it." In contrast, Wittgenstein's philosophy is organized around "the agony of skepticism" (*Wittgenstein and William James,* p. 23).

79. Ludwig Wittgenstein, *On Certainty,* trans. D. Paul and G. E. M. Anscombe (New York: Harper and Row, 1972), § 359.

80. Ibid.

81. Goodman, *Wittgenstein and William James,* p. 17.

82. Wittgenstein, *On Certainty,* § 422. Goodman, the author of the one book on James and Wittgenstein, is a useful commentator on Wittgenstein's relation to pragmatism, particularly in the first and sixth chapters of his book.

83. Wittgenstein, *On Certainty,* § 148.

84. Ibid., § 94.

85. Mulhall, *Inheritance and Originality,* p. 179.

86. Wittgenstein, *On Certainty,* § 370.

87. Ibid., §§ 94, 358, 308. This sentence draws on some of Linda Zerilli's formulations in her brilliant essay "Doing without Knowing: Feminism's Politics of the Ordinary," *Political Theory* 26, no. 4 (August 1998). I also have learned from Avrum Stroll's *Moore and Wittgenstein on Certainty* (New York: Oxford University Press, 1994).

88. Wittgenstein, *On Certainty,* § 476.

89. Ibid., §§ 538, 374.

90. Ibid., § 204.

91. Ibid., § 359.

92. Wittgenstein, *Philosophical Investigations,* § 219, p. 224.

93. Cavell, *Claim of Reason,* p. 431.

94. Cavell, "Interview," p. 50.

95. Cavell, *Claim of Reason,* p. 493.

96. Wittgenstein, *On Certainty,* § 475.

97. Wittgenstein, *Philosophical Investigations,* § 66.

98. Goodman, *Wittgenstein and William James,* p. 32.

99. James is still imprisoned in metaphor, still shackled to words as he tries to escape them, for he did not literally "return to life" and exit academia to pursue a world elsewhere, as Wittgenstein in fact did for a time.

100. Wittgenstein, *Culture and Value,* p. 31.

101. Wittgenstein, *On Certainty,* § 7.

102. Cavell, *Claim of Reason,* p. 125.

103. Conant, "Introduction," p. lxxiii.

104. See Kolakowski's essay of 1980, "Looking for the Barbarians: The Illusions of Cultural Universalism," in *Modernity on Endless Trial* (Chicago: University of Chicago Press, 1990). I am paraphrasing sentences on pp. 22–23. He argues that European culture's superiority (and also the source of its weakness and vulnerability) is its Enlightenment heritage of endless self-criticism and self-doubt.

4. *Pragmatism* and Death:
Method vs. Metaphor,
Tragedy vs. the Will to Believe

WILLIAM J. GAVIN

My analysis of *Pragmatism* begins with an observation, perhaps with a detour of sorts. The "manifest content" of *Pragmatism* concerns its image as a method and as a theory of truth. Both of these are important. However, there is also a "latent content" to *Pragmatism*. The method and the theory of truth are "situated" in a more nebulous "context." That context can be found in the first and last lectures of the text. Both of these turn to the subject of "death" as an important theme with which pragmatism must deal. "Dealing," it may be noted, does not necessarily mean "solving." Dealing may have to do with affirming, even if not wholly accepting, or, alternatively, declaring "tragic" and incomprehensible. Any view of pragmatism as a method or "problem solver" can be rejected or at least significantly limited in power and scope by noting domains where and how it does and does not apply. In sum, I wish to focus upon death (suicide) and tragedy, as these are found in *Pragmatism*. These seem not to be "solvable" via the pragmatic method because they are not problems to begin with. They may be "resolvable," that is, appropriated or rejected, but that entails utilization of "the will to believe."

The Beginning: *Pragmatism* and Death

Pragmatism begins with two examples about death. The two examples come from a publication titled *Human Submission* by the anarchist Morrison Swift, who was a little extreme for James's tastes, but with whom he nonetheless sympathized a great deal. In one of them John Corcoran, an unemployed clerk, "ended his life by drinking carbolic acid" (*P*, 21). He had found work as a snow-shoveler but was too weak from illness to sustain the pace after one hour. Upon returning home he found that his wife and children had no food and that he had been dispossessed. He ingested the poison the following day. James selected as a second example from Swift a Cleveland worker who kills his children and himself, and agrees with Swift that this type of case or situation discloses reality in all its elemental rawness, and that it cannot be explained by being explained away. This had oftentimes been the project of religion and of religious idealism, and its many treatises on God, Love, and Being (see *P*, 22).

But more than the rationalizations of religious idealism is at fault here. James opened his lectures on pragmatism by "inventing the problematic" or outlining "the present dilemma in philosophy." He divided the world of philosophy into two camps, the "tough-minded" and the "tender-minded," admitting that the division was rather oversimplistic in nature, and he has great difficulty in attributing "freedom" to either camp. He initially lists it under the tender-minded, but seems to remove it shortly thereafter, saying that tender-minded rationalism believes in systems, and that systems are closed. James finds it difficult to accept the findings of either camp exclusively. The tender-minded are too ethereal and abstract, the tough-minded too unromantic, even if they do seem to deal with this world. Neither camp is very "intimate" with life. The two examples from Swift's text are offered as examples from the latter, that is, of real experience with which, thus far at least, the abstract written treatises of philosophers had been unwilling or unable to deal.

The difference here is an important one. Have philosophers heretofore chosen to emphasize the abstract over the concrete? To replace and not reflect life as it is actually lived? Does language per se, or logic per se, or "thinking" per se necessarily do this? Or, on a deeper level, is it just the case that "humankind cannot stand very much reality"? If the first alternative is the case, then the situation can still be salvaged. And indeed James, in this first lecture, throws his philosophical hat in the ring, saying, "I offer the oddly-named thing pragmatism as a philosophy that can satisfy both kinds of demand [tough-minded and tender-minded]" (*P*, 23). But even if salvageable two important caveats are still in order. First, James stated at the very beginning of the first lecture that "the history of philosophy is to a great extent that of a certain clash of human temperaments" (*P*, 11). This indicates, on a self-reflexive level, that pragmatism involves an attitude or a stance toward reality, rather than a solving of the latter as if it were a problem. We too often fail to notice, as Hilary Putnam argues, "that [the will to believe] is meant to apply to the individual's choice of philosophy, including pragmatism itself."[1]

Second, accounts are interpretations, more akin to metaphors than descriptions, and limited in scope. This could be due to the nature of language, or to the nature of reality itself. Even if an account is possible, there are good and bad accounts—or "fat" accounts and "thin" accounts. "An outline in itself is meagre, truly, but it does not necessarily suggest a meagre thing. It is the essential meagreness of what is suggested by the usual rationalistic philosophies that moves empiricists to their gesture of rejection" (*P*, 25). Accounts then, due to the very nature of language itself, can provide only limited access to reality. In one sense of the term, empiricism is more concrete than rationalist religious systems. But in another sense both religion and science have explained reality, or at least some types of reality, by explaining it away. Accounts are limited, but some are more "intimate" with life than others. To be successful, James's account must be more than merely descriptive; it must be "directive," pointing beyond itself toward a return to life, a "leading that is worth while," rather than just a static correspondence. And it must deal with life in its "concreteness," not explain the concreteness away.

Let us return to our two examples from Swift and to James's offering of pragmatism as a mediator. Can pragmatism deal with the two deaths given in the text? And does "deal with" mean "explain" or "make meaningful"? Or does it rather mean appropriate, make one's own, even if not completely comprehensible? Both deaths are, in a sense, senseless, that is, unnecessary, avoidable. The death of the clerk and that of the Cleveland workman might be explained, or accounted for, in terms of an unjust socioeconomic system. Altering the system would, arguably, dissolve the perceived need to commit suicide out of despair. In other words, if the situation is perceived as a "problem" in Deweyan terms,[2] then a proposed solution can be offered. Both anarchism and Marxism, in all their variations, might be put forth as potential competing paradigms to solve it. Some "explanations" might be better than others, pragmatically speaking, for example, Marxism as opposed to Liebnitzian rationalism, because it offers an actual solution to a concrete problem in this world—as opposed to a rationalization of the status quo.

But if the specific examples of death alluded to here can be accounted for in one respect, death per se can not. That is, individual personal deaths cannot be rendered "acceptable" just because they can be understood "in the long run," as part of an ongoing evolutionary process. If this is so, every individual death is in some sense "tragic."[3] A situation is tragic not merely because good is pitted against good, but rather because it remains in some sense "unmediated." There are "dregs" left behind, so to speak. As Kathleen Higgins puts it, "the kind of suffering from which tragedy draws its material is not remedied by thinking the situation through."[4] However, James does flirt with "thinking the situation of death through" in *Pragmatism*. He offers a wedding, a mediation, a way of interpreting tragedy as provisional in nature when he discusses "spiritualism" versus "materialism." But ultimately he does not explain tragedy by explaining it away. We return to this in our conclusion.

James never returns to the two suicides offered as "exemplars" of what we need to deal with in the real world.[5] But he does offer pragmatism as a mediator, and, at the end, he does offer meliorism as a viable approach to the issue of salvation. However, sometimes mediation does not work, resulting in "forced" choices rather than marriage. Going further, James's offering of meliorism was quickly tempered if not rescinded as he wondered whether "the claims of tender-mindedness go too far" (*P*, 141). The self that emerges from this compromise is more fragile and tragic than just promethean in nature. James realizes that meliorism is not just a position to be intellectually proved, but rather that it needs to be passionately affirmed, even in the face of uncertainty. Furthermore, that affirmation must be continuously renewed—and we will not be equally successful in doing so each and every time. Finally, while meliorism on the surface remains a positive outlook, there remains, just beneath the surface, the threat that it may ask too much of us.

We should read *Pragmatism* keeping in mind that James himself seriously contemplated suicide in 1868–70, and that ultimately he did not solve the issue as a methodological problem, but rather "got over it" by exercising the "will to believe." James's thoughts of suicide were not "caused" exclusively by socioeconomic conditions, though his not having held a full-time job for any period of time did weigh heavily on his mind. There were bigger issues at stake: his realization that he was accomplishing nothing and was running out of time. In other words, he was finite, and would die.

We leave lecture one, then, with the request that philosophical texts deal with life, with two suicides as exemplars of what life looks like, with the promise of pragmatism, as yet undefined, as a mediator, marrying tough- and tender-minded aspects of reality to each other. *Pragmatism* will end with James returning to the theme of death, and with his realization that it has a "tragic" dimension to it. But before we go there let us turn to the "manifest content" of the text, the one that discusses pragmatism as a method.

The "Corridor": Description vs. Metaphor

In lecture two, "What Pragmatism Means," James states that "at the outset, at least, . . . [pragmatism] stands for no particular results. It has no dogmas . . . save its method. . . . [I]t lies in the midst of our theories, like a corridor in a hotel. Innumerable chambers open out of it" (*P*, 32). The corridor metaphor is one of the most famous to be found in *Pragmatism*. Another of equal importance is the image of pragmatism as a minister or mediator, wedding the present moment to past experience. "New truth is always a go-between, a smoother-over of transitions. It marries old opinion to new fact so as ever to show a minimum of jolt, a maximum of continuity" (*P*, 35). A third metaphor views our knowledge growing like a grease spot:

> Our minds . . . grow in spots; and like grease-spots, the spots spread. But we let them spread as little as possible: we keep unaltered as much of our old knowledge, as many of our old prejudices and beliefs, as we can. We patch and tinker more than we renew. The novelty soaks in; it stains the ancient mass; but it is also tinged by what absorbs it. Our past apperceives and co-operates; and in the new equilibrium in which each step forward in the process of learning terminates, it happens relatively seldom that the new fact is added raw. More usually it is embedded cooked, as one might say, or stewed down in the sauce of the old.
>
> New truths thus are resultants of new experiences and of old truths combined and mutually modifying one another. (*P*, 83)[6]

James seemed to be a philosopher incapable of not using metaphor.[7] Metaphors do not disclose their meaning in a straightforward manner. Rather, they are a way in which to comprehend something indirectly.[8] As with Nietzsche's use of aphorisms, the meaning and conditions of James's metaphors are not immediately apparent, but rather require an art of exegesis.[9]

The image of pragmatism as a corridor can be taken, that is, appropriated, in either a descriptive or a metaphorical manner. Taken descriptively or literally, the corridor metaphor promotes a view of pragmatism as a neutral, positivistic tool or instrument to determine what actually exists—that is, as not just one hermeneutic interpretation or appropriation among others. James is himself somewhat responsible for some of the confusion here, since he initially presents pragmatism as "a method only" (*P*, 31). This statement, taken uncritically, stands in some tension with his earlier point, made just a few pages earlier in the text, that philosophy "is only partly got from books; it is our individual way of just seeing and feeling the total push and pressure of the cosmos" (*P*, 9) and that this involves "a certain clash of human temperaments" (*P*, 11). John Smith long ago pinpointed this reference in James as one that can cause extreme difficulty. He notes:

> The corridor represents the method and what goes on in the individual rooms represents "doctrines" as distinct from the method. . . . The pragmatists were somewhat uncritical in their acceptance of this distinction; they often seemed to think that to specify a method does not involve presuppositions concerning what there is and what there must be if the method is to prove successful. . . . The underlying problem is of the utmost importance because of the widespread belief to be found not only among philosophers but among scientists as well that there is a "neutral" way of proceeding which is unencumbered by the biases inevitably expressed in "doctrines."[10]

Taken literally, the corridor narrative is the narrative to end all narratives, the ultimate meta-narrative. Taken metaphorically, the corridor is one of an endless series of linguistic attempts to portray reality in all its "fatness," that is, its richness and concreteness. Metaphors do not simply describe; they reveal and conceal simultaneously. If this is so, it becomes clearer that closure is not possible, so long as language is looked at as essentially metaphorical. Language, even in its ideal form, logic, will never capture reality completely.[11] For James, we can make progress, on a piecemeal level, but closure is not an option, even if it were desirable. Nonetheless, as James admits, closure remains tempting—at least for some of us, if not all of us some of the time.

On a self-reflexive level, one of the things metaphors reveal is James's ongoing love-hate relationship with language, and with its apparent inability to deal with reality. He once cried out that "language is the most imperfect and expensive means yet discovered for communicating thought."[12] In another place he says: "What an awful trade that of a professor is—paid to talk, talk, talk! I have seen artists growing pale and sick whilst I talked to them without being able to stop. . . . It would be an awful universe if everything could be converted into words, words, words."[13] On the other hand James realized that language, while often dysfunctional and misleading, also had a necessary role to play. And so he developed a more positive and nuanced view of language. From this perspective, words and sentences were seen as "signs of direction" rather than impartial descriptions. Metaphors pointed beyond themselves, alluding to but never completely capturing external realities. The inability of language to capture reality completely means, among other things, that life is not just a "problem" to be solved. Nor, for that matter, is death.

The Middle: Pragmatism as a "Problem Solver" vs. "The Will to Believe"

Pragmatism was offered by James in a manner somewhat different than it was conceived by Peirce. For the latter, pragmatism was a question of determining the meaning of, say, calling a given diamond "hard" or a given knife "sharp." It would also be able to show that some issues, specifically metaphysical ones, were, in fact meaningless. It was a matter of "dissolving" issues, so to speak.[14] For James, on the other hand, it was not a matter of showing that a given concept had no verifiable meaning, but rather one of "resolving" issues, especially metaphysical ones. James says: "The pragmatic method is primarily a method of settling metaphysical disputes that otherwise might be interminable" (P, 28). Stan Thayer asks that we note the ambiguity of the term "settling" here, "which can mean clarifying the meaning of questions under dispute, or resolving the disputes by providing a satisfactory answer."[15] The new view of pragmatism offered by James focuses more on "resolution." "Meaning," that is, consistency, may be necessary, but it is not sufficient, at least not sometimes. There is a sense of "urgency" involved that is either not found or not emphasized in Peirce. What difference does it make—to me, if the universe is viewed as one or as many? Is it better viewed, pragmatically speaking, as "concatenated?" What difference is there, pragmatically, between Locke's view and Berkeley's? None, it seems. Sometimes, as we shall see below concerning materialism versus spiritualism, the difference may seem to be more "psychological" than "logical" in nature—but James would be quick to reject this dualistic dichotomy. The history of philosophy is, after all, the clash of human temperaments. But while there is a sense of urgency here, this should not be interpreted to mean that, at some time in the future, the urgency is going to go away. In one sense we make progress by "resolving" issues, but in another sense there will always be issues to resolve. This realization demands much of us, and might even be seen as a bit pessimistic rather than naively optimistic in nature.[16]

Generally, James argues that, pragmatically speaking, an idea is true if it makes a difference, and making a difference means two things: coping with the present, and preserving as much of the past as possible, as one advances into the future. It is here that James gives us the metaphor of a wedding, with pragmatism as a "marrier" or minister. This is an outlook that tends to stress continuity over disruptiveness. As James says in the text, "[t]he most violent revolutions in an individual's beliefs leave most of his old order standing. Time and space, cause and effect, nature and history, and one's own biography remain untouched" (P, 35). Such an approach is gradualist in nature, and has rendered James seemingly open to criticism. As Cornel West has noted, "James's attempt to incorporate contingency and revision into a theory of truth is radical; yet in its gradualism his theory applies a Burkean notion of tradition to the production of knowledge and truth. Of course, new knowledge and truths must build on the old, but James's preoccupation with continuity minimizes disruption and precludes subversion."[17] However, while the wedding metaphor and the image of the grease spot may seem to privilege continuity over disruption, there is also evidence in the text of *Pragmatism* that the marriage may, at least occasionally, be more disruptive than initially meets the eye. Sometimes, as the poet William Carlos Williams says:

> Divorce is
> the sign of knowledge in our time,
> divorce! divorce![18]

To bring this out we turn to the issue of pluralism, as it appears in the text. In the fifth lecture on *Pragmatism,* "Pragmatism and Common Sense," James argues for a topology of "regional ontologies"[19] or multiple paradigms, with no underlying "bed of reality" to which they can be reduced. In an important passage at the end of the lecture, he says:

> There are . . . at least three well-characterized levels, stages or types of thought about the world we live in, and the notions of one stage have one kind of merit, those of another stage another kind. It is impossible, however, to say that any stage as yet in sight is absolutely more true than any other. Common sense is the more consolidated stage, because it got its innings first, and made all language into its ally. Whether it or science [the second stage] be the more august stage may be left to private judgment. But neither consolidation nor augustness are decisive marks of truth. . . . Vainly did scholasticism, common sense's college-trained younger sister, seek to stereotype the forms the human family had always talked with, to make them definite and fix them for eternity. . . .
>
> There is no ringing conclusion possible when we compare these types of thinking, with a view to telling which is the more absolutely true. . . . Common sense is better for one sphere of life, science for another, philosophic criticism for a third; but whether either be truer absolutely, Heaven only knows. . . . Profusion, not economy, may after all be reality's key-note. (*P,* 92–93)

This is a pregnant paragraph. It clearly advocates both pluralism and perspectivalism as necessary accompaniments to the pragmatic method. It warns against taking common sense for granted. Contrary to common sense, it suggests that there is nothing wrong with assuming that reality may lend itself to a number of "accounts." It may be richly "profuse" rather than reducible to a final or complete picture. What, it may be asked, is the role of the philosopher, given this regional and pluralistic account? Generally, it is to articulate, preserve, and nurture the "fattest" account possible, to highlight the "thick" as opposed to the "thin" account, as James noted in lecture one, to allow each realm its due, to espouse contextualism and perspectivalism and pluralism over absolutism and certainty. One possibility might be to stress that there are "disjunctive" and "conjunctive" transitions among the domains, resulting in a more "concatenated" picture. But the phrase "levels, stages or types of thought" requires more attention. The first two suggest a rather continuous approach wherein comparison is possible. But different "types" of thinking suggests different "paradigms," if you will.[20] Changing from one paradigm to another may be more "revolutionary" than gradualistic in nature, if common points cannot be identified. Differently stated, if there are radically different types of experience, or radically different regional ontologies, then the decision as to which of them to adopt in a given situation may be disruptive or "forced." It may involve "the will to believe." For most of the time, we can adopt a gradualist approach, or a concatenated one. But sometimes we are faced with experiences of different types, not reducible to one another and incompatible. This may be true on the macroscopic level of common sense versus science versus philosophy. But it may also be true on a more microscopic level of personal experiences. That is, not all experiences or situations may be of the same type, that is, solvable. Some may only be "dealt with," that is, not solved, by exercising the will to believe. Some may be "tragic," that is, reducible neither to problems nor to will-to-believe situations.

"The will to believe" sneaks into *Pragmatism* in the sixth lecture, "Pragmatism's Conception of Truth." There James is defending a view of truth as "agreement" but redefining agreement as other than copying. Here he tells us that we cannot "be capricious with impunity." We have to find something that will work, and that means it "must mediate between all previous truths and certain new experiences" (*P*, 104), keeping as much of common sense and of the past as possible. So far all seems smooth sailing, even if the "squeeze" is a tight one. But even here, there's a rub. "Yet sometimes alternative theoretic formulas are equally compatible with all the truths we know, and then we choose between them for subjective reasons. We choose the kind of theory to which we are already partial; we follow 'elegance' or 'economy'" (*P*, 104; see also *WB*, 13–33). Here James, even though seemingly stressing the continuity model of marrying the present to the past, and still allowing for the future, seems to say that there are decisions we will make where we have to color outside the lines. He seems to say that, after both sensory evidence and conceptual coherence are given their due, we will make exclusionary decisions based upon "our passional nature," as he did in "the will to believe" (see *WB*, 20). A pluralistic account might emphasize the fatness of the three levels, their irreducibility to an ultimate source. But a radical pluralism might suggest that sometimes we choose among these, running the existential risk of being wrong, but nonetheless willing to take the chance for "personal" reasons.

A similar outcome can be seen in the issue of "materialism" versus "spiritualism" earlier in the text. James, having asked "what difference does it make, if one adopts one or the other," says it makes no difference concerning the past, but a great deal of difference concerning the future. Spiritualism "means . . . the letting loose of hope" (*P*, 55). Somewhat surprisingly, the whole issue is couched in terms of "tragedy." For materialism, everything in the universe will dissolve; transient achievements will simply end, "[w]ithout an echo; without a memory.

. . . This utter final wreck and tragedy is of the essence of scientific materialism as at present understood" (*P*, 54). Spiritualism, on the other hand, upholds a world "with a god in it to say the last word . . . where . . . tragedy is only provisional and partial, and shipwreck and dissolution not the absolutely final things" (*P*, 55). James here seems to say that the world of materialism doesn't make sense, and also that tragedy can be allowed if it is only temporary. The issue is couched in terms of tragedy versus hope, or partial tragedy versus complete tragedy. What does this mean? It seems to mean that, ultimately, the world has meaning, at least in the long run, that it will go on. It could be taken to mean that ultimately, the tragic will disappear. This topic is taken up at the "end" of *Pragmatism*.

The End: *Pragmatism* and Death

Throughout the entire text of *Pragmatism* James has been worried that his position would be taken as a form of positivism, that is, as rejecting the claims of religion. And so he returned to the issue of religion several times in the text, for example, in lectures two and three, and he devotes the entire last chapter to preserving a place for religion. He does this by offering "meliorism" as an alternative theory to the absolutistic or fundamentalist positions that the world is definitely damned or that it will definitely be saved. "Meliorism treats salvation as neither inevitable nor impossible. It treats it as a possibility, which becomes more and more of a probability the more numerous the actual conditions of salvation become" (*P*, 137). He creates the image of the world's creator, aka God, presenting an offer or challenge to all of humanity, one which says that the world will be saved only on condition that each of us does our level best. He says that our acts are what create the world's salvation, and that "[m]ost of us . . . would . . . welcome the proposition and add our fiat to the fiat of the creator" (*P*, 140). This sort of life, for James, is a real adventure, with real danger; it is a social endeavor, of "co-operative work genuinely to be done" (*P*, 139). Here then is the challenge. And here is James, perhaps exercising his own form of the will to believe, in human nature. But this optimism is tempered just a page later, in a text highlighted by Cushing Strout, who says:

> We too often forget that in his mature work, the *Pragmatism* of 1907, he [James] cried out with a tragic sense that John Dewey never had: "Is the last word sweet? Is all 'yes, yes' in the universe? Doesn't the fact of 'no' stand at the very core of life? Doesn't the very 'seriousness' that we attribute to life mean that ineluctable noes and losses form a part of it, that there are genuine sacrifices somewhere, and that something permanently drastic and bitter always remains at the bottom of its cup?"[21]

Here, at the end of *Pragmatism*, James returns to the topic with which he began, namely, death. He admits that "in the end it is our faith and not our logic" (*P*, 142) that decides between affirming a dangerous and adventurous universe and selecting absolutism. He tells the reader: "I can believe in the ideal as an ultimate, not as an origin, and as an extract, not the whole. When the cup is poured off, the dregs are left behind forever, but the possibility of what is poured off is sweet enough to accept" (*P*, 142). So, *Pragmatism* begins and ends with death. James admits that our successes will be "dis-seminated and strung-along," and provides us with an image, an epigram, of one person who did not make it:

> A shipwrecked sailor, buried on this coast,
> Bids you set sail.
> Full many a gallant bark, when we were lost,
> Weathered the gale. (*P*, 142)

What does this mean? We have a metaphor of a dead sailor. Does the image have meaning? Can it be given meaning? Can the sailor's death be made sense of? Or, is it just tragic? The American president Theodore Roosevelt once said that "[d]eath is always and under all circumstances a tragedy, for if it is not, then it means that life itself has become one."[22] What makes a given death tragic anyhow? The sailor's death seems to have meaning only in the sense that others "passed him by." He serves, in a Nietzschean sense, as someone whose death is a "spur" to others.[23] His death is redeemed in the successes of others, in a cooperative ongoing effort. But all this sounds more Roycean than Jamesian in character. The death of the individual sailor is meaningful, that is, makes sense "in the long run," as Peirce would say. Dewey also can be brought to bear here. In "Context and Thought," he tells us that "every occurrence is a concurrence."[24] Applied to the topic of death, my death is not my own, though it is assuredly that; it is also an event for others. As the Dewey scholar Tom Alexander has noted, "[t]he finality of individual death opens up the possibility, even the necessity, of participating in a shared social project which transcends individual lives—culture. Everyone dies, but culture continues."[25] Going further, in *Democracy and Education*, Dewey tells us that "Life is a self-renewing process through action upon the environment. In all the higher forms this process cannot be kept up indefinitely. After a while they succumb; they die. The creature is not equal to the task of indefinite self-renewal."[26] This quasi-Hegelian stance of not being "equal to infinity" ultimately seems to have enabled Dewey to adopt an "acceptance" model of death, that is, one that enabled him to come to terms with personal mortality by subsuming the individual self in a broader social one. Defining "life" as covering "customs, institutions, beliefs, victories and defeats, recreations and occupations," Dewey notes that "[e]ach individual, each unit who is the carrier of the life-experience of his group, in time passes away. Yet the life of the group goes on."[27]

Dewey here offers a model of individual death as "acceptable" because it is understandable "in the long run."[28] But, in James, there is much more of the personal and individual. And on a personal level, that is, one stressing the uniqueness of each individual, the death is perhaps more "tragic," that is, less bearable or acceptable in nature. At the very least, the "strenuous life" being offered by James as the truly pragmatic one, asks a lot of us. James seems to admit as much in a response to a review of *Pragmatism* titled "The Absolute and the Strenuous Life." He says: "The pragmatism or pluralism which I defend has to fall back on a certain

ultimate hardihood, a certain willingness to live without assurances or guarantees" (*MT,* 124). The world of the pluralistic pragmatist "is always vulnerable, for
some part may go astray; and having no 'eternal' edition of it to draw comfort
from, its partisans must always feel to some degree insecure. If, as pluralists, we
grant ourselves moral holidays, they can only be provisional breathing-spells, intended to refresh us for the morrow's fight. This forms one permanent inferiority
of pluralism from the pragmatic point of view" (*MT,* 124). James here seems to
admit that too much is being asked,[29] and that this "is bound to disappoint many
sick souls whom absolutism can console" (*MT,* 124). He seems to say that we cannot live the strenuous life all the time. Life has its "unheroic days," as Royce would
say, or at least its bad moments.[30]

It may be that only some of us can live in this fashion and also that even
if we do live it, we must continually reaffirm it, and that we will fail in this endeavor at least some of the time. There will be losers; in a sense, we will all lose,
that is, die. Can one, in a Nietzschean sense, affirm the finitude of being human,
all too human, or does this require too much? The position advanced by James
in the first and last lectures on the topic of death is not one where he solves or
"resolves" the issue as if it were a problem. It is, rather, a portrait or an image or
an attitude that he "attests to." The intervening lectures may well concentrate on
resolving issues, but the first and last lectures seem to focus on something that is
not an issue or a problem: death. Death cannot be explained by being explained
away—in the long run. Or at least it is more than this. In one sense Roosevelt is
correct. Death, viewed in its immediacy, is tragic, that is, unintelligible, or is appropriated by exercising the will to believe, that is, exercising hope, unfounded
hope. The question then arises, how "typical" is the position on the strenuous
life advocated by James? Is it the rule, most of the time? Or is it the exception to
the rule? Alternative paradigms might be found in Dostoevsky's "Legend of the
Grand Inquisitor" and Kafka's *The Trial,* both of which seem to say that humankind cannot live without certainty or without meaning. Joseph K., the anti-hero
in *The Trial,* wants "definite acquittal," and seems unable, not just unwilling, to
act without prior knowledge. As a result, he does nothing throughout the text,
which consequently dissolves into a meaningless process. He dies, "like a dog,"
that is, on a subhuman level.[31] Dostoevsky's Grand Inquisitor confronts Christ
with the accusation that most people can't bear the freedom offered by him; they
require instead "miracle, mystery, and authority."[32] Dostoevsky's "underground
man" is worried that he will be "understood," perhaps even loved, by Lisa. As
Dostoevsky portrays him, he can preserve his freedom only by paying a terrible
price—by remaining constantly "unpredictable" through spitefulness and lying.[33]
In short, if James appropriates and highlights the strenuous life, Dostoevsky and
Kafka remind us of how difficult it is to live it on a continual basis.[34]

Conclusion

James "framed" the issue with which pragmatism was to deal as
"the dilemma of the tough-minded vs. the tender-minded." These terms mean

various things; one of them important to James was that of science versus religion. But he also wanted philosophy to return to life, and life does not come in neatly disciplinary parcels. Nor does it arrive as a set of issues that can be solved. Some of life's experiences are "problematic" in nature. They can be solved via the use of the pragmatic method. That method is not neutral in nature, but has metaphysical presuppositions. James realizes this as he proceeds through the lectures. James also has trouble placing freedom or free will in either of the camps. That is because freedom is more than the calculation of probabilities for him—although freedom sometimes functions in this fashion. Pragmatism as a method should be looked at within the context of the examples James brings up at the beginning and the end of the text. *Pragmatism* begins with death and *Pragmatism* ends with death. Pragmatism can make some sense of death by replacing tragedy with meliorism, but there remains a sense in which death on a personal level remains inexplicable, perhaps tragic.

There are different types of experience in the universe; some of them are problematic in nature and can be "solved" via the pragmatic method. However, some of them are not problematic in nature. These include tragic situations and situations involving the will to believe. While the focus of *Pragmatism* might seem to be on method, a method for undercutting or resolving many of the problems of traditional philosophy, we should keep in mind that not everything is a problem—or even a potential problem. This can be seen in the text itself, at the beginning and at the end. *Pragmatism* does require pluralism, and an unfinished universe. The pluralism it espouses must be one that can allow different types of experience—tragic, will-to-believe, and problematic ones. If this happens, pragmatism will never achieve the definitive triumph of a general way of thinking precisely because it will be espousing an outlook where there are only partial, that is, perspectival, solutions, and sometimes no "solutions" at all.

This realization, however, when taken with James's admission that his position would be a hard one to uphold and sustain, has resulted in that "recrudescence of absolutistic philosophies" that Dewey was so prenascent about in "The Influence of Darwin on Philosophy."[35] Pragmatism may, at first glance, have seemed to be an optimistic, progressive position, taking small steps but going forward, nonetheless. But in a sense, it has perhaps not been tried at all, on a large scale. James's initial optimism about pragmatism, and his efforts to show that it was not too radical but, rather, a new term for old ways of thinking, were tempered as he began to realize that it seemed to demand too much of us. Specifically, it seemed to demand that we live not only with probability (uncertainty) but also with the realization and affirmation, that, at least from one perspective, not everything is a problem. Specifically, neither will-to-believe-type situations nor tragic situations per se are problematic ones. In the middle of *Pragmatism* James comes rather close to explaining tragedy by making it temporary. But at the end of *Pragmatism,* the shipwrecked sailor stands not only for a spur for the future, but for the realization, and affirmation, that, from an individual perspective, there will also be dregs. "The providence of tragedy," Kathleen Higgins reminds us, "is related to an extreme subset of the actual—the part of actual human experience that is painful and not susceptible to relief through analysis."[36] Tragic situations cannot be solved, but they can, perhaps, be countered by offering, as an alternative, will-to-believe-type situations. Experience comes in many types; not all of them are "problematic" in nature. If the fact of "no" does "stand at the very core of life," then on an individual personal level we are all, in a sense, "dregs." The example or metaphor of the shipwrecked sailor, James states, requires the "acceptance of loss as unatoned for, even tho the lost element might be one's self" (*P*, 142). The self can be incorporated into a larger picture, and, consequently, death can be "accepted." But to the extent that the personal is emphasized, and the uniqueness, that is, non-replacability, of the specific individual in question is stressed, to that extent death remains inexplicable, perhaps "tragic." Perhaps it can be countered only by constant reaffirmation through the will to believe, and this both unevenly and continuously.

NOTES

1. Hilary Putnam, *Renewing Philosophy* (Cambridge, Mass.: Harvard University Press, 1992), p. 191.

2. See John Dewey, "The Pattern of Inquiry," *LW*, 12.105–108. All references to Dewey's work are to *The Collected Works of John Dewey*, ed. Jo Ann Boydston (Carbondale and Edwardsville: Southern Illinois Press, 1969–91), and published as *Early Works*, *Middle Works*, and *Late Works*, hereafter referred to as *EW*, *MW*, and *LW*.

3. On this topic, see John Stuhr, "Persons, Pluralism, and Death: Toward a Disillusioned Pragmatism," in *Genealogical Pragmatism: Philosophy, Experience, and Community* (Albany: State University of New York Press, 1997), pp. 277–95.

4. Kathleen Higgins, *Nietzsche's Zarathustra* (Philadelphia: Temple University Press, 1987), p. 19.

5. For the notion of "exemplar," see Thomas Kuhn, *The Structure of Scientific Revolutions*, 2nd ed. (Chicago: University of Chicago Press, 1970), pp. 187–91.

6. See also the metaphor of truth evolving "like a snowball's growth," *P*, 108.

7. Stan Scott notes that James "appears to have accepted the premise that to understand is to generate metaphors of understanding." See *Frontiers of Consciousness: Interdisciplinary Studies in American Philosophy and Poetry* (New York: Fordham University Press, 1991), p. 56.

8. Charlene Haddock Seigfried has noted that James's style is no mere accident. She says: "William James's use of analogy and metaphor is more than a rhetorical device. It is integral to his hermeneutics and reflects his concrete analysis of human thinking" (*William James's Radical Reconstruction of Philosophy* [Albany: State University of New York Press, 1990], p. 209).

9. To quote Seigfried again, "metaphors better reflect . . . the contextuality and revisability of discourse than language does" (p. 210).

10. John E. Smith, *Purpose and Thought: The Meaning of Pragmatism* (New Haven, Conn.: Yale University Press, 1978), p. 44.

11. James was later to renounce the ability of logic to encompass reality, saying it could touch the surface of reality but not plumb its depths. "For my own part, I have finally found myself compelled to *give up the logic*, fairly, squarely, and irrevocably. It

has an imperishable use in human life, but that use is not to make us theoretically acquainted with the essential nature of reality. . . . Reality, life, experience, concreteness, immediacy, use what word you will, exceeds our logic, overflows and surrounds it" (*APU*, 96).

12. Ralph Barton Perry, *The Thought and Character of William James,* vol. 2 (Boston: Little, Brown, 1935), p. 203.

13. *The Letters of William James,* edited by his son, Henry James, vol. 1 (Boston: Atlantic Monthly Press, 1920), pp. 337–38

14. See Robert Talisse, and Micah Hester, *On James* (Belmont, Calif.: Wadsworth, Thompson Learning, 2004), p. 44.

15. H. S. Thayer, *Meaning and Action: A Study of American Pragmatism* (Indianapolis: Bobbs-Merrill, 1973), p. 77n.

16. Talisse and Hester catch this point well in their book *On James:* "While not strictly pessimistic, it may seem that James has painted a thoroughly bleak picture of human life: We are caught in a fight that we cannot win; we must participate in an ongoing struggle between good and evil, but we have not the resources to secure a decisive victory; we are called to commit to the meliorist project of improving the world, but we have no guarantee that even our very best efforts can succeed. What kind of life is this?" (p. 71).

17. Cornel West, *The American Evasion of Philosophy: A Genealogy of Pragmatism* (Madison: University of Wisconsin Press, 1989), p. 65.

18. William Carlos Williams, *Paterson* (New York: New Directions, 1946–58), p. 18.

19. For the notion of "regional ontology," see Edmund Husserl, *Ideas,* trans. W. R. Boyce Gibson (New York: Collier Books, Macmillan, 1962), p. 57.

20. For the notion of paradigm, see Thomas Kuhn, *The Structure of Scientific Revolutions.*

21. Cushing Strout, "William James and the Twice-Born Sick Soul," *Daedalus* 97 (1968): 1079. Original reference is to *P,* 141.

22. Theodore Roosevelt, "Letter to Cecil Spring-Rice," March 12, 1900, in *The Works of Theodore Roosevelt,* vol. 2, ed. H. Hagedorm (New York: Charles Scribner's Sons, 1926), p. 102. Quoted in Stuhr, "Persons, Pluralism, and Death: Toward a Disillusioned Pragmatism," p. 278.

23. For the notions of "dying at the right time," and death as a "spur," see Friedrich Nietzsche, *Thus Spoke Zarathustra,* trans. and with an introduction by R. J. Hollingdale (New York: Penguin Books, 1961), pp. 97–99.

24. Dewey, *LW,* 6. 9.

25. Thomas Alexander, *John Dewey's Theory of Art, Experience and Nature: The Horizons of Feeling* (Albany: State University of New York Press, 1987), p. 159.

26. Dewey, *MW,* 9.5.

27. Ibid., 9.5.

28. For a very different view of Dewey, one emphasizing that "self-realization is self-depletion," see Stuhr, "Persons, Pluralism, and Death: Toward a Disillusioned Pragmatism," pp. 277–95.

29. As John Stuhr has noted, in the years following the publication of *Pragmatism,* "James increasingly and insightfully recognized that pragmatism, immensely right in theory, was unlikely to be a 'definitive triumph' in life because it constituted in practice a philosophy that is insufficiently a live option or is a far too demanding and strenuous an option for many persons." "Pragmatism, Pluralism, and the Future of Philosophy: Farewell to an Idea," in John Stuhr, *Pragmatism, Postmodernism, and the Future of Philosophy* (New York: Routledge, 2003), p. 172.

30. See Josiah Royce, *The Religious Aspect of Philosophy* (Boston: Houghton Mifflin, 1885), p. 385.

31. See Franz Kafka, *The Trial* (New York: Schocken Books, 1968).

32. See Fyodor Dostoevsky, *Notes from the Underground and the Grand Inquisitor*, selection, translation, and introduction by Ralph Matlaw (New York: E. P. Dutton, 1960), pp. 117–41.

33. Ibid., pp. 3–115.

34. See William J. Gavin, "'Problem' vs. 'Trouble': James, Kafka, Dostoevsky and 'The Will to Believe,'" *William James Studies* 2, no. 1 (2007).

35. See Dewey, *MW*, 4.13.

36. Higgins, *Nietzsche's Zarathustra*, p. 19.

5. William James's Pragmatism: A Distinctly Mixed Bag

Bruce Wilshire

They picture pragmatism a priori (I don't know why) as something that must necessarily be simple . . . I repeat . . . pragmatism is one of the most subtle and nuanced doctrines that have ever appeared in philosophy (just because the doctrine reinstates truth in the flux of experience), and one is sure to go wrong if one speaks of pragmatism before having read you as a whole.

—Henri Bergson, letter to James, 1909

William James is a tragic figure. I will try to fully explain what I mean by that. But right off the bat, we can point out a feature of this tragic stance. It's fairly widely believed that James is a major philosopher. Yet in no other such philosopher's work, I believe, are great strengths so vividly mixed with major defects. His famous, often read—too often read, I think—popular lectures, *Pragmatism,* gaudily illustrate this claim.

What does it take to be a major philosopher? A most difficult question. Wilfrid Sellars's one-liner statement of what philosophy seeks to discover is hard to better: how things, in the broadest sense, hang together, in the broadest sense.

But how does one start a process of discovery without begging crucial questions that philosophy should endeavor to answer? How does one begin to comprehend the farthest reaches of complexity without prejudging things—or occluding whole horizons of possibilities and viewpoints—stupidly? James's description in *Pragmatism* of expertness in philosophy is arresting: "Expertness in philosophy is measured by the definiteness of our summarizing reactions, by the immediate perceptive epithet with which the expert hits such complex objects off" (*P,* 25). The summarizing that emerges through perceptual epithet! A taking in at a glance that delivers the first sketch of the whole lay of the land. Is there any better way to avoid getting lost in the details of some corner of the subject matter, any better way to begin doing philosophy unprejudiciously?

Asserted are deep points of affinity between philosophic and artistic intuition. It should not greatly surprise us that James studied art seriously for a time. In an expertly done self-portrait as a young man, James shows himself looking sidewise and sharply at viewers, as if he would take us in at a glance.

James did not finally take the career route of the professional artist. But, thankfully, his artistic proclivities never totally left him—the definiteness of summarizing reactions, the immediate perceptive epithet with which the expert hits such complex objects off. Art gave him a grip on what confronts us from every side every instant, on what confronts us viscerally and concretely, on what he calls the much at once. Look very carefully, he says, at the actual color of the shade under the trees on this sunny day here and now in the fields. Hackneyed thoughts suggest immediately and automatically that that shade be painted black or some shade of gray. But the color that actually appears is purple! That is, the total circumpressure of the situation here and now makes the shade appear purple, and to this the good painter—and the philosopher—must try to adhere.

James's vitality is plain enough: his racy, many-allusioned, colorful prose, his common touch, as if he were just one person talking to another. But this frequently conceals another deeper layer of vitality. I mean his energy of mind that cuts through the periphery to the center of its subject, and—holding that center fast— still keeps in its grasp the manifold aspects of that same subject that prevent any false simplification.[1] At his best, he sees how things, in the broadest sense, hang together, in the broadest sense. He learns to keep his poise in the midst of the much at once pulsing and moving unpredictably on every side and within him.

Not to be omitted from our initial account is James's personal experience of an overwhelming much at once. Following his earning of an M.D. degree from Harvard, he was struck down in a nearly total existential collapse. Something "gave way in his chest," and he was bedridden for about a year in his parents' house. He described it as "a terror at his own existence" that paralyzed him. Despite all his advantages—his family's wealth, his father's social and intellectual circle that included Emerson, his own advanced degree from Harvard—he saw no point in trying to do anything. He felt determined and shackled by the much at once, the blind impress of events of which he knew so little.

But before he became a chronic invalid, something else appeared to him in the primal mother lode of his experienced field. It was the reality of possibility, and in deeply committed and emotionally loaded reasoning about it. If freedom exists—says James with notable scientific caution—it's illogical to wait for evidence of freedom. If freedom exists, the first act of the free will should be to freely believe in freedom. It's no exaggeration to say that James thought his way out of bed and into a greatly productive life. This leap of faith in thought was part and parcel of a leap of behavior and a leap of and in his being.

At close to sixty he was back in bed again, this time with heart failure caused by getting lost in the mountains and by overexertion in response. Once again, the much at once overwhelmed him, but he turned into gold this experience of being flattened: his account became *The Varieties of Religious Experience*. He discovered a basal feeling, mood, or sense of "the whole residual cosmos" and its "circumpressure" (which he believes everyone has but most lack means of articulating). This is that "solemn but glad" feeling, this feeling of being touched by that which we hadn't known we didn't know, the mysterious cosmos. It is "the more than reason can say" and gives birth to relentless efforts to codify, tame, and institutionalize it in traditional religious groups.

Why, then, caught in the grip of "the More" didn't James become a devotee of the ineffable, a mystic of the experience of the One? Because, again, of his nearly incredible many-sidedness and his deep vitality. He is greatly respectful of particularity, individual differences, and hard facts. Also respectful of the history of philosophy, and the traditional need to formulate experience in concepts: those of truth, meaning, individual, species, cause, reality, Being. If I am right, his balance at the center of himself and his hold on the manifoldness of experience comes partially undone in his famous *Pragmatism*.

* * *

James is artist, psychologist, philosopher. He is also scientist. His urge toward fluidity and continuity and the building of momentum across the board is immensely strong. But how to keep it all arranged!?

The monumental *The Principles of Psychology* occupied him from 1878 to 1890 (to 1892 if we include the shocking Abridgment). He intends, he says, to produce a scientific psychology. Thus he will simply assume that there are both physical and mental states, and that the point is to discover laws of functional co-variation between brain states and mental states. He realizes, he says, that philosophical issues can be raised—for example, how does anything get "known into" a mental state?—but he will just not raise them. In the best tradition of nineteenth-century materialism and positivism, No metaphysics!

He gradually and painfully discovers that the chief metaphysical issue is—What are mental states?—and that it must be raised if we are even to barely specify what such a state is; and if we can't do that we can't begin to discover explanatory scientific laws of functional co-variation. In fact, a horde of philosophical (or metaphysical) issues and assumptions keep raising themselves. He must run backward to uncover, acknowledge, inspect them. *The Principles* teaches that James, the avowed empirical scientist, can't run backward fast enough to keep up with himself.

James's powers of description never desert him, and place him as a great phenomenologist-proponent of the principle that description must precede explanation. His chapter "The Stream of Consciousness" in *Principles* is justly famous. What he describes as actually presenting itself might prompt a revision of the chapter's title, so that it reads "The Streaming of Consciousness." We need a verb or a gerund, not a noun. All is activity, formation, re-formation, flow and fusion. We can't precisely tell where one "mental state" ends and another begins; or we can't tell if there is one, or more than one, mental state occurring. If we look really closely we also see that some streaming of awareness is occurring in the focus of the "field of consciousness," whereas much more is occurring on the margins. How much more? We cannot tell, for if we name what's almost out, way out there on the fringe, it has become clearly in. A strange boundlessness presents itself.

Why aren't we simply carried away in this vast, rushing streaming? (Recall Heraclitus, *panta rei*, everything flows, we can't step into the same river twice.) Well, if we are sane, we aren't. And we are not, James realizes, because "mind" has a "keel." We can think of the same thing twice, or thrice, or as many times as we wish (see *PP*, chapter 12). There must be at least two major dimensions of "consciousness": the momentary experiencing and the recur-able experienced—

recur-able perhaps only in memory or anticipation. (Imagine that we think again of the latest measurement of the diameter of the Earth, pole to pole.) Edmund Husserl, much influenced by *The Principles,* writes of the flowing act of thinking (noesis) and what it is of or about (noema), and that the former cannot be specified without the latter (or as the medievals said, *obiect specificat actum*). James comes to acknowledge (though not with perfect clarity) this pivotal dependency, this "intentionality," but remains very skeptical that the conditions of identity of "the act" of thinking can be discovered. Here all is flowing and fusion.

James calls "the keel of the mind," its object directedness and redirectability, "conception." This certainly seems to suggest some "whatness," some universal quality in the object of thought. We think again of that instance of that sort of thing. But I think it's fair to say that the role of conception is never fully cleared up before his death in 1910. Concepts, he acknowledges, form a coordinate realm of reality, but this is never fully developed, which prompts him to say at the end of his life that his thought is too much like an arch built up on only one side. Inevitably, then, his insight into the two essential dimensions of awareness—experiencing and experienced—is not completely clarified either. James (and John Dewey as well) knew that we should not use atomic, or "single-barreled," terms such as experience, percept, concept, but rather dynamic "double-barreled" ones, for example, experiencing-experienced, perceiving-perceived, conceiving-conceived. But James did not hew consistently to his own insight (nor did Dewey).

As I will argue, this knotted conceptual inadequacy is most glaringly evident in the popular lectures, *Pragmatism,* and creates an opening for the bludgeoning criticism that his theory of truth received, and to his rage over it. James remains heavy on flow and light on object, heavy on ever-ongoing experiencing and light on the integrity of the experienced. If I am right, his hunger for fame was disastrous.

We must remember, however, just how multi-sided, creative, perceptive, and philosophically ambitious he was. James cannot tell a lie, though he tries hard sometimes to do so. What is this floating, reified abstraction "mental state"? All he can really discover, he finally admits, is Object of thought—thus capitalized because it is so vastly encompassing. All particulars or topics must be picked out within it. For example, we don't hear thunder alone or pure, but thunder-breaking-in-upon-silence-and-contrasting-with-it. Now, we can think of that whole phenomenon again. But what's the "cash value"—the actual phenomena presented to us—when we say of any of our forms of thinking, "I am thinking that"?

Calling it a digression, he nevertheless concedes in *Principles* that all he can garner in the way of actual phenomena are various sectors of Object, in particular various movements of and in his body, all directed at something or other. It is that peculiar "warmth" of that body which is always with us, though usually not focused, the continuity of which is essential for the experienced continuity and identity of one's own self. It is object—in some variable sense—that is also subject. It is only sometimes conceived—though for the sane it must always be recur-able, or collectable, or recollectable. James is allergic to any form of mentalism, intellectualism, ego-logy, Cartesianism.

The Abridgment of *The Principles* is commonly interpreted—when read at all—as James's textbook version, with money uppermost in mind. But it is one of the great turn-abouts and confessions in the history of philosophy. First, we notice with bafflement that a previously conceived essential characteristic of thought—that it have an ("intentional") object—is missing from the list of characteristics. Second, the final short chapter is stunning, nearly unbelievable. James maintains that psychology is no science, that the waters of metaphysical criticism leak into it at every joint, and that he is an incompetent. His twelve years of effort have delivered a "bloated, tumified, dropsical mass." And, then, twelve years before his official announcement of his anti-dualistic metaphysics of radical empiricism, we get a rough sketch of it. Key phenomenal characteristics constitute both the world known and the knower. Any distinction between the two amounts only to different arrangements of phenomena, different interdigitating contexts of the same phenomenal characteristics.

Admittedly, James never rounded out his metaphysics of radical empiricism. There are gaps. But the gaps are so placed that a sympathetic and intelligent reader can fill them in and piece together a philosophical view that significantly mitigates the harsh criticisms that his theory of truth in *Pragmatism* prompted. In that book he claims that he advances a general theory of truth that is independent of his metaphysics. James harbors a kind of messianic urge: he wants to help wandering, stumbling, suffering humanity regardless of anyone's metaphysical commitments. But I believe that the best case can be made for his theory of truth only when that is seen to be an integral feature of his metaphysics.

Briefly now, his metaphysics. His empiricism is radical, not the mentalistic variety spawned originally by Descartes and refashioned by the British empiricists. At his clearest, James writes of "specific natures," sorts of characteristics (species, "whats"), that arranged in one context of specific natures constitute the world known, and in a somewhat altered context constitute the knowing and the knower. For example, take the hardness, roughness, and positioning, or sitedness, of a stone wall. Such characteristics constitute the wall itself. When the wall is known, the knowing can take several forms. When the wall is directly perceived, its characteristics of hardness, roughness, and sitedness form a context that is joined by the perceiving body of the perceiver. A perceiving body, and not a remembering, anticipating, or theorizing body, is one that is directly engaged with the wall itself here and now. When knowing occurs in these other modes, the body is semi-detached from whatever present and actual situation holds it, but it is focused on what it would experience if it were directly perceiving the wall.

Though sketchy, or worse, one can fill in the gaps so that distinctions can be drawn between the passing experiencing of the wall and the wall itself experienced, and experienced as stationary, durable, not passing away at all. The undeveloped key is the different stances of the knowing organism that correlate essentially with different modes of knowing. James gives us a beginning in these words about the body in an extensive footnote from "The Experience of Activity" in *Essays in Radical Empiricism*:

The individualized self, which I believe to be the only thing properly called self, is a part of the content of the world experienced. . . . The body is the storm centre, the origin of co-ordinates, the constant place of stress in all that experience-train. Everything circles round it, and is felt from its point of view. The word "I," then, is primarily a noun of position, just like "this" and "here." Activities attached to "this" position have prerogative emphasis, and, if activities have feelings, must be felt in a peculiar way. The word "my" designates the kind of emphasis. I see no inconsistency whatever in defending, on the one hand, "my" activities as unique and opposed to those of outer nature, and, on the other hand, in affirming, after introspection, that they consist in movements in the head. The "my" of them is the emphasis, the feeling of perspective interest in which they are dyed. (*ERE,* 86)

But it is only a beginning.

Nevertheless, particularly in the essay "A World of Pure Experience" that emphasizes leading and continuity in the context of knowing, we can see how a thinker embroiled in working out a new metaphysics might have been led to deliver the popular lectures published as *Pragmatism.* But we have already anticipated, in part, other features—key ones—that must be brought into play if James is to have any chance of avoiding his critics' most destructive shots (which, as we will see, targeted his apparently straight-out claim that truth is created). Ironically, these key features were brought into play in "Humanism and Truth," published in *Mind* in 1904, the very year that James officially introduced his radical empiricism! But, alas, they were not included in the popular lectures of 1907, and it is these lectures that gained by far the most attention (even, scandalously, from most professional philosophers). In a sad working of history, these became paradigmatic, with greatly baneful consequences for the culture and the world.

Let us sketch the high points of *Pragmatism,* and how the whole caper left James vulnerable—and enraged. First, these high points are very high: they are glistening pinnacles. James was writing what had been, or was to be, spoken. I know of no other philosopher who has delivered his thought more movingly or brilliantly. James has an artist's sensibility and style.

Soon in the lectures James makes a daring rhetorical move. It's clearly an attempt to disarm with candor. He will deliver, he says, "a monstrously over-simplified and rude" set of "popular lectures" (*P,* 24). Possibly because of its daring and audacity, most people have manifestly not taken it seriously. "It must be mere performance." In any case, it helps us clarify James's use of the pragmatic theory of meaning. When he states, as he often did, that the meaning of anything is a matter of its concrete consequences for our experience, does he mean the anticipated or envisaged consequences, or just the consequences, whether envisaged or not? If he made this daring admission seriously and envisaged people taking it seriously—that is, responding to his lecture with due caution—then he was mistaken, and we'd have to say that his meaning misfired, or did not lead to truth. On the other hand, if meaning means consequences, whether envisaged or not, then his words are a nearly meaningless and dangerous rhetorical gesture.

James's very eloquence becomes a problem. What he wanted to accomplish is fairly clear. Truth matters. Truth is not merely a stunningly pretty word that people reify and then claim to revere. Truth is a matter of being led effectively through the shoals, pitfalls, very real dangers of the world: it is not to be misled. Truth is a species of goodness. It is no exaggeration to say that some of his pronouncements can be placed on the page as we would Aeschylean verse:

> Woe to him whose beliefs
> play fast and loose with
> the order which realities
> follow in his experience;
> they will lead him nowhere
> or else make false connexions. (P, 99)[2]

Truth for James is a great human accomplishment. Given his construal of the philosophical position called Absolute Idealism, its theory of truth is no more than verbal mumbo-jumbo, a kind of spell that he intends to break. In its shuttling of airy abstractions, it is supposed that reality must consist of an array of sorts of things; these sorts must have some structure or meaning; so they must be knowable in some way; so why not say that they are known by some Absolute Mind? This vacuous correspondence between Mind and Reality is, of course, a human invention, one designed to give solace in a dangerous world: "Someone knows—Someone is in charge." It is a quasi-accomplishment that absolves many, they think, from the hard work of formulating meaning in terms of actual consequences for concrete human experience. Then of following out these intended consequences to see if the expectations are actually fulfilled, that is, to see if the meaning becomes truth.

To those who doubt that a "mere" human organism could achieve truth, James responds with a kind of blinding brilliance. If one doubts the miracle of matter, then:

> To anyone who has ever looked on the face of a dead child or parent, the mere fact that matter could have taken on for a time that precious form, ought to make matter sacred ever after. It makes no difference what the principle of life may be, material or immaterial, matter at any rate cooperates, lends itself to all life's purposes. That beloved incarnation was among matter's possibilities. (P, 50)

But one brilliant expression of one brilliant glimpse, glance, or insight will not always be sufficient for doing philosophy.

Some of the misunderstandings of what James was getting at are so gross that one must suspect that some hidden desire not to understand him must be at work. Thus one professional philosopher of the period characterized pragmatism this way: Whatever pleases one to call truth is truth. But James's first great paper in philosophy, "Remarks on Spencer's Definition of Mind as Correspondence" (1878), would annihilate such an interpretation. Truth cannot be contingent upon personal advancement of any sort, so of course not even upon human survival. The question must be, does the idea, belief, claim advance, survive? In the very process of veri-fying (James's spelling) a belief, the person with the belief may die (e.g., in the very act of verifying my idea that there's a burglar downstairs, I may be shot by him). James goes so far as to repeat an old Roman's words, *Fiat justitia pereat mundus:* Let the law be justified though the world perish. Or, "I bet my life that the law is the truth."

In this early article James also wrote that truth is the fate of thought over the long haul. That word suggests strongly that the career of an idea is constrained by opaque and obdurate realities in the world that obtrude upon an idea, that it is quite powerless to fight against, avoid, or even predict. But no mention is made in *Pragmatism* of this early article.

Other widespread misunderstandings of James's theory of truth contained in this famous book are not so easily dispelled. Crucial dimensions of his thought are missing in the piece. The misunderstandings stem not merely from habitual, sleepy adhesion to cliché, so "self-evident": "Reality is a set of determinate happenings, right?, so truth is just a mirroring of these happenings in some actual or potential mind—it is 'what is the case.' This cannot come to be or pass away. James must be wrong in thinking that truth is created through beliefs being created and verified—through veri-fication—a supposed truth-making."

In fact, as many philosophers have pointed out, "truth" is a tenseless predicate, and this certainly seems to be more than a merely verbal point. When, say, I believe that my friend's mother's eyes are blue, and this belief leads me right into my friend's mother's presence and the belief is verified, her eyes were really blue before I believed anything about them. It is simply true that her eyes are blue. If she should die and be cremated, it is simply true that her eyes were blue.

Now, as I've briefly mentioned, James had pretty well covered himself against this objection three years earlier in "Humanism and Truth." But no clear statement of this occurs in the famous book! He had covered himself in a way that follows from the germ of his metaphysics of radical empiricism and from his tacit phenomenology. In his dynamical and organismic view, reality is a matter of interweaving histories. They must be distinguished but not disconnected. There is the history of the knower's believing—and of course what's believed—and the history of the thing or things about which one is believing something. This is how he puts it in "Humanism," after setting the scene as that discerning of the pattern of nearly equally bright second-magnitude stars that form for us the shape of a dipper, and then counting their number to be seven:

> A fact virtually pre-exists when every condition of its realization save one is already there. In this case the condition lacking is the act of the counting and comparing mind. But the stars (once the mind considers them) themselves dictate the result. The counting in no wise modifies their previous nature and they being what and where they are, the count cannot fall out differently. It could then always be made. Never could the number seven be questioned, if the question once were raised. . . . We have here a quasi-paradox. Undeniably something comes by the counting that was not there before. And yet that something was always true. In one sense you create it, and in another sense you find it. (*MT,* 56)

Looked at one way, truth is created. Looked at another, truth is found or discovered. That is, the concept of truth is ambiguous—though essentially and beneficently so. James should have emphasized more—I believe—that the two ways of looking must always both be employed. In any case, what is discovered—if it's true discovery of something that really happened and had or has a career—is discovery of what is the case. This just IS the case. It is tenseless.

In this key article, "Humanism and Truth," James clarifies the whole situation quite nicely:

> As in those circular panoramas, where a real foreground of dirt, grass, bushes, rocks, and a broken-down cannon is enveloped by a canvas picture of sky and earth . . . continuing the foreground so cunningly that the spectator can detect no joint; so these conceptual objects, added to our present perceptual reality, fuse with it into the whole universe of our belief. In spite of all berkeleyan criticism, we do not doubt that they are really there. Tho our discovery of any one of them may only date from now, we unhesitatingly say that it not only is but was there, if, by so saying, the past appears connected more consistently with what we feel the present to be. This is historic truth. Moses wrote the Pentateuch, we think, because if he didn't, all our religious habits will have to be undone. Julius Caesar was real, or we can never listen to history again. Trilobites were once alive, or all our thought about the strata is at sea. (*MT,* 54)

All our thought cannot be at sea. That is, thought must think whatever is necessary for thought to occur at all. This definitely includes the integrity of the world about which we sometimes discover things. For example, Charles Lyell, the geologist, looked in 1845 at trilobite fossils and hypothesized that they once lived millions of years ago in the sea. When this was confirmed at a somewhat later date, what is the case is confirmed.

And in what respect is truth created? Here James is at his most obviously and blazingly brilliant. The truth we can garner is only as extensive and as good as the questions we can create and ask, the actual difficulties we can face, the effectiveness of the methods of inquiring we can devise. That day dawns only for those who are awake.

The most dramatic case of truth being created is when the believing and the thing about which one is believing something is one and the same being—one's own self. When one is believing something positively and passionately about one's own capacities then of course the capacities themselves are affected. Very often that makes the difference between success and failure in one's ventures. This might also apply to the success or failure of one's group's ventures. Above all, as mentioned, was James's creation of his own life as he thought and acted his way out of nervous collapse, terrible paralysis. I believe that he freely—in a leap—created his freedom and his life. What was discovered thereby? Himself.

Nearly all this was compellingly laid out in "The Will to Believe" (1897). But no more than other of James's great work was this really included in the famous *Pragmatism.* Bedazzled by his opportunity to perform (for a thousand at Columbia University in one case), he began losing his grip on the many strands of his thought and his life. He instanced one of his own statements in *Varieties of Religious Experience:* Life finally runs the robustest of us down.

* * *

James is a tragic figure, at least in crucial respects. His critics threw out the precious baby with the dirty bathwater. He was furious. He declared that his critics showed an inability to understand him that was "almost pathetic." But I imagine that some of his rage was actually directed at himself—that he had allowed himself to be drawn into the excitement of the popular arena.

Why would he give the lectures? In 1906 or '07 he was already a widely heralded thinker in both Europe and America. Why would he dumb down his thought and throw away his hard-earned reputation? Didn't the great psychologist know that the masses cannot tolerate any ambiguity—not even the essential and beneficent ambiguity of his concept of truth? Well, he may have known on one highly intellectual level of awareness, but it was not enough to stop him. I have just mentioned the effects of illness and age. Probably more important was ontological anxiety about his own being that he could never completely shake.

Here James's tragic dimension appears in wider, cultural scope. James was as aware as Nietzsche was of the vast change that has occurred in the world with "the death of God." The old authorities have toppled—at least for many, many people—been displaced. But if our identity as selves is to solidify we must be authorized by some authority. The only authority that many can find is approval from the masses, for example, gaudy displays of power, popularity, prestige. If I am right, James himself felt acutely the need for approval of this kind, and dumbed down his ideas on at least one crucial occasion.

Again, James discerned the sea change in the world, and the dangerous shoals and maelstroms that we must try to navigate around. Most of his critics could not see this about him, could not see what he saw. Abysmally enough, his illuminating and biting metaphors drawn from economics were construed by some on the literal level only. When, say, he spoke of the cash value of ideas, they thought that he thought of the commercial value of ideas! Or when he compared life to a boarding house where "the butter, the pancakes, and the syrup seldom come out even." This wasn't just charming and piquant writing, but a biting assessment of the modern world, where problems of distributive justice will not forever be swept under the rug. Or when he spoke of the credit system that more and more takes over things. Yes, our lives have always been predicated on expectation and promise, but who is really trustworthy today?[3]

Not all of *Pragmatism* is disastrous. Notice his assessment of the new secular age of science and technology, which antedates critiques by Karl Jaspers or Aldous Huxley, say:

> The scope of the practical control of nature newly put into our hand by scientific ways of thinking vastly exceeds the scope of the old control grounded on common sense. Its rate of increase accelerates so that no one can trace the limit;

one may even fear that the being of man may be crushed by his own powers, that his fixed nature as an organism may not prove adequate to stand the strain of the ever increasingly tremendous functions, almost divine creative functions, which his intellect will more and more enable him to wield. He may drown in his wealth like a child in a bath-tub, who has turned on the water and who can not turn it off. (P, 91)

As I've said, James began losing his grip on the many strands of his thought and his life. This is tragic, because it prevented him from sending out the best signals to so many in the twentieth and twenty-first centuries who wander disoriented, without pole stars, emotionally flattened and vaguely but really demoralized. Tellingly, James wrote "The Energies of Men": he knew that we cannot be vitally alive without the excitement of the ideal, or of the strange, without the engagement with that which lies just over the horizon, the unknown and the unknown unknown. Friedrich Schiller had spoken of the disenchantment of the world. James felt this acutely.

There is a highly relevant strand in his own thought that he might have developed much more than he did. In "The Many Worlds" section of *Principles* he writes of the mythic world: the world of mythic horses, say, a world holding Pegasus and excluding "Maggie in her stall." Some of the strands comprising one context or world are different from those comprising another, but the worlds are not simply sealed off from each other.

His metaphysics of radical empiricism, though never completely clarified, is a complex system of variously interweaving histories. Moreover, in his very last work he wrote of "vicious intellectualism," which he defined this way: to assume that what is not explicitly included in the definition of something is excluded from that thing. That is, things variously ooze into what intellectualist logic says they are not. And the consequence? We can much better understand how the mythic and the factual merge into each other, to a surprising extent, in everyday life. Much better understand how the experienced world without living mythic strands tends to dry out and fall apart. Much better understand why people create myths as best they can: sports contests, Hollywood celebrities, gamblers' hauls, Michael Crichton's conspiracy novels, fundamentalists' revivals, national displays of corporate power. The spectacular latter case in his day: the annexation of the Philippine Islands and the national celebration of same. James added mordantly that little brown men are too remote from us to be grasped and felt as the bodily subjectivities that they are, living forward in the light of their future.

* * *

Since the most dismissive critiques of James's theories of meaning and truth issued from professional philosophers, it should not surprise us that his reputation has suffered most in academic-philosophical circles. I have already touched on the scandal of professional philosophers relying mainly on his popular lectures for their information about him. In any case, in most of the "best" philosophy departments William James has become a byword for slovenly "unprofessional" philosophical thinking.[4]

Toward closing this piece, let us revert to James's words, "Expertness in philosophy is measured by the definiteness of our summarizing reactions, by the immediate perceptive epithet with which the expert hits such complex objects off." Accepting this description, the best perceptive epithet for analytic philosophy, I think, has been supplied by Eugene Halton: ascetic.[5] It is mentalism, Cartesianism in some form, aversion to the immediate presence of our bodies as our selves. James's attempts to grasp us in our histories as minding organisms interlacing with a plethora of other histories have been dropped. It is a matter not of the grip loosening, but of not having been attempted. James's thoughtful balancing act over the abyss goes inadequately appreciated.

Halton nicely exposes the background role of logical positivism in recent and ongoing analytic philosophy—most of it. For example, he locates this positivism in Charles Morris's *Foundation of the Theory of Signs* (1938). Typically, Morris sees much of the history of philosophy as a tower of Babel. He would "debabelize" it.[6] For example, salvage something of James, say, shrink the nearly incredible richness of the whole "pragmatic" tradition into a mere arm of a "scientific semiotics" called "pragmatics." No longer is attention to be paid to the pre-reflective domain of what James called sciousness, the realm of common sense and its limits where philosopher-phenomenologists delve into the gritty and messy domains of human-organic life that hold before scientists can do their work: that is, get out of bed in the morning, discuss house repairs, get to the lab, not mistake the coffee-urn for the cyclotron, and so on. After reading James, warts and all, there's detectable a zombie-like and eerie quality in so much recent academic philosophy. As if we see people walking around, all right, but not quite touching the ground.

I hope this volume in your hands prompts a serious reconsideration of William James.

NOTES

1. See William Barrett's foreword to my *William James and Phenomenology: A Study of "The Principles of Psychology"* (New York: AMS Press, 1977).

2. I am indebted to John J. McDermott for this way of laying out the words on the page.

3. See James Livingston, *Pragmatism and the Political Economy of Cultural Revolution, 1850–1940* (Chapel Hill: University of North Carolina Press, 1994).

4. See the first essay of my *Fashionable Nihilism: A Critique of Analytic Philosophy* (Albany: SUNY Press, 2002).

5. See his *Bereft of Reason: On the Decline of Social Thought and Prospects for Its Renewal* (Chicago: University of Chicago Press, 1995).

6. Ibid., p. 3.

6. The Deconstruction of Traditional Philosophy in William James's Pragmatism

RICHARD M. GALE

William James's *Pragmatism* was intended to effect a revolution in philosophy, a radical reorientation in the way philosophy is to be done. Like Hume before him and the later logical positivists, James views the history of philosophy with horror, as a scandal, since it consists of disputes that are not only perennial but apparently intractable as well since the disputants cannot even agree upon any decision-procedure for resolving their disagreements. Past philosophy, therefore, resembles a crap game played with unmarked dice. It was the mission of *Pragmatism* to find a method for putting marks on the dice so that these disputes would become tractable.[1] What is this method that will enable us to resolve these disputes after two thousand years of fruitless bickering? How does James deploy it to resolve these problems? And with what success? These are the questions that this essay will attempt to answer.

The Method

The method, as you might garner from the title of the book, consists in applying the pragmatic theory of meaning to thoughts and conceptions so as to ascertain their true meaning. James credits Charles Sanders Peirce with having first formulated this theory:

> Mr. Peirce, after pointing out that our beliefs are really rules for action, said that, to develop [*sic*] a thought's meaning we need only determine what conduct it is *fitted* to produce: that conduct is for us its *sole* significance. . . . To attain perfect clearness in our thoughts of an object, then, we need only consider what conceivable effects of a practical kind the object may involve—what sensations we are to expect from it, and what reactions we must prepare. Our conception of these ef-

fects, whether immediate or remote, is then for us the *whole* of our conception of the object, so far as that conception has positive significance at all. (*P*, 28–29; my italics)

Before considering how James employs this pragmatic theory to clean out the stables of traditional philosophy and with what success, some problematic features of it must be addressed. First, James begins by speaking of the "conduct that it [the thought] is fitted to produce" but subsequently adds sensations when he speaks of "what sensations we are to expect from it and what reactions we must prepare." This raises the question of whether actions and sensations are each necessary and together sufficient or whether each is alone sufficient for a conception or thought to have a meaningful content.

We know that Peirce required both conduct and sensations. The reason is that his account of meaning is modeled on the operationalistic concepts that are employed by working laboratory scientists. For them the content of a conception is a set of conditionalized predictions as to what sense experiences will be had in the future upon performing various actions. For example, "If you place this substance in aqua regia, then you will have sense experiences of its dissolving." Think in this connection of a physicist's conception of momentum or energy based on the operations by which these quantities are measured. James broadened the application of Peirce's account so that it applies to all concepts, even those of a metaphysical, religious, and moral sort. Although James usually went with Peirce's conditionalized prediction account, we shall see that sometimes he was willing to go with actions alone. He also sometimes went with experiences alone, but, as will be seen, he then was unwittingly switching to a non-pragmatic version of empiricism.

Another problematic feature is that this pragmatic theory of meaning identifies the *whole* or *sole* meaning of a thought with this set of conditionalized predictions. But this has the counter-intuitive consequence that the whole meaning of a proposition reporting a past event, that Caesar crossed the Rubicon, for example, consists in the future experiences that will be had upon performing different actions, such as finding certain sentences inscribed in books in the library. This is what A. O. Lovejoy aptly characterized as the paradox of the alleged futurity of yesterday. This problem will be considered later.

Yet another problem is that the claim that "our beliefs are really rules for action" is a potentially misleading ellipsis, for neither the psychological belief state, the believing, nor the what-is-believed, the content of the belief, can be identified with a rule without absurdity. Whereas the believing is temporally locatable, a rule is not itself so locatable, although its being followed or enforced is. Furthermore, what is believed when one believes that snow is white is not a rule, such as the rule to assert "snow is white" when asked what is the color of snow; for one could believe that there is such a rule but have no disposition to follow it. What Peirce and James meant, no doubt, is that to believe that snow is white is to have the disposition to follow this rule, as well as other rules that specify how one ought to act toward snow, such as to infer that one will have white visual images when confronted with snow under standard conditions.

There is another problem that concerns the nature of the relation between the thought and the subsequent behavior. James unwittingly gives both a normative and a nonnormative account of this relation. The former makes room for evaluating the believer's behavior, whether intentional or nonintentional, as being correct or incorrect in respect to the way in which it is connected with the original belief or thought, but the latter does not, being confined to a mere causal or temporal account of the relation between the belief and the subsequent behavior. James's use of "conduct [the thought] is *fitted* to produce" in the above quotation favors the normative interpretation, as does his use of "conduct to be *recommended*" in Baldwin's *Dictionary* (EP, 94. See also VRE, 351). There are other normative-sounding expressions that James uses to characterize the behavioral disposition of the believer. He speaks of the conduct that a belief "dictates" or "calls for" (EP, 124). He also speaks of the "conduct that *should* be followed" by the believer or that is "*required*" by the belief (EP, 335, and WB, 32; my italics). What a believer ought or is demanded to do is different from what she will be caused to do by her having the belief in question.

Unfortunately, James often characterizes the behavioral disposition in purely causal terms, devoid of any type of oughtness or shouldness. He says that a belief "inspires" (EP, 124, and WB, 32) and "instigates" (P, 97) certain behavior. "We know an object by means of an idea, whenever we ambulate towards the object under the *impulse* which the idea communicates" (MT, 80; my italics). Sometimes James describes the relation between a belief and the attendant behavior in purely temporal terms, as when he speaks of the "conduct consequent upon" or that "follows on" a belief (EP, 125, and MT, 34). There is not even a hint of anything normative in these causal and temporal accounts.

The problem with the causal and temporal accounts is that the behavior that is *caused by* or *follows* a given belief or thought is notoriously variable among persons because it is determined by features of the believer's psychological makeup. This results in a subjectivistic, Protagorean nightmare in which meanings become so person-relative that communication becomes practically although not theoretically impossible, since in principle enough could be known about a person's external behavior so that his behavior upon hearing certain words could be predicted. This is nicely illustrated in the "Niagara Falls" comedy routine in which every time Lou Costello would innocently mention "Niagara Falls" it would cause Bud Abbott to go berserk and start pounding on him. James is well advised to go with the normative account, and for the most part he does.

Unlike Peirce, who found the source of the normative in the way in which the community of scientists agreed upon the use of general terms, James eschews any appeal to normatively rule-governed human practices to explain the normative. His account of the normative basis for the proper use of general concepts, for example, is in terms of an intention to follow a "private rule," and thus he winds up with relativism and subjectivism. With regard to general concepts he writes that it is a fundamental psychical peculiarity which may be entitled "*the principle of constancy in the mind's meanings,*" and which may be thus expressed: "*The same matters can be thought of in successive portions of the mental stream, and some of these portions can know that they mean the same matters which the other portions meant.*" One might put it otherwise by saying that "the mind can always intend, and know when it intends, to think of the Same." (*PP,* I, 434)

This principle rests on a fundamental law of psychology: "That we can at any moment think of the same thing which at any former moment we thought of is the ultimate law of our intellectual constitution" (*PP,* II, 920). This principle or law is of a subjective character, since it is the subject's "intention . . . to think of the same," about which he cannot be mistaken, that determines the extension of his general concept over time (*PP,* I, 435). "Each thought decides, by its own authority," whether its present content is an instance of what it formerly intended to count as an instance of some concept. In other words, each subject follows an in-principle private rule in determining which individuals count as instances of a given general concept. She and she alone knows whether she is correctly following her intention to call these experiences instances of this concept.

This commitment to an in-principle private language in *The Principles of Psychology* becomes fully explicit in his last publication, *Some Problems of Philosophy.* A general word for a sensible quality, say for white, can collect together into its extension instances of white that differ in their color-qualities, provided "we mean that our word *shall* inalterably signify" a color common to them. "The impossibility of isolating and fixing this quality physically is irrelevant, so long as we can isolate and fix it mentally, and decide that whenever we say 'white,' that identical quality, whether applied rightly or wrongly, is what we shall be held to *mean.* Our meanings can be the same as often as we intend to have them so" (*SPP,* 57). James uses "we" in this passage in the distributive sense, since each one of us must adhere to her own private intention always to call things "white" that have the same color as the specimen she has mentally isolated and officially dubbed as the standard of whiteness. James does allow for the possibility of the speaker "rightly or wrongly" applying "white," but only the speaker is able to determine whether this correctly adheres to his own or her own private rule. The reason is that his paradigm of whiteness, which is a mental image private to herself, is not in principle accessible to anyone else. It is Wittgenstein's beetle in the matchbox that is observable only by the matchbox's owner. Therefore no one else can check up on the speaker to determine there is consistent adherence to the rule always to call things white that have the same color as his or her mental paradigm of whiteness. It was this commitment to an in-principle private language that made James the major whipping boy of the later Wittgenstein. Whether James's account of what qualifies an individual as being the proper referent of a singular concept also is mired in subjectivism is less clear and will not be pursued here.[2] With this preliminary sketch of James's pragmatic theory of meaning in hand, it can now be asked how he applied it to outstanding debates in the history of philosophy for the purpose of deconstructing them.

Pragmatic Meaning and Content Empiricism

James initially applies his pragmatic method to a nonphilosophical dispute that concerns whether a man succeeds in walking around a squirrel when he circles the tree on which the squirrel is affixed but the squirrel moves in such a manner as always to keep the tree trunk between itself and the man (*P*, 27–28). He attempts to resolve the dispute by deploying his pragmatic theory of meaning. The upshot is that the disputants agree about all the relevant empirical facts but use different definitions of "walking around," and thus their dispute is a merely verbal one. The implication is that many of the outstanding philosophical disagreements are only verbal, which is a thesis that would have been heartily endorsed by the logical positivists and linguistic analysts. But James's description of these empirical facts is in terms of what can be observed *at the time of the past circling*, not, as his pragmatic theory would have it, what can be observed in the *future* after certain verifying steps are taken, such as, if you check the tree in the future, you will find tiny claw marks and if you check the ground, human footprints and squirrel droppings.

To be sure, James is giving an empirical rendering of the rival claims, only it is a different species of empiricism than is his pragmatism since, unlike the latter, it is not exclusively future oriented. It is the species of empiricism that was championed by the British empiricists from Locke to Hume, whom James frequently credits, along with Socrates, with being early pragmatists (*P*, 30), and could aptly be called "content empiricism" because it analyzes an idea of *X* in terms of the experiences that would be had upon experiencing *X*. James's subtitle of *Pragmatism, A New Name for Some Old Ways of Thinking*, confounds his pragmatic theory of meaning with their content empiricism. A more accurate subtitle, though hardly a grabber, would be *A New Name for a New Way of Thinking That Is a Different Species of Empiricism Than an Old Way of Thinking*.

That James recognized both of these species of empiricism helps to explain the relation between his pragmatism and his radical empiricism, an issue on which he never was clear. Pragmatism is a theory of both meaning and truth. An idea's meaning is a set of conditionalized predictions, with its truth consisting in the actual fulfillment or verification of these predictions, as is required by this assumption. Pragmatism, therefore, is a conjunction of a pragmatic species of empiricism (M for short) with a theory of truth (T for short) based on it. "Radical empiricism," on the other hand,

consists first of a postulate, next of a statement of fact, and finally of a generalized conclusion.

The postulate is that the only things that shall be debatable among philosophers shall be things definable in terms drawn from experience. . . .

The statement of fact is that the relations between things, conjunctive as well as disjunctive, are just as much matters of direct particular experience, neither more so nor less so, than the things themselves.

The generalized conclusion is that therefore the parts of experience hold together from next to next by relations that are themselves parts of experience. The directly apprehended universe needs, in short, no extraneous trans-empirical connective support, but possesses in its own right concatenated or continuous structure. (*MT*, 6–7; my italics)

James was none too clear about the relation between radical empiricism and his pragmatism—the conjunction of M and T. At first he says "that there is no logical connexion between pragmatism, as I understand it, and a doctrine which I have recently set forth as 'radical empiricism'" (*P*, 6). But later he says that the establishment of the pragmatic theory of truth "is a step of first-rate importance in making radical empiricism prevail" (*MT*, 6). Both remarks are correct, but they need further explanation.

Some commentators have mistakenly thought that radical empiricism entails pragmatism but not vice versa. The reason for this is that they thought that radical empiricism's postulate of empiricism *is identical with* the M conjunct of pragmatism, its operationalist theory of meaning; and, since M entails T and radical empiricism entails M, radical empiricism entails the conjunction of M and T, which together constitute pragmatism. Pragmatism, thus, is a logically necessary condition for radical empiricism, since one of the conjuncts in radical empiricism, its postulate of empiricism, entails pragmatism. What these commentators failed to realize is that pragmatism's pragmatic theory of meaning, M, is only one species of empiricism; and, since the empirical postulate refers to a generic empiricism, of which content empiricism and M are different species, this postulate does not entail M. For, whereas a species entails the genus, the converse does not hold: that something is a tiger entails that it is an animal but not vice versa.

The reason why the establishment of the pragmatic theory of truth "is a step of first-rate importance in making radical empiricism prevail" is that it eliminates certain prominent counter-examples to the empirical postulate of the latter, consisting in the truth, correspondence, and reference relations. The pragmatic theory of meaning shows how these relations can be empirically analyzed in terms of a succession of experiences that terminates in a percept of the correspondent or referent in the truth or reference relation. Thus, pragmatism, although it does not entail radical empiricism, helps it to prevail by protecting its flank against some seemingly powerful counter-examples. Just how it does this will be considered shortly.

James often makes an unannounced shift from his official pragmatic species of empirical meaning to the content empiricism species. A good example of this is his account of the meaning of a concept. Initially, he gives his pragmatic account: Once we know what "difference . . . [a claim's] being true will make in some possible person's history, we shall know, not only just what you are really claiming, but also how important an issue it is, and how to go to work to verify the claim" (*SPP*, 38). But he then immediately countenances content empiricism as bringing out part of the meaning of a concept when he says that in obeying this pragmatic rule for determining meaning "we neglect the *substantive* content of the concept, and follow its function only" (*SPP*, 38; my italics). The *function* of a concept or idea—what it portends for future experience and conduct—is only a part of its meaning; it has in addition a *substantive content*. This content will be, for James, an experiential one, as is required by content empiricism. "To understand a concept you must know what it *means*. It means always some *this,* or some abstract portion of a *this,* with which we first made acquaintance in the perceptual world, or else some grouping of such abstract portions. All conceptual content is borrowed: to know what the concept 'colour' means you must have *seen* red, or blue, or green" (*SPP,* 46). In this passage James espouses Hume's concept empiricism, which requires that all concepts be derived by a process of abstraction from sense experience. These sense experiences constitute the "substantive content" of a concept's meaning. They need not be future experiences that are attendant upon the performance of certain operations.

A similar distinction between function and content underlies James's remark that "[t]he meaning of a concept may always be found, *if not in some sensible particular which it directly designates,* then in some particular difference in the course of human experience which its being true will make" (*SPP,* 37; my italics). The sensible particular that is directly designated supposedly constitutes its substantive content. The distinction between a concept's pragmatic function and its substantive empirical content also is found in his account of the three forms that a concept can take. "The concept of 'man,' to take an example, is three things: 1. the word itself; 2. a vague picture of the human form which has its own value in the way of beauty or not; and 3. an instrument for symbolizing certain objects from which we may expect human treatment when occasion arrives" (*SPP,* 36). Condition 3 concerns the function or pragmatic meaning of the concept, which in the case of abstract contents is the only form that the concept takes. Condition 2, on the other hand, is the substantive content since it involves the "vague picture" or the image part of the concept. James goes on to add that "however beautiful or otherwise worthy of stationary contemplation the substantive part of a concept may be, the more important part of its significance may naturally be held to be the consequences to which it leads." But, in spite of giving pride of place to a concept's pragmatic meaning, this countenances the substantive content as part of the meaning of certain concepts (*SPP,* 37). This distinction between the substance and the function of a concept gives reason to think that James had a theory of pragmatic meaning rather than a pragmatic theory of meaning, given that he recognized a non-pragmatic cognitive or substantive meaning in addition to a pragmatic one, namely, content empiricism.

And it is well that he did recognize content empiricism as part of the meaning of a concept or thought since the problem posed by the paradox of the alleged futurity of yesterday for James's exclusively future-oriented pragmatic theory of meaning can be neutralized only by supplementing this theory with that of content empiricism. Let us get back to our sample proposition reporting a past event, that Caesar crossed the Rubicon. It violates common sense to equate the *whole* meaning of this proposition with a set of conditionalized predictions that specify what experiences one would have in the future upon performing different actions. This future-oriented account of meaning must be supplemented by the content empiricist's analysis of this proposition in terms of the sense experiences that would have been had by an ideal but possibly nonexistent observer who was at the Rubicon at the time in question, this being similar to James's above content empiricist's account of the meaning of the claim that a man walked around a squirrel. This account of the meaning of a proposition about the past can be recast in terms of a distinction that was made by subsequent logical positivists. Schlick distinguished between a statement's actual and logical verification, Carnap between its practical and theoretical verifiability, and Ayer between its practical and in-principle verifiability. The latter member of each of the three distinctions corresponds to James's content empirical meaning, since it concerns what an ideal observer who was suitably equipped and stationed in space and time would have observed. The former concerns how it is practically possible for a present person to verify a statement, this often involving indirect verification with respect to propositions about the past and other minds.

James does not think that the mere "logical," "theoretical," or "in-principle" possibility of verification is enough for meaningfulness. There also must be the practical possibility of verification by a present person. He is prepared to fight in the last ditch for it being *necessary* that propositions about the past have a pragmatic meaning. The reason is that James is an empiricist first, last, and always. Thus, he will not countenance a non-empirical truth or a correspondence or reference relation, called a "salutatory relation," between a thought or idea and its worldly correspondent. This is the nub of James's response to John E. Russell, who held that the law of bivalence held for propositions about the past even when they were not in principle verifiable.

> Dear Russell: We seem now to have laid bare our exact difference. According to me, "meaning" a certain object and "agreeing" with it are abstract notions of both of which definite concrete accounts can be given.
>
> According to you, they shine by their own inner light and no further account can be given. They may even "obtain" (*in cases where human verification is impossible*) and make no empirical difference to us. To me, using the pragmatic method of testing concepts, this would mean that the word truth might on certain occasions have no meaning whatever. I still must hold to its having always a meaning, and continue to contend for that meaning being unfoldable and representable in experiential terms. (*ERE*, 153; my italics)

If we were completely causally cut off from the past Caesar, so that no future indirect verification is practically possible, the belief that Caesar crossed the Rubicon, in spite of having a content empirical meaning, would not be meaningful.

In order to be able to know that Caesar crossed the Rubicon we must be able to refer to him. James gives a pragmatic account of how singular reference is secured. It will be seen that the paradox of the alleged futurity of yesterday applies to this account and can be neutralized only by supplementing it with content empiricism. For James, the aim of a singular reference is to enable the referer to come into experiential contact with the referent, to grab it by the lapels in the *future*. Toward this end, the referer has a causal recipe that will guide her through a succession of experientially vouchsafed steps that will terminate in this direct contact, or indirect contact if the referent should be the contents of another mind or a theoretical entity of science. This is in accord with the underlying Promethean spirit of his philosophy, in which our whole way of conceiving the world is geared to furthering our quest to gain control and mastery over objects so that we can use them to maximize desire-satisfaction. Toward this end we must be able to concoct recipes that will lead us to these objects so that we can effectively use them. This exclusively future-oriented causal theory of reference stands in stark contrast with the past-oriented causal or historical theories of singular reference championed in recent times by Kripke, Donnellan, Putnam, and Burge in which the causal chain begins in the past with a baptismal-type bestowal of a proper name that then gets continuously passed on from one referer to a subsequent one in an ongoing linguistic community that terminates in a present use of the name. Whereas this theory of reference fails to do justice to the pragmatic aspect of reference, James's theory seems to make it impossible to refer to a past object, given that the referent of a singular concept always is some object in the future.

That it is impossible to refer to a past individual creates the following problem for reference to individuals in the future, which I owe to Henry Jackman. Imagine that I have a cap that I have continuously owned since I purchased it seven years ago. I left it on a table in the next room and now entertain a thought of it. According to James the meaning of this thought for me is a recipe that will guide me step by experiential step from where I now am to the cap on the table in the next room so that I can grab it by the "lapels." I follow this recipe and reach a cap that exactly resembles my initiating thought of it, even down to having a dark spot on its bill where the dog had an accident, but unbeknownst to me some practical joker, out to give a counter-example to James, had replaced it with an exact duplicate. I take the cap to be the referent of my initiating thought because it not only resembles my original cap but also satisfies all of the pragmatic functions of the original cap, such as discouraging panhandlers from approaching me for money. But it isn't my cap, and there seemingly is no way to explain why it is not without tracing the past history of this cap against that of my original cap in order to show that it is not spatio-temporally continuous with the original cap. Thus, unless it is possible to refer to a past object qua past object, it is not possible to determine that a present object is the referent of a past act of reference.

In order to show how a past object can be referred to he must again supplement his pragmatic account of meaning with that of content empiricism. In the case of my cap that is now in the next room, my causal recipe for getting my hands on it must be supplemented by a content empiricism description of the cap's past history, its continuous history since I purchased it seven years ago, that is, a description of the experiences that would have been had were an observer to have continuously observed it over this seven-year interval. And this is content empiricism.

Deployment of Pragmatism to Philosophical Disputes

Now for some of James's *philosophical* deployments of his pragmatic method. The clearest and most dramatic application of this method is to the long-standing dispute between theism and atheism, misleadingly called "materialism" by James. He attempts to unearth the pragmatic meaning of these rival theories by considering what happens if there should literally be no future. The result of this thought-experiment supposedly can be generalized to all philosophical disputes between rival theories, thus giving great significance to his discussion. In accordance with his pragmatic theory of meaning, the differences between theism and materialism are to be found in differences between their conditionalized predictions. Theism predicts that good will everlastingly win out over evil if we collectively exert our best moral efforts, and materialism that, regardless of what efforts we make, all will end in death and destruction because the lower forces are ultimately in control.

James claims that if there is no future, the world popping out of existence at this very moment, these seemingly opposing theories would have the same meaning—namely, none at all.

> He [the pragmatist] asks us to imagine how the pragmatic test can be applied if there is no future. Concepts for him are things to come back into experience with, things to make us look for differences. But by hypothesis there is to be no more experience and no possible differences can now be looked for. Both theories have shown all their consequences and, by the hypothesis we are adopting, these are identical. The pragmatist must consequently say that the two theories, in spite of their different-sounding names, mean exactly the same thing, and that the dispute is purely verbal. (P, 50–51)

James also says that "it makes not a single jot of difference so far as the *past* of the world goes, whether we deem it to have been the work of matter or whether we think a divine spirit its author" (P, 50). "Thus if no future detail of experience or conduct is to be deduced from our hypothesis, the debate between materialism and theism becomes quite idle and insignificant" (EP, 127).

There are problems with James's way of neutralizing the dispute between theism and atheism under the hypothesis that there is no future. First, there is a problem of internal consistency, for James so defines theism that it is refuted if there should be no future since it requires that "an ideal order . . . shall be *permanently* preserved" (EP, 130; my italics). Let us not worry about this, for there are even more serious difficulties.

That "the debate between materialism and theism becomes quite idle and insignificant" without a future, as lacking in emotional interest, does not entail that these theories are completely devoid of meaning. James is expressing only his personal dislike for such debates. This becomes clear when he says that "in every *genuine* metaphysical debate some practical issue . . . is involved," the "genuine" qualification being a tip-off that an evaluatively based, disguised linguistic innovation is in the offing (P, 52; my italics). James adds that such debates are of "purely intellectual" interest and urges his reader to avoid them (EP, 126). But such a debate, no matter how unworthy of a Promethean agent's attention, must have some meaningful content since it has at least an "intellectual" interest. By his use of "intellectual" and "idle and insignificant," James is begrudgingly recognizing an additional species of meaning to that of pragmatism.

The same objection applies to James's remark that "when a play is once over, and the curtain down, you really make it no better by claiming an illustrious genius for its author, just as you make it no worse by calling him a common hack" (*EP*, 127). It would seem that, for James, your claim that the play's author is a genius must issue in conditionalized predictions, such as, if you should meet the author at a cocktail party and question him about his play, what he says will attest to his genius. The proper response to this is that although your passing judgment on the worth of the author in no way alters the aesthetic value of the completed play, the intrinsic qualities of the play themselves serve as evidence for whether it has an author at all, and, if so, how good a one. Thus, the choice between the author–no author hypothesis or the good author–hack author hypothesis is decidable even if the world comes to an end when the curtain comes down. But this requires that these hypotheses have genuine *past* empirical content, as content empiricism would have it. Otherwise, the paradox of the alleged futurity of yesterday arises.

Another flaw in James's treatment of the no-future case concerns his claim that if there is no future, then "no future detail of experience or conduct is to be deduced from our hypothesis" of theism (*P*, 52). Whether there be a future or not does not make any difference in respect to what predictions a hypothesis entails, but only in respect to the truth of these predictions, it being assumed by James that all predictions are false if there be no future. If having predictive consequences is necessary for a hypothesis to be meaningful, then a hypothesis can possess such pragmatic meaning even when there is no future.

Maybe the most decisive refutation of James's claim that there is no difference in meaning between atheism and theism in the no-future case is that it winds up violating the principle of the temporal homogeneity of *being evidence for*—namely, If *E* counts as evidence for or confirms proposition *p* at time *T*, then *E* counts as evidence for or confirms *p* at any time. *Being evidence for* must not be confounded with *being taken to be evidence for*. The former, in spite of being an epistemic relation, is existentially grounded in an objective relation between two worldly states of affairs, whereas the latter is relative to the epistemic state of a subject—what she knows and believes at a certain time. A certain type of rash is taken by a doctor, but not a layman, as evidence of a certain disease; but nevertheless the rash is evidence for both of them of this disease. *Being evidence for* is homogeneous among not only times but persons as well. James seems to violate the temporal homogeneity of *being evidence for* when he says that a benevolent course of events in the future would serve as evidence for, even be verificatory of, theism, but this very same course of events in the past would not.

There are indications that James saw serious difficulties with his discussion of the theism-materialism debate in the no-future case in his 1898 "Philosophical Conceptions and Practical Results"; for when he repeated it eight years later in *Pragmatism*, he added, "I am supposing, of course, that the theories *have* been equally successful in their explanations of what is" (*P*, 51). Thus, James seems to be assuming, although he does not explicitly state it, that the past of the no-future world in his example is an ambiguous mixed bag of good and evil that does not speak clearly either for atheism or for theism. But if he is to handpick his example in this manner, while he escapes the foregoing charge of relativizing *being evidence for* to a time, he cannot generalize from his example, as he plainly does; for immediately after completing his discussion of the no-future example, he draws this general conclusion: "Accordingly, in *every* genuine metaphysical debate some practical issue, however conjectural and remote, is involved," in which the "issue" concerns what is future *quoad* now (*P*, 52; my italics).

We do not have just to infer that James saw a difficulty in his 1898 address. In *The Meaning of Truth* he comes right out and tells us what it is: "I had no sooner given the address than I perceived a flaw in that part of it; but I left the passage unaltered ever since, because the flaw did not spoil its illustrative value" (*MT*, 103). James not only mislocates the source of the difficulty, failing to see that it temporally relativizes *being evidence for* and makes meaning wholly prospective, but makes a concession to the content empiricist that undercuts his claim that an idea's pragmatic consequences exhaust its meaning. He finds the difficulty with his former identification of the whole meaning of theism with what is outwardly observable in the future to be analogous to what we find missing in a soulless "automatic sweetheart" whose outwardly observable behavior is "absolutely indistinguishable from a spiritually animated maiden, laughing, talking, blushing, nursing us, and performing all feminine offices as tactfully and sweetly as if a soul were in her" (*MT*, 103). What we find woefully inadequate is its lack of inner conscious states, because its outward behavior "is valued mainly as an expression, as a manifestation of the accompanying consciousness believed in" (*MT*, 103). James's worry about whether it is good for her too shows him to be a closet Cartesian, as does his use of the Cartesian argument from analogy for the existence of other minds (*MT*, 24 and 30, and *ERE*, 36 and 38). Analogously, what we sorely miss in his former rendering of theism in terms of the future triumph of goodness, provided we do our moral best, is the inner conscious states of God, for humans desire a being "who will inwardly recognize them and judge them sympathetically." Herein what is outwardly observable, whether future or not, cannot constitute the whole meaning. A wedge is being driven between the inner states of consciousness that constitute at least part of the meaning of a statement about God or the real sweetheart and what is outwardly observable. These inner states would constitute part of the content empirical meaning of states about the two individuals.

James's change in the way he interpreted the concept of God, in which the pragmatic view of God as being nothing but our ally in our efforts to make good win out over evil in the future gets supplemented with his being the possessor of inner consciousness, mirrors a change in the way he conceived of the idealist's Absolute. On the basis of his pragmatism—that the only "test of probable truth is what works best in the way of leading us, what fits every part of life best, and combines with the collectivity of experience's demands, nothing being omitted" (*P*, 44)—he infers that the sole meaning of belief that there is an Absolute is that we may take a moral holiday; and, although this is a good thing, it clashes with our other of our beliefs concerning the reality of evil and pluralism. The difference between absolutism and pluralism is that whereas both permit leading the morally strenuous life, only pluralism "demands [it] since it makes the world's salvation depend upon the energizing of its several parts, among which we are" (*MT*, 123). James's pragmatic rendering of the Absolute is of a piece with his pragmatic reduction of the concept of Nirvana according to which "Nirvana means safety," which would justify our calling a pill that was able to impart a sense of safety to those who ingest it "Nirvana."

Needless to say, this pragmatic rendering of the meaning of the Absolute was stoutly rejected by Absolute Idealists. In *The Meaning of Truth,* in which James attempts to rebut objections to *Pragmatism,* he responds in the following tongue-in-cheek way to their rejection: "I had shown the concept of the absolute to *mean nothing but the holiday giver, the banisher of cosmic fear. . . .* Apparently my absolutist critics fail to see the workings of their own minds in any such picture, so all that I can do is to apologize, and take my offering back. The absolute is true in no way then, and least of all, by the verdict of the critics, in the way which I assigned" (*MT,* 5).

But this is not the end of the story, for subsequently, in *A Pluralistic Universe,* James supplements his reductive pragmatic analysis with a substantive content. "On the debit side of the account of the absolute, *taken seriously and not as a mere name for our right occasionally to drop the strenuous mood and take a moral holiday,* introduces all those tremendous irrationalities into the universe which a frankly pluralistic theism escapes" (*APU,* 57; my italics). It is typical of James to make this major change in his theory of meaning in an offhand remark, without any indication that it involves a countenancing of another species of meaning in addition to his official pragmatic one. Supposedly, since the Absolute is a mind, it has the same sort of inner consciousness as does his theistic God and, hopefully, his sweetheart.

One aspect of taking the Absolute seriously, of which James was well aware, is the theoretical role that it plays in explaining how reference is possible. Herein he supplements his pragmatic meaning not with that of content empiricism but with the theoretical explanatory role that a concept plays. Royce argued that the only way in which an idea could have a referent is if the referent is an idea in the same mind as is the referring idea, from which it is a short skip and a jump to the conclusion that every idea is contained in the same mind—the Absolute. James completely agreed with Royce that the referential relation must hold between ideas contained in the same mind, the only difference being that whereas Royce required that the ideas be simultaneous, James allowed them to be successive. The earlier idea contains a recipe for leading to its referent idea through a sequence of empirically vouchsafed steps.

There are other examples of James countenancing a theoretical role for a concept. Most of the time James favored an instrumentalist theory of theoretical entities in science, according to which they are only convenient heuristic fictions that aid our ability to make inferences and calculations. But when it came to the Soul and God, James did not give his typical reductive pragmatic account, according to which "'God,' 'freedom,' and 'design,' mean the same thing, viz., the presence of 'promise' in the world" (*MT*, 5–6). He claimed that the substantive Soul, although lacking any experiential content and being devoid of explanatory power in psychology, did help to make sense of the moral life and certain extraordinary conscious states. That he is even willing to ask the question whether the theory of the Soul, understood as "both immaterial and simple," has "advantages as a theory over the simple phenomenal notion of a stream of thought accompanying a stream of cerebral activity, by a law yet unexplained," shows that he is countenancing another species of meaning in addition to the above two empirical species, since this sort of soul is accessible to neither external nor internal sense (*PP*, I, 325). Although "the Soul-theory is, then, a superfluity, *so far as accounting for the actually verified facts of conscious experience*," it could have an explanatory value in metaphysics when understood as a transcendent 'more'" (*PP*, I, 329; my italics). "For my own part I confess that the moment I become metaphysical and try to define the more, I find the notion of some sort of an anima mundi thinking in all of us to be a more promising hypothesis, in spite of all its difficulties, than that of a lot of absolutely individual souls" (*PP*, I, 328). "The reader who finds comfort in the idea of the Soul, is, however, perfectly free to continue to believe in it; for our reasonings have not established the nonexistence of the Soul; they have only proved its superfluity for scientific purposes" (*PP*, I, 332).

The most dramatic departure from his pragmatic theory of meaning is found in James's sympathetic account of mysticism in *The Varieties of Religious Experience*. Mysticism challenges James's pragmatic theory of meaning and truth. The pragmatic theory of meaning, as contrasted with the theory of pragmatic meaning, holds that the meaning of X is a set of conditionalized predictions of what experiences we shall have upon performing certain operations, with a belief in the reality of X becoming true when these predictions are verified. But the mystic's conception of the Absolute, the undifferentiated unity, the eternal one, or God is not based on how we can ride herd on it, for there is nothing that we do to or with this mystical reality, or ways in which it is expected to behave if we perform certain operations. It doesn't dissolve in aqua regia. It simply *is*, and is just what it *appears* to be in the immediate experience of the mystic. A door-to-door salesman of mystical reality, therefore, would be stymied when asked, "But what does it do?" or "What can I do with it?" Herein the content of the proposition that this reality exists is not reducible to any set of pragmatic conditionalized predictions. The star performer finally gets into the act, unlike the case of the pragmatically favored melioristic religion, which reduced "God exists" to the conditionalized prediction that good will win out over evil in the long run, if we collectively exert our best moral effort. The reason James chose meliorism as his example of a religion in the final lecture of *Pragmatism* is that it can be shown to employ the same pragmatic theory of meaning and truth as does science, which fits his program of reconciliation through methodological univocalism.

In order to account for the meaning of mystical reality-claims, James will have to resort to content empiricism, which was found to be his other species of empiricism to that of pragmatism. Since the meaningful content of the mystic's reality-claim is based on the manner in which she is phenomenologically appeared to in an of-God type experience, the truth of the claim will depend on whether her experience is objective or cognitive. The spiritual and moral benefits that the experience occasions become relevant, but only as a means of indirect verification, there now being, as there wasn't for meliorism, a distinction between direct and indirect verification, with an assertion's meaning being identified primarily with the former, that being the apparent object, the intentional accusative, of the mystical experience. James seems to recognize this when he says that "the word 'truth' is here taken to mean something additional to bare value for life" (*VRE*, 401). This crucial qualification of his former pragmatic theory of truth deserved to be put up in bright lights rather than to be buried in a footnote. Accordingly, James makes the issue of the cognitivity or objectivity of mystical experience a central issue in *The Varieties of Religious Experience.* Concerning them, he asks about their "metaphysical significance" (308), "cognitivity" (324), "authoritativeness" (335), "objective truth" (304), "value for knowledge" (327), their "truth" (329), and whether they "furnish any *warrant for the truth* of the . . . supernaturality and pantheism which they favor" (335), or are "to be taken as *evidence* . . . for the actual existence of a higher world with which our world is in relation" (384). James is quite explicit that the answer to the "objectivity" question is independent of the biological and psychological benefits that accrue from mystical experiences.

Conclusion

James's attempt to use his pragmatism to deconstruct traditional philosophy is, thank God, a complete failure, as are all attempts to do this. The major cause of failure is that along the way to establishing the deconstructionist conclusion the deconstructionist must do a lot of hard-core, traditional philosophizing of just the sort that is outlawed by this conclusion; for the theories of meaning and truth that the deconstructionist must utilize are of a piece with the most wildly speculative metaphysical theories, disputes about them being perennial and intractable. Philosophy is all of a piece. Fortunately, James's actual practice as a philosopher violated his pragmatically based strictures. This is what is missed in Richard Rorty's claim that "as long as we see James or Dewey as having 'theories of truth' or 'theories of knowledge' or 'theories of morality' we shall get them wrong."[3] Instead, James had a "therapeutic conception of philosophy familiar from Wittgenstein's *Philosophical Investigations*" that showed us a way of avoiding the fruitlessness of doing philosophy in the traditional manner.[4] Rorty seems not to have noticed that James devoted two books, *Pragmatism* and *The Meaning of Truth*, to developing a theory or account of truth and that Dewey wrote books, such as *Experience and Nature* and *Art as Experience*, that were exercises in hard-core traditional philosophy of just the sort that his official metaphilosophy exorcized.

The deconstructionist's strategy is to challenge those who do philosophy in the traditional manner to describe the rules of their philosophical language-game in virtue of which we can keep score and determine who wins and loses. And when they are unable to do this, it is inferred that their language-game is a bogus one. This demand for a cognitive discipline to have a decision procedure for determining who is right smacks of scientism, in which the methods employed by the sciences, as well as the way in which they use concepts, are taken to be legislative for all contexts and disciplines, a discipline's failure to measure up to these scientific standards showing that it is bogus. The only effective response to the deconstructionst's challenge is to do more traditional philosophy. For there are many language-games that we play which are central in our lives but for which we cannot specify the rules of the game. And this brings us back to the unmarked dice with which this paper began. The dice are not completely devoid of markings, but the markings are blurry. Often it can be determined who wins and money will change hands, but there always will be occasions on which the markings are not clear enough to determine a winner. The result of this partial indeterminability is that although money changes hands and there are temporary increases and decreases in the bankrolls of the crap shooters, no one ever gets permanently wiped out. Yes, the South shall rise again!

NOTES

1. In his posthumously published *Some Problems of Philosophy,* James identified philosophy with the residuum of unanswered problems or questions but immediately adds that although "they have *not yet been answered* . . . it does not follow that . . . no answer will ever be forthcoming" (*SPP,* 18; my italics).

2. For a full discussion see my book, *The Divided Self of William James* (London: Cambridge University Press, 1999), pp. 166–74.

3. Richard Rorty, *Consequences of Pragmatism* (Minneapolis: University of Minnesota Press, 1982), p. 160. See also p. 139.

4. Richard Rorty, *Objectivity, Relativity, and Truth* (Cambridge: Cambridge University Press, 1991), p. 3.

7. James on Truth and Solidarity: The Epistomology of Diversity and the Politics of Specificity

José M. Medina

Given William James's thoroughgoing individualism, it may seem peculiar—even implausible—to use his philosophy to bring together the notion of truth and the notion of solidarity. James's philosophy seems oriented toward the individual and her experiences, but not so much toward interpersonal relations. However, despite his recalcitrant and unqualified individualism, I want to argue that there is a strong social element in James's philosophy. I see this impetus toward the interpersonal and social in his pluralism and relationalism. James's radical pluralism is based on a theory of relationality according to which nothing can be understood in and by itself, but rather in relation to other things, in a network of relations. On this relational view, the identity of things is concocted in a network of interdependences; and to have a sense of self is to have a sense of the dependences that compose one's life, for we can understand the identity of something only by grasping the fabric of relations in which that thing appears. It is essential to distinguish this relationalism from the holism that is often attributed to figures such as Ludwig Wittgenstein, Wilfrid Sellars, Nelson Goodman, and W. V. O. Quine. Whereas the Jamesian relationalism is based on open-ended networks of relations that are typically unfinished and indeterminate, the holism that circulates in contemporary philosophy of language requires finished and complete wholes (whether they are frameworks, webs of beliefs, or language-games). James's relationalism is beyond the usual dichotomy between atomism and holism and actually undercuts it, for, without assigning priority to the component parts or to the whole, it prioritizes relations and calls attention to their formative and transformative character in shaping the relata. From a relational perspective, to understand the identity of something is to understand how that thing is related to many other things, but also how it can become entangled in many other potential relations. For it is not only the factual relations that are already given that matter, but also those other potential relations that can unfold or be created.

The identity of each thing is bound up with diversity, for each thing enters into constitutive relations with many other things and becomes entangled with a wild diversity of entities to which it is related in a network of interdependences. From this point of view, issues of identity have to be understood as issues of diversity: the others are essential to the self, for it is in networks of relations that individuals and groups are formed. Diversity is not a multicultural invention of postcolonial and globalized societies. On this view, diversity is the condition of denizens of this world and, therefore also, the human condition. We are diverse and heterogeneous beings who are shaped and reshaped through diverse and heterogeneous networks of interpersonal relations. James's conception of the self underscores this deep sense of relationality and involvement with those around us. For James, the self is a bundle of relations: the self is formed in and through the relations in which it becomes involved; we negotiate our identity in these relations. As he puts it: "Every bit of us at every moment is part and parcel of a wider self, it quivers along various radii like the wind-rose on a compass, and the actual in it is continuously one with possibles not yet in our present sight" (*APU*, 1977). As McDermott has shown, despite James's unflinching individualism and his explicit rejection of sociality as a constitutive aspect of the self, the Jamesian Promethean self is not a solitary self but a member of a community of experience and interpretation that cannot help but be enmeshed in social networks, for it is a relational unit that shrinks and grows as it relates to others.[1]

In James's view truth is a value that regulates our normative engagements with others. Truth is therefore the source of solidarity, for it contributes to the sharing of experience and the coordination of action. When James defines truth as "whatever proves itself to be good in the way of belief" (*P*, 42), he is referring not only to what we believe individually but also to what we believe together. For, as James puts it, "all human thinking gets discursified [. . .] by means of social intercourse" (*P*, 102); and in the "discursification" of our thinking our beliefs get articulated and evaluated in social negotiations that are regulated by truth. In other words, truth is a value that regulates our epistemic practices for the fixation of belief. Our truth negotiations are oriented toward the configuration of a common vantage point from which we can survey the world together. They aim at the sharing of experiences and at the coordination of action. In these negotiations we have to take responsibility for the beliefs we hold to be true. On the Jamesian view, holding a belief as true is holding that it is good to live by it; and this allegiance to a particular belief makes one responsible for its practical consequences in one's life and in the lives of others. In this way, as we shall see, James's conception of truth underscores the epistemic and social responsibility of believers and their accountability to others.

It is important to note that the normative engagements that truth regulates are open-ended negotiations that involve not only actual but also possible others with whom we may share our cognitive life. That is, the normative negotiations concerning truth are open to indefinitely many others who can become our interlocutors. And what is crucial to note here is that these potential interlocutors are specific others who pose specific challenges and demands. They cannot be properly understood as a Generalized Other à la Mead or as a formal universal community of communication à la Habermas. As I will try to show in what follows, the notion of solidarity that derives from James's view of truth is very different from Mead's cosmopolitanism or from Habermas's universalism.

The central goal of this essay will be to use James's conception of truth to make explicit the connections between the epistemic reconstruction of beliefs and the sociopolitical critique of our practices and ways of life. In the next section, I will examine the normative and performative aspects of truth, bringing to the fore the social and political implications of James's view. In the section after, using as an illustration the critical reconstruction of our beliefs about the past, I will try to show that, according to James's radical pluralism, epistemological analysis is always at the same time social critique. This discussion will try to make clear that, far from falling into relativism, James's pluralistic conception of truth makes room for a robust notion of objectivity, which is at the same time a notion of justice. Finally, I will explore the implications of the convergence between the epistemic and the political that I see in James's view. I will argue that the Jamesian insights about truth have a prolific (and yet untapped) critical potential and can be used to set the agenda of a critical epistemology for the twenty-first century.

The Living Truth of Pragmatism

As I have argued elsewhere,[2] along with Nietzsche, James is responsible for posing the most fundamental questions about truth that contemporary philosophers will have to address. These radical critical questions concern the very value of truth: What is the nature of our obligations with respect to truth? And why are we obligated to seek the truth, to tell the truth, to respect the truth, to live up to the truth, and so on? Why should we value truth rather than falsity? These questions make us critically conscious of a crucial aspect of the concept of truth that had traditionally been either assumed or denied in philosophy,[3] namely, the normativity of truth. James warns us that we should be suspicious when it is built into the very notion of something that that thing is valuable. He encourages a skeptical attitude toward any alleged built-in normativity. James criticizes the appeal to truth as an end in itself, which turns truth into an arbitrary stopping-point of explanation and justification. In this way James warns us to beware of those properties that are said to have intrinsic value and cannot be called into question; for making a value absolute and self-evident is the best way of protecting it while hiding a dogmatic attitude toward it. Rejecting the absolutist conception of truth, James argues that truths are desired for their consequences, for the impact they can have on our life-experiences and practices. So his view of truth can be understood as an alethic consequentialism and instrumentalism. He himself describes his position as an "instrumental" conception of truth that follows the footsteps of the instrumentalist views put forth by Schiller and Dewey (see *P*, 34). But although he calls this conception "a theory," it is worth noting that his view is actually closer to contemporary minimalism and deflationism than to substantive theories of truth that postulate truth-makers and defend universal theses about the underlying nature of all truths.[4] James's instrumentalist view of truth is profoundly contextualist and pluralist and calls for piecemeal elucidations, rather than for a unified and substantive theory. Indeed, for James, the search for a single substantive property that makes all true beliefs and ideas true is misguided, for there are many ways in which truth functions as a value in our practices. However, he does identify some general pragmatic features that the value of truth has in our practices. But we should understand his pragmatic theory of truth not as a doctrine, but rather, as a practical orientation toward the value of truth and as a methodology for the elucidation of the practices in which that value figures. For, as James emphasizes, for a pragmatist theories are "instruments, not answers to enigmas, in which we can rest" (*P*, 32). Pragmatism, James underscores, has a marked procedural character, being first and foremost an attitude or orientation (a way of approaching problems) and a set of methods, not a set of doctrines.

James's discussions of truth constitute a reconstruction of the ways in which truth functions as a value in our practices. The goal of his reconstructive account is the rehabilitation of the value of truth on pragmatic grounds. Following Schiller and Dewey,[5] James conceives of truth as "one species of good," namely, "good in the way of belief" (*P*, 42). He characterizes truth as "the expedient in the way of our thinking" (*P*, 106). Denouncing the idealizations and abstractions of rationalism that led philosophers to despise "the muddy particulars of experience" (*P*, 110), he wants to explain "the cash-value of truth" in experiential terms. His empiricist and pragmatist view tries to bring the concept of truth back to the world of concrete experience and praxis (to the lifeworld) in which it functions. It is important to note that in his experiential and pragmatic justification of the value of truth, James depicts our obligation toward truth as "part of our general obligation to do what pays" (*P*, 106). On James's view, truths are reliable guides of our life and practice: we value truths for their "agreeable consequences," for their action-guiding role. Rejecting the traditional notion of truth as formal *adequatio* (or passive copying), James emphasizes the relation of truth to our agency and our life. As he puts it, the value of true ideas lies in their "useful leading": they lead to consistency, stability, and solidarity, and away from "eccentricity and isolation."

On James's view, consistency is a crucial part of the role that truth plays in the fixation of beliefs and ideas: new ideas and beliefs become accepted as true through their coherence with a body of already accepted beliefs and ideas. Hence the crucial importance of coherence, both internal and external, individual and social. As James puts it, "ideas (which themselves are but parts of our experience) become true just insofar as they help us to get into satisfactory relation with other parts of our experience" (*P*, 34; emphasis dropped). We are constantly engaged in a process of epistemic negotiation that aims at the consistency of new experiences with our existing beliefs as well as with those of others. This is the process "by which any individual settles into new opinions": "The individual has a stock of old opinions already, but he meets a new experience that puts them to a strain"

(*P,* 34). The strain, he adds, may also come from the experience of others who contradict our opinions or add new facts that have to be reconciled with them. In these negotiations we try to preserve "the older stock of truths with a minimum of modification, stretching them just enough to make them admit the novelty" (*P,* 35). According to James, the role of "older truths" in our epistemic life should not be underestimated ("Their influence is absolutely controlling. Loyalty to them is the first principle" [*P,* 35]). But at the same time James also insists on the crucial importance of our openness to experiential novelty: in order to have an epistemic life at all, in order to be alive as thinking and experiential subjects, we must open ourselves to new experiences and ideas that can alter the stock of accepted truths and become new truths. Our body of truths must grow.⁶ James warns us against the danger of relying uncritically on fixed truths, for this means relying on the experiences and valuations of others or of our past selves, which may have lost their force and appropriateness in our current experiential contexts. Fixity is a property that human truths cannot have; those recalcitrant truths that take the appearance of being permanent and fixed simply hide ossified valuations and rigidified beliefs. The fixation of truth once and for all would mean mental death; it would mean putting an end to our epistemic lives. Our body of truth always has to be critically revisited in the light of new experiences. Truths cannot simply be taken for granted, because they become inert or dead truths, truths that have been removed from the stream of life and are presented in complete independence from particular experiential contexts and particular experiential subjects. As James puts it in a brilliant passage: "Truth independent; truth that we find merely; truth no longer malleable to human need; truth incorrigible, in a word; such truth exists indeed superabundantly [. . .]; but then it means only the dead heart of the living tree, and its being there means only that truth also has its paleontology and its 'prescription', and may grow stiff with years of veteran service and petrified in men's regard by sheer antiquity" (*P,* 37).

Although for James the fixation of true beliefs is not a private and individualistic process, it does have an essential individual dimension, for the process of negotiation between old truths and new experiences is ultimately "a matter for the individual's appreciation" (*P,* 36). Truths have to be related to the individuals in whose life they make a difference, to their experiences and valuations. Truths, insofar as they are reliable guides for action, have to be tied to the experiential sources from which they spring. When truths are detached from the life-experiences that gave them birth, they lose their vital force and they become rigid, ossified, dead. Truths cannot be simply found; they have to be created or recreated to be alive. A new idea "makes itself true, gets itself classed as true, by the way it works" (*P,* 36). This live quality and potency of truth resides in what we can call the performativity of truth. Living truths are truths of our own making. James emphasizes that truths are not just there, inert and given, but that they have to be produced. In his critique of the copy theory of truth, he argues that true ideas and thoughts are not mere copies but symbols and, therefore, they involve more than a passive mirroring: they require an active making. Ideas and thoughts are not veridical in themselves (veridicality is never an intrinsic quality); they have to be made true. In this sense the focus of James's discussions is on Making True, rather than on Being True.[7] For James, truth is a value that emerges from and remains inscribed in human agency and human creativity: it regulates our creative transactions with the world around us and with each other. As he puts it, "In our cognitive as well as in our active life we are creative. We add, both to the subject and to the predicate part of reality. The world stands really malleable, waiting to receive its final touches at our hands. [. . .] Man engenders truths upon it" (P, 123).

Of course, the living truths we make today will be the dead truths of tomorrow. By contrast with the fixity of truth underscored by traditional views, James's view emphasizes the transient character that is conferred upon truths by their dependence on our experience and agency. James warns us against relying uncritically on the truths of the past—the truths of others (or of our former selves)—that is, against accepting inherited truths independently of the life-experiences from which they were drawn. Truths cannot simply be recirculated in our epistemic practices, for they lose their action-guiding value and productivity when they are detached from concrete life-experiences, becoming ossified by habitual use. But this does not mean that we cannot rely on those beliefs that have been previously accepted as true. Our epistemic activities need to rely on a stock of truths that have been previously established in our transactions with the world (our own as well as those of others). But the older truths on which we rely cannot be simply taken for granted; they have to be subject to a critical epistemic examination that traces them back to their experiential sources. This is why James claims that, besides a method, pragmatism is "a genetic theory of what is meant by truth" (P, 37; my emphasis). We have to uncover how truths have been made. We need to recover "the trail of the human serpent" that is left "over everything" (P, 37) and is often erased or forgotten. It is in this sense that the Jamesian approach to truth is essentially genealogical.[8] James tells us that we should keep in mind that even the most ancient truths "also once were plastic. They also were called true for human reasons. They also mediated between still earlier truths and what in those days were novel observations" (P, 36–37). Truth has "its paleontology" (P, 37).

On James's view, the epistemic analysis of our beliefs requires the genealogy of those ideas and thoughts that have been made true in our practices. But of course genealogy is driven by present concerns and interests and, therefore, it is both backward-looking and forward-looking simultaneously. The genealogy of truth tries to uncover what our truths have done so far and what they can still do for us. It traces the practical trajectories along which the lives of those truths have run their course, trying to determine if there is still some life left in them and what paths their present and future lives can take. Our epistemic analyses must be both retrospective and prospective: they must assess the truth of our beliefs at the crossroads between the life-experiences and actions of the past and those of the future; that is, they must evaluate how these beliefs can guide us in mediating the interface between the actualities and the potentialities of our life. Thus understood, our epistemic analyses constitute a critical enterprise: they involve the critical examination of the practical and experiential conditions and consequences that truths have in our life. Through a critical appraisal of the conditions from which they arise and the conditions to which they lead, our analyses investigate how truths can shape our forms of life, exploring the prospects of our life in common from an epistemic point of view. The general aim of the genealogical analysis of our stock of truths is to establish a solid epistemic ground for a shared life. The critical examination of our epistemic life has the potential to create relations of solidarity with fellow thinkers and inquirers whose epistemic appraisals can be coordinated with ours, even if our valuations and theirs don't coincide or even converge. A community of thought and interpretation is a community of solidarity, that is, a community of subjects who are prepared to think and believe together as they act upon their beliefs through collaborations, and who are ready to be responsive and accountable to each other as they try to share their experiential vantage points and to coordinate their actions. For this reason, the critical examination of our epistemic perspectives has a marked sociopolitical dimension. The Jamesian view strongly suggests that an epistemic analysis properly conducted is always an exercise in social critique with definite political implications. I will elaborate this point in the next section through a discussion of our individual and collective memory and the epistemic analysis of our beliefs about the past.

Epistemic Analysis and Social Critique: Objectivity and Justice

Beliefs have a contrastive character: we believe one thing as opposed to many other things. Accordingly, the analysis and evaluation of beliefs should also be contrastive and proceed by comparison with epistemic alternatives. It is not surprising that James defined philosophy as "the habit of always seeing an alternative": "Philosophic study means the habit of always seeing an alternative, of not taking the usual for granted, of making conventionalities fluid again, of imagining foreign states of mind. In a word, it means the possession of mental perspective" (EP, 4).

We can understand an idea or a belief only by putting it in perspective; and we can properly assess its value only by comparing it with all possible alternatives that we can envision. Note that this comparative and contrastive exercise remains always open-ended, for it concerns not only the epistemic alternatives that have been already articulated and are readily available, but also those we can create or imagine. Hence the crucial role that creativity and imagination play in our epistemic explorations.[9] But of course our creative and imaginative powers are always limited, and, therefore, we must always remain committed to the pursuit of new epistemic alternatives that can put our current epistemic appraisals in a different light. Different cultural groups, new generations, eccentric individuals, or perhaps even our future selves, can come up with alternatives that had escaped us before. We must deem our epistemic valuations tentative, transitory, and always open to revision. We must reject any alleged final judgment of our epistemic contents because our epistemic appraisal of epistemic contents remains always open to negotiation and cannot have complete finality or closure.

An important aspect of the openness of epistemic analyses and evaluations relates to the fallibilistic attitude cultivated by all pragmatist thinkers. But James's relationalism offers more than an unflinching epistemic fallibilism. On his view, the always tentative understanding and appraisal of our ideas and beliefs must be pluralistic: it must contain a multiplicity of perspectives that speak to each other and engage one another. Epistemic contents are not properly examined until they have been considered from different angles (as many as possible) in relation to each other, that is, as they reflect each other in complex ways. On this pluralistic view, epistemic analyses and evaluations must be polyphonic and kaleidoscopic. In order for us to be able to assess beliefs and determine which ones we want to live by and deem true, these beliefs must be exposed to the challenges posed by different perspectives and confront the resistances that arise from different view-points. It is important to note that this thoroughgoing pluralism does not lead to a radically relativistic model of epistemic appraisal, but rather, to a negotiating model that leaves room for objectivity. On this model, validity is not relativized to individual perspectives, but it is conceived as something relational that emerges from normative engagements among different perspectives. Different epistemic standpoints engage each other and enter into negotiations. There are of course normative tensions among competing standpoints; but their engagements and the resolutions of their epistemic negotiations can display more or less degrees of objectivity. As an illustration, I will examine how the negotiating model of epistemic appraisal works in the domain of (individual and collective) memory. I will try to show how James's relational and pluralistic suggestions can shed light on our beliefs about the past, where they can be appreciated perhaps more clearly than in any other epistemic domain.

It is not difficult to see that our beliefs about the past are perspectival and that they are formed and articulated through selective emphasis. Given the selective nature of our memory, we have to subject to constant critical scrutiny what we remember and forget, as well as how we remember and forget. And the critical examination of how our beliefs about the past are formed and maintained in our memory should be open to a plurality of diverse perspectives in order to avoid limitations and distortions as much as possible and improve their objectivity. The idea that retrospection can proceed through the meshing of diverse perspectives suggests a negotiating model of memory. According to this pluralistic negotiating model, memory is not something that can be fully monopolized, and, therefore, it always remains beyond the exclusive control of any singular perspective, be it the perspective of a particular individual or that of a particular group or institution. Our memory, both individual and collective, is forged and maintained through negotiating processes (often unconscious) in which different experiential stand-points intersect and different agential perspectives are coordinated. The past of individuals and peoples is not something fixed and inert; our epistemic relation with the past is always in the making through our agency and negotiations. The past is constantly being recreated in our everyday practices through a plurality of heterogeneous interpretative activities, formal and informal, conscious and unconscious. These diverse interpretative activities that recreate the past and maintain our memories alive include heavily regulated practices designed for this purpose: for example, writing and reading historical narratives (memoirs, biographies, history books, etc.), celebrating commemorations, and creating and consuming historical artworks (movies, paintings, novels, songs, etc.); but also more informal activities that have a historical or retrospective component: for example, habits and customs that reproduce how things had been done previously; ways of talking (naming, describing, praising, etc.) that echo in particular ways past subjects, events, and cultures; and ways of using and interpreting symbols from the past (e.g., the confederate flag, the cross, the pink triangle, etc.). There are many institutions (museums, historical societies, universities, governments, etc.), many artifacts (archives, libraries, public commemorative objects such as statues, plaques, etc.), and many disciplines (history, anthropology, museology, cultural criticism, etc.) that actively participate in the epistemic practices that shape our beliefs about the past; but even more importantly, there is always an irreducible plurality of experiential and agential perspectives involved in these practices. For the agents who participate in the interpretative practices that recreate the past have (or at least can have) differently organized and differently situated selves with different temperaments, and they go about differently in the assessment of their memories and in the reconstruction of their past. Our beliefs about the past maintain their vital force, if they do, thanks to day-to-day epistemic negotiations embedded in a complex network of interpretative practices that always involve a multiplicity of perspectives. It is within these plural and diverse interpretative practices that our epistemic negotiations about individual and collective memories take place, and the objectivity and truth of our beliefs about the past is established.

A full discussion of the epistemic negotiations that take place in our interpretative practices about the past is beyond the scope of this paper. What I want to call attention to with this discussion is an important point about our epistemic life that James's pluralistic and performative view of truth underscores: namely, that the openness to negotiation with an irreducible plurality of experiential and agential perspectives is a precondition for the objectivity and justice of our epistemic practices. When we assess the objectivity of our beliefs about the past and of the interpretative practices in which they were formed, we have to consider whether there has been an unbiased process of negotiation among differing perspectives, that is, whether our beliefs and interpretations have been compared with others in a negotiating process in which each perspective has been given an equal voice and treated with equal respect. In this sense, our assessments of objectivity are at the same time assessments of the fairness of the relevant epistemic practices in which beliefs are articulated, interpreted, and justified. In these practices agents are differently situated and sometimes excluded. Therefore, in our epistemic analyses we have no option but to examine whether the social and political conditions for fair comparison and contrast among alternative interpretations are given. On this view, epistemic analysis cannot be properly conducted without a sociopolitical critique in which issues of inclusion, exclusion, marginalization, and oppression are raised and addressed. The idea that openness to negotiation is required for objectivity and justice suggests that our practices should be guided by a cluster of desiderata that contain both cognitive and political elements such as: the inclusion of alternative viewpoints, the equality of voices and opportunities to speak, and the need of genuine normative engagements with conflicting positions. The desirability of these elements in our practices derives from their epistemic and political benefits: for example, removing biases and exclusions, reducing inequalities among participants, improving people's capacities to speak and to listen to others, and so on. In this view epistemic and sociopolitical melioration go hand in hand; and a lack of openness to negotiation results in a double deficit: the lack of objectivity and the lack of justice.

It is important to note that the critical reconstruction of one's past is a never-ending task. No matter how much critical reflection goes into the establishment and evaluation of our memories, the critical reconstruction of our beliefs about the past cannot reach an end-point and be declared final. Our epistemic negotiations and appraisals cannot have complete closure or finality because that would mean to foreclose the possibility of ever reopening our conversations about a shared past, of inviting new voices and perspectives to participate in the critical reconstruction of shared memories. Although the process of evaluation and critique will certainly come to a halt for all kinds of contingent reasons, it has to remain open and ready to be resumed because there can always be new forms of epistemic engagement and unforeseeable negotiations that can have an impact on our beliefs. James's thoroughgoing fallibilism and radical pluralism suggest that the genealogy of our beliefs can always be revisited. Remember that James's genealogical approach to truth calls for a critical examination of how our beliefs were established, but also (and simultaneously) for a critical reflection on how they could be established differently. According to this view, different experiential and agential standpoints can make different contributions to the genealogy of our beliefs and even offer alternative genealogical histories. Given the right sociopolitical conditions, the critical reconstruction and reevaluation of our beliefs can (and should) be reopened and resumed whenever new standpoints appear on the scene, but also whenever we discover that certain voices or perspectives were never considered or were not given equal weight. Thus it is not surprising that populations sometimes feel compelled to reopen the conversation about their past when the sociopolitical conditions change in such a way that voices and perspectives that had previously been ignored or not fully taken into consideration can now participate differently in the reconstruction of their past because they enjoy a different kind of agency. For example, this has been happening periodically in different ways and on different fronts in the public debates about past dictatorial regimes that have taken place in Argentina and in Chile. In these countries different sectors of the population (as well as particular individuals) have demanded a sustained effort to critically revisit the reconstruction of a shared past in the light of evidence, testimony, and articulations or interpretations of facts that challenge established beliefs or are simply not integrated in the collective memory and "official history" in circulation. This has happened also in Spain, where there have been new public debates (still ongoing) about how to remember and talk about the civil war and Franco's dictatorship and how to deal with the legacy of this historical period. In Spain these multifaceted debates about collective memory have raised questions about objectivity and justice simultaneously, covering many diverse issues that range from reparations and restitutions, to modifying the historical narratives available so as to include other voices and perspectives, and to changing all kinds of elements in public life that echo past events and past subjects in particular ways: sometimes celebrating or commemorating, sometimes stigmatizing, through street names, the display of symbols, public art, and the like.[10]

The reinterpretability and renegotiability of our beliefs about the past have been viewed by many as an obstacle to historical objectivity and historical truth, the thinking being that (at least in principle) we should be able to determine and fix the veridicality of our memories once and for all, so that we reach a point where we can no longer change our minds through reinterpretation and renegotiation. However, James's radical fallibilism and pluralism suggest that, far from being at odds with objectivity and truth, the openness to reinterpretation and renegotiation of our beliefs is in fact what makes it possible to improve their objectivity, to correct their biases and mistakes, and to maintain their truth alive, that is, dynamic, adaptable, and integrated in our lives. The openness to negotiation that James's pluralism recommends calls attention to the kind of accountability and responsiveness to others required by our epistemic agency. As more perspectives are taken into account in our epistemic negotiations, we can improve the articulation and justification of our beliefs, and our epistemic appraisals thus become more objective. The reinterpretation and renegotiation of our beliefs should be thought of as opportunities for learning from each other and correcting each other.

But, on this view, however, what is considered objectively true is not identified with whatever is agreed upon at the time. On the Jamesian view, the open-ended epistemic negotiations through which we establish and reevaluate the truth of our beliefs are not driven toward unification and consensus (at least not always and necessarily); the goals that guide them are, rather, coordination and cooperation through genuine normative engagements.[11] In other words, what matters is that views are compared, contrasted, and critically evaluated vis-à-vis each other, but not that they converge and merge into a single, unified perspective. At the end of the day, our negotiations may yield a multiplicity of heterogeneous truths. In fact, such multiplicity should be expected since, according to James's pluralism, there is an irreducibility plurality of different epistemic perspectives, and different epistemic perspectives are likely to yield different truths. In some cases, we may find out that the different truths in the running are different but combinable or at least capable of coexisting in coordination. In other epistemic disputes, we may find out that there is a radical clash in which different epistemic assessments remain at odds with each other.[12]

The status, scope, and implications of these epistemic differences cannot be decided a priori, prior to the actual engagements among competing perspectives.

At any rate, however deep or shallow differences turn out to be, what the Jamesian view emphasizes is that they cannot be erased, overcome, or subsumed under some (more abstract) unity of a higher order. It is for this reason that James's radical pluralism cannot support a consensus theory of truth, whether relativistic or universalistic. For when the harmonization of epistemic differences takes the form of a mandatory consensus, differences become something purely transitory that must be eliminated for epistemic success. On the Jamesian view, truth is not identified with agreement at all: neither with the current agreement of particular communities à la Rorty,[13] nor with the ideal agreement of a universal community à la Habermas.[14] Both Rorty and Habermas, like James, argue for a deep connection between objectivity and justice, linking the epistemic and the sociopolitical. Rorty does it by rooting this connection in the local agreement in values and ways of life that happens to rule the day in a particular community. By contrast, Habermas argues for purely formal and abstract notions of objectivity and justice that are grounded in the notion of universalizability (i.e., the capacity to become part of the universal consensus of all rational beings who can be communication partners). James does neither. James's pragmatic view of truth recommends an attitude or temperament in epistemic practices, but it does not provide a method for resolving disputes or a general account of the epistemic and sociopolitical force that our truths can have in all contexts. The pluralistic and genealogical view of truth defended by James offers a piecemeal approach that is not in the business of identifying what makes all our truths true. And, indeed, agreement (whether local or universal) becomes the general truth-maker in consensus theories of truth. By contrast, the piecemeal approach of pluralistic genealogy is in the business of examining, case by case, the diverse ways in which particular truths are settled, challenged, negotiated, evaluated and reevaluated in particular contexts.

James argues that we should always talk about truths in the plural. He defends the diversification of truth according to plural contexts, plural practices, and plural interests. On this view, truths are relative to the always changeable reality we cope with in our experiences and practices. But James's alethic pluralism should not be conflated with radical relativism.[15] Such relativism would clearly be inadequate for the epistemology of retrospection discussed above. A community cannot simply make up the facts and choose whatever revisionary history is most convenient for them. It is not the case that if people continue negotiating long enough, they may be able to establish by consensus any belief they wish about past events and past subjects (e.g., that the Holocaust never happened), and that they can make this belief true. The Jamesian approach rejects this naïve constructivism and revisionism. For one thing, James's pluralism demands that we give normative weight to all subjects and their experiences; and this includes subjects of the past, whose experiences we cannot simply choose to disregard or shape at will without compromising the objectivity of our beliefs and epistemic appraisals. On this view, there is an irreducible plurality of centers of experience and agency that function as a center of resistance and contestability in our epistemic negotiations. All experiential subjects have the capacity to contest and resist our truth claims and epistemic assessments. And insofar as our predecessors are treated as subjects—and not as objects we can manipulate at will—we need to take into account their perspectives. The reconstruction of the past must include the experiences and valuations of past subjects, in which we can find questions, challenges, and resistances of all sorts.

The reconstruction of our past—both individual and collective—has to contend with a plurality of perspectives and must, in that sense, be polyphonic. The memory of an individual or of a people cannot be monopolized, that is, it cannot be completely unified and fully controlled by a single perspective. Hegemonic unifications of memories do exist both at the collective and at the individual level, effected and policed by oppressive regimes and oppressive personalities. But no matter how successful these hegemonic unifications happen to be in erasing tensions and repressing differences, there are always alternative interpretations and possible contestations even if they remain implicit or unconscious, that is, even if the possibility of epistemic dissent cannot yet be realized. Our genealogical exercises situate truth claims and narratives in and among different experiential and agential perspectives; and thus they open us to possible contestations and resistances, inviting us to enter into epistemic negotiations. It is in this sense that epistemic genealogy is a critical exercise that has the potential to change not only our understanding of our past and of ourselves, but also our social and political relations to others with whom our lives are entangled, that is, those with whom we share a past, a present, or a future. Critical genealogy has both epistemic and sociopolitical efficacy since it has the transformative capacity to reshape both epistemic and political communities simultaneously through critical interventions that affect both shared interpretations and shared values.

Diversity and heterogeneity are ubiquitous and inescapable features of our cognitive life and therefore also of our beliefs about the past. Our memory (both individual and collective) always remains open to reinterpretation and renegotiation. The articulation and interpretation of memories (as well as their critical reconstruction) require the weaving of past and present experiences and their projection into the future, that is, the delineating of trajectories: our beliefs about the past get articulated and interpreted in relation to the present and future; and this means through the mediation of our understanding of the present and our vision of the future (or of possible futures in the plural). This task of articulating and interpreting by delineating trajectories can always be carried out in multiple and varied ways since subjects and groups are differently situated with respect to their past, given the different circumstances of their lives. This suggests that there will be as many accounts of the past as there are conceptions of the present and visions of the future. In this sense, there are always alternative pasts. As G. H. Mead suggested, with changing conditions and new visions of the future, we encounter novel pasts. As he puts it: "the novelty of every future demands a novel past."[16] But of course this doesn't mean that every present can reinvent the past without any constraints. The past cannot be simply instrumentalized and put at the service of our interests without any consideration for the subjects and peoples of the past. Following Mead as well as critical theorists as different as Jürgen Habermas and Walter Benjamin, James Bohman and Max Pensky have argued against the instrumentalization of the past and for the need to give moral recognition to past subjects and moral weight to their experiences and perspectives. As Bohman puts it, "we do not just deliberate about the past, but rather *with* the past."[17] There are constraints on our selective memory. We are not free to remember or forget in whatever way seems most convenient to us. We have to open our memories to the challenges and contestations of various subjects—the subjects in our present and in our future as well as those in the past[18]—with whom we compare and contrast our views of the past and with whom we form a community of solidarity. This community is held together not by shared interpretations—since differences and disagreements are encouraged in it—but by shared concerns.

As I hope it has been illustrated by my application in this section of the Jamesian view of truth to beliefs about the past and their reconstruction, epistemic genealogy and political critique work together in the production of knowledge and in the construction of communities. The critical reconstruction of beliefs through genealogy suggested by James can function as a source of objectivity and solidarity simultaneously, contributing to the improvement of understanding and to the reconfiguration of communities, that is, to epistemic and social melioration. James's radical pluralism underscores these deep connections between the epistemic and the sociopolitical aspects of our lives. In the concluding section I will briefly elucidate the notion of solidarity that, on my interpretation, can be derived from James's pluralism and its relevance for today.

Diversity, Solidarity, and the Politics of Specificity

James's radical pluralism yields a very specific conception of solidarity in which bonds and shared commitments are established on the basis of (rather than at the expense of) an irreducible diversity of experiential and agential perspectives, and with an eye to fostering and strengthening this diversity. As argued in the previous section, this is a view of solidarity in which differences are not overcome, abstracted, unified, or subsumed under a more general viewpoint. Pace unitary accounts of solidarity that erode diversity and stifle dissent and epistemic contestation, James's pluralism underscores the importance of arranging our practices so as to cultivate diversity, encouraging us to establish sociopolitical structures that promote diversity and to develop investigative and justificatory practices that invite differences. Both in its epistemic and in its political dimensions, the Jamesian view of solidarity has clear analogues or descendants in contemporary epistemology and contemporary social and political philosophy. On the one hand, one of the places where we can see the Jamesian insights being explored in the contemporary literature is in feminist epistemology (especially in so-called Standpoint Theories). In particular, the James-inspired view of solidarity I have sketched here is strikingly similar to the pluralistic view of objectivity that Helen Longino has developed in the philosophy of science.[19] Although Longino does not cite James or give any indication that he may have inspired her, she emphasizes that pluralism and (a somewhat eccentric form of) empiricism are the pillars of her view of objectivity, and, therefore, it is not surprising that this view can be easily linked to Jamesian ideas. Although Longino doesn't use the expression "epistemic solidarity," her pluralistic negotiating model of objectivity can be understood as an account of it. On this model, objectivity is explained as the achievement of a critical dialogue among genuinely different perspectives, a dialogue guided by epistemic and political values that relate to diversity. Among these values that are simultaneously epistemic and sociopolitical, especial prominence is given to those that cluster around the multilayered notion of equality among participants and perspectives: equal access to education, cultural capital, and disciplinary power; equal authority in scientific disciplines, journals, and institutions; equal distribution of resources among groups, and so on.

On the other hand, there are many theories of solidarity in contemporary social and political philosophy that can be seen as congenial to the Jamesian approach. Especially important here is Carol Gould's recent work on solidarity. In "Transnational Solidarities" she criticizes the homogenizing and essentializing tendencies of traditional views of solidarity according to which you could have solidarity with others only insofar as you were the same in some respect, that is, insofar as you enjoyed similar attributes or shared a standpoint.[20]As an alternative to these traditional views, Gould proposes a network conception of solidarity. Unlike those views that base solidarity on sharing an identity, a set of properties, or a perspective, "network solidarity" is achieved not at the expense of differences, but rather, through relations that preserve differences, that is, through the construction of networks of heterogeneous elements. Networks of solidarity are formed by weaving together problems, values, and goals that, though often irreducibly different, can overlap, converge, or simply be coordinated so that they can be addressed simultaneously and enjoy mutual support. As Gould puts it, on this view "solidarity is a disposition to act toward others who are recognized as different from oneself, in the sense of being differently situated."[21] This view undermines misconceived restrictions that have been imposed on solidarity, such as Rorty's claim that in order to have solidarity with others, we must recognize them as "one of us." More generally put, pluralistic views of this kind unmask (and show how to overcome) the misconception that solidarity requires assimilation, which is central to the American multicultural model based on the image of "the melting pot."[22] In recent race theory there has been also a movement toward pluralistic views, that is, a movement away from a conception of racial solidarity based on shared properties and toward a conception based on common problems and concerns. Criticizing racial and cultural essentialism, critical race theory has shown how we can have solidarity without unification or homogenization. The most exhaustive and detailed exposition and defense of a pluralistic view of racial solidarity along these lines is the one articulated in Tommie Shelby's recent book *We Who Are Black*.[23] Similar pluralistic and non-essentialist views of solidarity have also been defended by other philosophers in the recent feminist literature, especially by feminists of color.[24]

As argued in previous sections, when we combine James's radical pluralism with his genealogical approach to truth, we find a way of bringing together objectivity and justice: through genealogical critique we can identify and correct biases and exclusions and thus improve simultaneously the degrees of objectivity and justice that our practices exhibit. Epistemic and sociopolitical critiques can make important contributions to the formation of pluralistic communities in which different understandings and interpretations as well as different values and political commitments are coordinated. Another way to put the suggestion of the pluralistic view I have sketched is to say that epistemic and political solidarity should be promoted through a critical genealogy that uncovers the specificity of human experiences, the concreteness of human life, and the distinctiveness of individuals, groups, and cultures. The critical and liberating power of genealogical approaches that uncover and release repressed differences has been underscored by postcolonial theory. The crucial importance of the specificity and concreteness of diverse forms of life and human experiences is the centerpiece of Said's groundbreaking critique of colonialism and neo-colonialism,[25] which—in his analysis—rest on an insidious form of oppression that works by erasing differences and their historical development. In detailed historical studies Said criticizes the processes of orientalization through which Europeans and North Americans have created this imaginary Other—the Orient and its peoples—which they then contrast with the West. Through the homogenization of human groups and the erasure of their history, orientalizing discourses have constructed a monolithic conception of The Other, where all others are thought of as being the same everywhere and at all times. This essentializing of The Other is combined with its exoticization, which turns others into completely foreign beings, radically unlike ourselves, with whom we have nothing in common and therefore nothing to share or discuss.[26] By repressing diversity and erasing local histories, orientalism turns solidarity into an impossible task. For, when we are under the sway of orientalism, we lose sight of the specificity of the life and experiences of others. As Said puts it, as a result of orientalist discourses that have come to dominate the public life of our contemporary, "what has really been lost is a sense of the density and interdependence of human life."[27] This is due to the anti-empirical attitude of orientalism, which is nothing more than a "self-reinforcing mythology"[28] that refuses to look into the empirical specificity of particular ways of life, their histories, and their complex relations. James's radical empiricism and radical pluralism can be used as antidotes against the anti-empirical attitude that leads to the essentialization and exoticization of non-Western cultures. James's empiricist and pragmatist pluralism underscores the importance of paying attention to the specificity of concrete experiences, and gives normative weight to irreducibly different experiential and agential perspectives. On this view, a proper understanding of the significance of human experiences requires understanding the lives in which they occur, their repercussions (the difference they make in people's lives), and the complex networks of relations in which they are embedded. And, as we have seen, the Jamesian view of truth suggests that we must engage in critical genealogical reconstructions in order to uncover the specificity of each perspective and its experiences. These genealogical reconstructions make important contributions to the politics of specificity.[29] The politics of specificity is interested in critical genealogies based on plural analyses of cultural diversity and local histories, for these genealogies can be used as weapons of resistance against hegemonic powers, against their totalizing narratives and their official histories, which marginalize differences and erase dissent. We can exert epistemic and political resistance[30] through the genealogical recovering of the specificity of particular histories and cultural contexts, which can disarm the divisive processes that essentialize and exoticize human groups and their experiences. In this way, the Jamesian framework can be used to recuperate the lost "sense of the density and interdependence of human life" that Said talks about.

We have to move beyond anti-empirical and divisive frameworks (such as orientalism) and toward a genuinely pluralistic framework in which intracultural and intercultural diversity are properly understood and solidarity becomes possible at all levels, local as well as global. In order to properly appreciate the diversity of human forms of life and their interdependences, we need an epistemology of diversity and a politics of specificity. As Gould puts it, a genuinely pluralistic solidarity "requires an effort to understand the specifics of the other's concrete situation, to imaginatively construct for oneself their feelings and needs, and to listen to their own account of these, where possible."[31] And the epistemic commitment to understanding different perspectives in their specificity and concreteness should be supplemented and combined with the political commitment to create and sustain contexts and practices that foster the flourishing of genuinely plural perspectives and voices that can contend with one another and critically engage each other without having to suppress their differences. In this way an epistemology of diversity requires, and at the same time gives support to, a politics of specificity—both must work in tandem, supporting and reinforcing each other. The Jamesian framework can be read as providing the basis for an epistemology of diversity and a politics of specificity for the contemporary world. James's radical pluralism and relationalism teaches us to develop a sense of mutual dependence, for a pluralistic and relational understanding of experience requires that we view the experiences of others as alternatives to and for us, not as completely alien, foreign perspectives that cannot mesh with our interests, values, and, in short, with our life. The importance of developing a sense of interdependence and mutual engagement cannot be overestimated, especially today. For, indeed, becoming aware of the interdependences that compose our life is crucial for maintaining an epistemically and politically responsible agency in the multicultural societies and the globalized world of the twenty-first century.

NOTES

1. See John J. McDermott, *Streams of Experience: Reflections on the History and Philosophy of American Culture* (Amherst: University of Massachusetts Press, 1986), esp. pp. 52 and 55–56.

2. See especially José Medina and David Wood, eds., *Truth: Engagements across Philosophical Traditions* (Oxford: Blackwell, 2005), pp. 9–12. See also Barry Allen, *Truth in Philosophy* (Cambridge, Mass.: Harvard University Press, 1993) for a more detailed historical argument that also assigns this central critical role to James's and Nietzsche's views of truth.

3. In many discussions of truth in the history of philosophy its normative dimension was simply ignored, but in many others it was considered and denied. The latter is the case in so-called *descriptivist* views of truth. Relying on a strong separation between the factual and the normative, these views treat "true" as a purely descriptive predicate. Although the fact-value distinction has come under heavy attack on various fronts, descriptivism still survives in naturalist approaches defended in the contemporary literature (see, for example, Hartry Field, "Disquotational Truth and Factually Defective Discourse," *Philosophical Review* 103, no. 3 [1994]: 405–52).

4. See Simon Blackburn and Keith Simmons, eds., *Truth* (Oxford: Oxford University Press, 1999), for a sampler of minimalist and deflationary positions on truth and their debates with substantive theories of truth.

5. Cf. John Dewey, "Propositions, Warranted Assertibility, and Truth," *Journal of Philosophy* 38 (1941): 169–85, and F. C. S. Schiller, *Studies in Humanism* (London: Macmillan, 1907).

6. James uses the metaphor of growth when he describes how new ideas become true: the new idea "makes itself true, gets itself classed as true, by the way it works; grafting itself then upon the ancient body of truth, which thus grows much as a tree grows by the activity of a new layer of cambium" (*P*, 36).

7. For different perspectives on this distinction, see parts 2 and 3 of Medina and Wood, *Truth*.

8. By emphasizing this aspect of James's view I am facilitating the convergence of his framework with what has been called *genealogical pragmatism*. John Stuhr has articulated this brand of pragmatism through Dewey and Foucault, developing an account of the role that genealogy can play in a pragmatist philosophy. See Stuhr, *Genealogical Pragmatism: Philosophy, Experience, and Community* (Albany: SUNY Press, 1997).

9. I have discussed in more detail the critical role that the imagination should play in epistemology in "Pluralism and the Epistemology of *Resistance*" (paper presented at the International Conference on Identity and Memory, Mérida, Mexico, September 2006). I have used both James and Wittgenstein to explain this critical role of the imagination.

10. All of these issues are addressed by the new legislation (the so-called Ley de Memoria Histórica) proposed by the socialist government in Spain, which passed in July 2006. This new legislation has sparked more heated debates, being criticized by some for not going far enough (e.g., for simply recommending, instead of demanding, the removal of fascist symbols) and being criticized by others for unnecessarily "reopening wounds" that should be left undisturbed because they can heal only with time (or, some have even suggested, through *forgetting*).

11. That is, through engagements in which the different parties enjoy a minimal amount of equality and respect and they really take into account and address each other's concerns.

12. There can be different kinds of clashes and incompatibilities. The competing truths under consideration can be uncombinable because they contradict each other or because they occupy different and non-overlapping spaces. The former case raises issues relating to the bivalence of truth; the latter case raises issues of incommensurability.

13. See especially Richard Rorty, "Universality and Truth," in *Rorty and His Critics,* ed. Robert Brandom (Oxford: Blackwell, 2000), pp. 1–30.

14. See especially Jürgen Habermas, "Richard Rorty's Pragmatic Turn," in Medina and Wood, *Truth,* pp. 109–29.

15. Besides what I say below, there are other considerations that can be used to distinguish James's pluralism from radical relativism. For James, no matter how diverse and heterogeneous our epistemic practices happen to be, there is always the possibility of coordinating the truths that emerge from those practices. On James's view, this ever-present possibility is guaranteed by the general interests of mankind, that is, by the interests that relate to adaptation and the survival of the species. These general interests constitute the ground for what James calls our "general obligation to do what pays," which is what brings us all together as truth-seekers. On this naturalistic perspective truth is viewed as what proves to be reliable and adaptive in the long run. Although James calls attention to the relativistic elements in our assessments of truth, his empiricist and pragmatic relativism in conjunction with his naturalism make room for a strong notion of objectivity, which goes well beyond the strictures of radical relativism.

16. George Herbert Mead, *Philosophy of the Present* (Indianapolis: Hackett, 1949), p. 33. In this work, Mead developed a social constructivist view of the past. His view has strong affinities with the Jamesian pluralistic view of memory I have articulated in this section. Mead proposed *inclusion* as the guiding epistemic and political value for our reconstructions of the past. He suggested that we should judge the adequacy of our accounts of the past in terms of their inclusivity: the more perspectives we manage to integrate in these accounts, the more objective they should be considered. This view is grounded in Mead's account of communication and social agency as well as in his cosmopolitanism (see his *Mind, Self and Society* [Chicago: University of Chicago Press, 1934]). For Mead, the reconstruction of the past seems to function as a source of *solidarity*: the past should be in constant redescription so that more and more perspectives are brought together and thus an open and ever-expanding community is formed.

17. James Bohman, "Deliberating about the Past: Decentering Deliberative Democracy" in *Pragmatism, Nation, and Race: Community in the Age of Empire,* ed. Chad Kautzer and Eduardo Mendieta (Bloomington: Indiana University Press, 2009), p. 123.

18. We have epistemic as well as moral obligations not only to our contemporaries, but also to subjects of the past. As Pensky puts it, in our critical examinations of the past, what is important is "the acknowledgement and efforts to fulfill an *obligation* to past persons, which may be discharged by any number of practices: the disavowal of older social norms, the requirement of collective processes of reflection, new modes of historiography, the inauguration of commemorative practices, or claims for restitution of various kinds. The normative orientation to a shared past, in other words, consists in establishing and maintaining normatively relevant *relationships with past fellow members of a democratic society*" ("Pragmatism and Solidarity with the Past," in Kautzer and Mendieta, eds., *Pragmatism, Nation, and Race,* p. 79).

19. Helen Longino, *Science as Social Knowledge: Values and Objectivity in Scientific Inquiry* (Princeton, N.J.: Princeton University Press, 1990).

20. Carol C. Gould, "Transnational Solidarities," *Journal of Social Philosophy* 38, no. 1 (2007): 148–64.

21. Ibid., pp. 156–57.

22. See my "Pragmatism and Ethnicity: Critique, Reconstruction, and the New Hispanic," *Metaphilosophy* 35 (2004): 115–46, in which I criticize assimilationist models and non-pluralistic views of ethnic and racial solidarity.

23. Tommie Shelby, *We Who Are Black: The Philosophical Foundations of Black Solidarity* (Cambridge, Mass.: Harvard University Press, 2005).

24. See María Lugones, *Pilgrimages/Peregrinajes: Theorizing Coalition against Multiple Oppressions* (Oxford: Rowman and Littlefield, 2003), and Cherríe Moraga and Gloria Anzaldúa, eds., *This Bridge Called My Back: Writings by Radical Women of Color* (New York: Kitchen Table Press, 1981). For an account of the convergence between race theory and feminist theory on a pluralistic conceptualization of solidarity and group identity, see my "Identity Trouble: Disidentification and the Problem of Difference," *Philosophy and Social Criticism* 29 (2003): 655–80.

25. Edward Said, *Orientalism: 25th Anniversary Edition* (New York: Vintage Books, 1979/1994).

26. This is what Said calls the establishment of "radical differences" among human groups that are divided (often quite arbitrarily) into static categories. And, as Said asks, "can one divide human reality into clearly different cultures, histories, traditions, societies, races, and survive the consequences humanly? [. . .] I mean to ask whether there is any way of avoiding the hostility expressed by the division, say, of men into 'us' (Westerners) and 'they' (Orientals)" (*Orientalism*, p. 45).

27. Ibid., p. xvii.

28. As Said puts it, "the Orientalist attitude [. . .] shares with magic and with mythology the self-containing, self-reinforcing character of a closed system" (ibid., p. 70).

29. I borrow this label from Uma Narayan, *Dislocating Cultures: Identities, Traditions, and Third World Feminism* (New York: Routledge, 1997), see esp. pp. 49–52. Following Said, in her account of Third-World feminism, Narayan has underscored the political value of uncovering *specificities* that are erased or repressed. As she puts it: "Attending to these specificities of incidence serves to counter a colonialist Western tendency to represent Third-World contexts as uniform and monolithic spaces, with no important internal cultural differentiations, complexities, and variations" (p. 50).

30. I have discussed in more detail this notion in my *Speaking from Elsewhere* (Albany: SUNY Press, 2006).

31. Gould, "Transnational Solidarities," pp. 156–57.

8. Pragmatism, Nihilism, and Democracy: What Is Called Thinking at the End of Modernity?

JAMES LIVINGSTON

I have elsewhere argued that the original American pragmatists revolutionized twentieth-century European philosophy by determining or re-shaping the intellectual agendas of Edmund Husserl, Ludwig Wittgenstein, Emile Durkheim, Georges Sorel, Jean Wahl, and Alexandre Kojeve. I have also argued that the "critique of the subject" proposed by post-structuralist feminists—particularly by Judith Butler—becomes more coherent and consequential when we rewrite its Nietzschean genealogy to include its pragmatist antecedents.[1]

In this space, I want to argue that William James and John Dewey are better guides to the end of modernity than Friedrich Nietzsche and Martin Heidegger, who still reign as the court poets of the so-called linguistic turn. I will claim that because the pragmatists do not abstain from the universalization of the commodity form (that is, from "objectification," reification, exchange value, modern credit, etc.), and do not indulge an idealization of artisanal labor, they are more useful philosophers for our own time—the time of "globalization"—than Nietzsche or Heidegger, and, for that matter, Horkheimer, Adorno, or Habermas.[2]

I begin by rehearsing the adjournment of modern subjectivity accomplished in James's essays on radical empiricism. Then I enlist José Ortega y Gasset, a close reader of Heidegger, to ask why that accomplishment has not been adequately acknowledged—which is to ask why Heidegger's version of an end to modernity has kept its accreditation. At this stage of the argument, the critics of pragmatism, who invariably emphasize that metaphors of money, commerce, and credit disfigure the philosophical discourse of James and Dewey, turn state's evidence and make my case for pragmatism. In concluding, I will suggest that these metaphors, and the nihilistic discourse we call pragmatism, are the linguistic resources we need to escape the "pathos of authenticity," and to address, accordingly, the universalization of the commodity form as both an impediment to and the condition of democracy.

In my view it is almost self-evident that pragmatism dwells in, and on, the end of modernity, simply because it gives up the ghost of modern subjectivity—that is, the historically specific compound of assumptions, ideas, and attitudes which convenes each individual as a set of radical discontinuities (e.g., mind vs. body) that are in turn projected outward, as language and work, and which meanwhile confers an ontological priority on the individual whose freedom resides in release from identities and obligations determined by the past (that is, by historical time). Almost, but not quite self-evident. Sometimes changes are so profound, so complete and effective, that we do not recognize them as events that have already occurred.[3]

Donald Davidson suggested as much in 1986, in an influential essay titled "The Myth of the Subjective." Here he noted that the ideas associated with "the relation between the human mind and the rest of nature, [or] the subjective and the objective as we have come to think of them, . . . are now coming under critical scrutiny, and the result promises to mark a sea change in contemporary philosophical thought—a change so profound that we may not recognize that it is occurring." The change he had in mind was the "demise of the subjective," which would derive from the collapse of the ontological division between mind and world, thought and thing, or, as Davidson once put it, between scheme and content. "What we are about to see," he claimed, "is the emergence of a radically revised view of the relation of mind and the world."[4]

Until that happened, most philosophers would cling to a Cartesian "myth of the subjective," which Davidson summarized as follows: "Since we cannot be certain what the world outside the mind is like, the subjective can keep its virtue—its chastity, its certainty for us—only by being protected from contamination of the world." Myth or not, it had determined the intellectual agenda of modernity: "To a large extent this picture of mind and its place in nature has defined the problems modern philosophy has thought it had to solve." Or again: "Instead of saying it is the scheme-content dichotomy that has dominated and defined the problems of modern philosophy, then, one could as well say it is how the dualism of the objective and the subjective has been conceived. For these dualisms have a common origin: a concept of the mind with its private states and objects." So the impending changes—"these dualisms are being questioned in new ways or are being radically reworked"—would presumably signify the end of modernity in the discipline of philosophy and perhaps in the culture at large.[5]

Davidson's admirers among pragmatists depict him as a new branch on the family tree. Richard Rorty, for example, suggests that "what Davidson added to Dewey is a non-representationalist philosophy of language that supplements, and in some measure replaces, Dewey's non-representationalist account of knowledge." But the fact is that James formally proposed the first version of this account of knowledge in 1904 and 1905, in the first two essays on radical empiricism. So the genealogical question must be addressed by reference to these essays and their impact—on Dewey among others. In 1903, to be sure, James himself believed that the "Chicago School" was developing an alternative to the modern dualisms of subject and object, and, in the long run, he would be correct. Meanwhile, however, that alternative emerged as a result of his own return to themes he had been exploring in courses at Harvard since 1897.[6]

And it is not as if no one noticed what James was doing. He spent a great deal of time and energy after 1904 simply replying to the critics of radical empiricism, who believed, with good reason, that pragmatism was its cause and effect. Certainly Alfred North Whitehead noticed what he was doing. He dated "the entailed revolution in our ways of thinking about philosophy," as Davidson names the consequence of "the demise of the subjective," from 1904, when the new *Journal of Philosophy, Psychology, and Scientific Methods* published "Does Consciousness Exist?"—the first installment of radical empiricism and the down payment on pragmatism. "The scientific materialism and the Cartesian ego were both challenged at the same moment, one by science [as represented by Einstein] and the other by philosophy, as represented by William James and his psychological antecedents," Whitehead wrote in 1925, "and the double challenge marks the end of a period which lasted for about two hundred and fifty years."[7]

The ways in which Dewey used, cited, and responded to this same essay suggest that he concurred with Whitehead's verdict on its importance and implications. In a flurry of articles published between 1905 and 1909, he repeatedly invoked its challenge to the Cartesian ego as the warrant for his own arguments—the "realism of pragmatism," for example, became the "obvious deduction from his [James's] denial of the existence of consciousness." In his later writings of the 1920s and 30s, he pondered the historical and political consequences of that denial by sketching the lineaments of a "social self" that could not exist prior to its association with others. And when Dewey returned in 1940 to the question of this subject as pragmatism presented it, he suggested that the essays on radical empiricism were an autodidactic reading of *The Principles of Psychology* (1890)—an autobiographical reckoning, as it were, with the dualisms still inscribed in an earlier intellectual stage.[8]

The title of the piece in which Dewey reinterprets radical empiricism is "The Vanishing Subject in the Psychology of James." It indicates both the author's purpose and the origins of Davidson's announcement regarding "the demise of the subjective." In concluding, Dewey noted that "psychological theory is still the bulwark for all doctrines that assume independent and separate 'mind' and 'world' set over against each other." But he also pointed out that this dualism "originally came into psychology from philosophy." He had already shown why James's psychology should be read as symptom and cure of this reciprocal contamination—how *The Principles* contained both "official acceptance of epistemological dualism" and a subversive account of self-knowledge "in which the 'subject' [notice the scare quotes] of dualistic epistemology disappears." But Dewey claimed the essays of 1904–1905 as the warrant for his new reading of *The Principles,* according to which the subversive account of self-knowledge became the privileged truth of the earlier text: "What he finally said in 1904, after he had thrown over his knowing Thought or Consciousness as a mere echo of a departed soul, was, after all, but an expression of ideas put forth in his Psychology, freed from hesitation and ambiguity."[9]

Now if we suppose that Davidson is correct to believe that the impending changes in philosophy are profound, even revolutionary, because they would dissolve the dualisms specific to the modern epoch by certifying the death of the subject (aka "the demise of the subjective"); and if we further suppose that Whitehead and Dewey were correct to trace the beginnings of this end to James's essays of 1904–1905; then we should ask why the subject in question has taken so long to die, and why the cultural revolution residing in the chronicle of its death remains unfinished or unnoticed. The question is worth asking even before we gather evidence of a death foretold from the essays of 1904–1905. For the mere resilience of modern subjectivity suggests that it is something more plausible and durable and actionable than a myth—and that we might, therefore, want to learn to live with it. With these possibilities in mind, I would answer the question in two ways.

First, the expectation that the Cartesian ego will disappear was, and is, no more realistic than the expectation that any given moment of infantile development will disappear insofar as a child grows and matures. The return of the repressed is much more likely, for cultures as for personalities, simply because each new moment of development will recall and recast the significance of past moments. In one of the essays on radical empiricism, "How Two Minds Can Know One Thing," James quoted Kierkegaard to explain this process: "We live forward, but we understand backward" (ERE, 65n6). Moreover, the political economy of the sign specific to late (corporate) capitalism clearly thrives on what social theorists have called desublimation or deterritorialization, that is, on the mobilization of "archaic" desires—these are quite literally forces of production—in the name of intensified subjectivity and increased profitability. The society of the spectacle, where cyborgs dream as if they were Cartesian egos, teaches us to live backward and understand forward.[10]

Second, and more important, modern subjectivity is not a form of "false consciousness" that we can exorcise by naming it the "myth of the subjective." For it is a discrete historical event as well as an idea. It is more real than God in this sense because it happened. As the sources of radical doubt about the evidence of the senses multiplied after 1500, and as the immediate, affective links between emotions and environments were severed, the European ego became a singular "point of view" on or above the world and the body rather than an undivided dimension of both: "the age of the world picture" arrived. The problem of perspective— where to position oneself in relation to the world and the body now conceived as external objects—accordingly became the metaphor of personal identity as well as the central, or rather founding, issue of epistemology and moral philosophy. The modern subject was born, in short, when "the logic of the gaze" became the paradigm of knowledge. The problem of perspective was quite genuine because this logic both required and accommodated new spaces and greater distances between subject and object—the relationship between human beings and their earthly or embodied environments had in fact changed drastically—and did, therefore, make the nature of reality, and, for that matter, the reality of nature, open questions.[11]

Certainly it was not obvious that the reality in question could be apprehended from any point of view or subject position. So anxiety about the subject's position in relation to the world became anxiety about the subjective as such, and that in turn created demand for rules or procedures that would formalize and guarantee its integrity. In retrospect, we can, then, see that the subject(ive) becomes "mythic" only insofar as we treat it as something more or less than historically contingent. To treat is as something more is to mistake it for a transhistorical attribute of human nature—to posit, in a neo-Kantian spirit, precisely the subjectivity or consciousness or transcendental ego that European phenomenology, from Husserl to Heidegger, tried to explain as the result, not the origin, of experience, as the effect, not the cause, of engagement with the world. But to treat it as something less, as Davidson does by denying or forgetting that that it was both cause and effect of the epochal transition to what we call the modern condition, is to remove philosophical conversation from the conditions and sources of its development in actually existing historical circumstances.[12]

Let us turn, then, to the essays of 1904–1905, to see if we can find the primary sources of a radically pragmatic empiricism that will permit the annulment and preservation of modern subjectivity—and so will let us live less anxiously with it. In "Does Consciousness Exist?"—the first installment—James begins by quoting an unnamed text that is almost certainly Emerson's *Nature*: "'Thoughts' and 'things' are names for two sorts of object, which common sense will always find contrasted and will always practically oppose to each other." Then he equates the "thought" of common sense and the "consciousness" of modern philosophy; having done so, he can announce the imminent death of the "transcendental ego" that represents modern subjectivity: "I believe that 'consciousness,' when once it has evaporated to the [neo-Kantian] estate of pure diaphaneity, is on the point of disappearing altogether. It is the name of a nonentity, and has no right to a place among first principles. Those who still cling to it are clinging to a mere echo, the faint rumor left behind by the disappearing 'soul' upon the air of philosophy" (*ERE*, 3–4).

James does not claim that there are no thoughts; instead he insists that the notion of "consciousness" and its more or less subjective bearers are unnecessary to explain the existence and effects of thoughts. "There is, I mean, no aboriginal stuff or quality of being, contrasted with that of which material objects are made, out of which our thoughts of them are made." A phenomenological reduction could not go any farther. Thoughts are real, James insists, because "there is a function in experience which thoughts perform." This function is knowing, through which the "portions" of the "one primal stuff in the world"—pure experience, the "instant field of the present"—are related in retrospect; but knowing is only "a particular sort of relation" between these parts of pure experience, in which knower and known are continuously reconstituted by new alignments of thought and thing, not bound by the inertia of subject and object (*ERE*, 4, 13).

James proposes, then, to discard the neo-Kantian version of the theorem that "experience is indefeasibly dualistic in structure"—not to deny any distinction between mind and matter, thoughts and things. He objects to the subject-object dualism that inevitably accompanies the notion of consciousness as toasted by "belated drinkers at the Kantian spring"; for it somehow subsists outside of time, and so cannot move, change, or develop: "Souls were detachable, had separate destinies; things could happen to them. To consciousness as such nothing can happen, for, timeless itself, it is only a witness of happenings in time, in which it plays no part." In this sense, James suggests that philosophical dualism has a history, in which "neo-Kantism" appears as the highest evolutionary stage. He cites G. E. Moore (of Cambridge-Bloomsbury fame) and Paul Natorp (later a friend and colleague of Heidegger's) as representatives of that stage, in which philosophers cannot define or describe "consciousness"—"it seems to vanish," said Moore— and yet insist that it remains after "mental subtraction" removes the content of thought (the object) from the agent of thought (the subject), thereby distinguishing the knower (mind) from the known (world) (*ERE*, 5).

"Experience, at this rate," James notes, "would be much like a paint of which the world pictures were made," that is, something with a "dual constitution," dividing naturally into particular pigments (content) and universal oil or solvent (consciousness). He then turns to his own argument:

> Experience, I believe, has no such inner duplicity; and the separation into consciousness and content comes, not by way of subtraction, but by way of addition. . . . The paint will also serve here as an illustration. In a pot in a paint-shop, along with other paints, it serves in its entirety as so much saleable matter. Spread on a canvas, with other paints around it, it represents, on the contrary, a feature in a picture and performs a spiritual function. Just so, I maintain, does a given undivided bit of experience, taken in one context of associates, play the part of a knower, of a state of mind, of "consciousness"; while in a different context the same undivided bit of experience plays the part of a thing known, of an objective "content." In a word, in one group it figures as a thought, in another group as a thing. And, since it can figure in both groups simultaneously we have every right to speak of it as subjective and objective at once. (*ERE*, 6–7)

Things like paint acquire meaning and significance—they become the recognizable emblems of experience—only in terms of human purposes or thoughts. So far the neo-Kantian account might work. But such purposes or thoughts are not given or revealed by "consciousness" as such, that is, by a subject conceived as prior or external to the particular events of experience, by a mind or self that is somehow exempt from the vicissitudes of time. At any rate that is the substance of James's retort to "neo-Kantism" in section 2 of the essay. Here it becomes obvious that he wants above all to situate "the function of knowing" in historical time, and accordingly to annul by explaining—to preserve by reinterpreting—the inherited dualisms of subject and object. But he doesn't want to reject or overcome this inheritance; he wants to contain it within his new narrative of philosophical difference.

James notes that "the whole philosophy of perception," which I take to mean epistemology, "has been one long wrangle over the paradox that what is evidently one reality should be in two places at once, both in outer space and in a person's mind." He has already encouraged the reader to relive the experience of seeing and perceiving the room in which he sits—that is, to experience the room as thing, as "a physical object, his actual field of vision," but also as thought, as "those self-same things which his mind, as we say, perceives." So the paradox is close by, and not at all abstruse or abstract. One way to solve it is by recourse to the strictly spatial metaphors of geometry (in effect by recourse to the most ancient of philosophies): "The puzzle of how the one identical room can be in two places is at bottom just the puzzle of how one identical point can be on two lines. It can, if it be situated at their intersection" (ERE, 7–8).

But the experience of the room is clearly more complex than an intersection that occurs in a merely logical or mathematical universe. What kind of crossroad would contain that increased complexity? "If the 'pure experience' of the room were a place of intersection of two processes, which connected it with different groups of associates respectively, it could be counted twice over, as belonging to either group, and spoken of loosely as existing in two places, although it would remain all the time a numerically single thing." The question then becomes, "What are the two processes, now, into which the room-experience simultaneously enters in this way?" James argues that the answer appears when we acknowledge the dimension of historical time to which the geometer's point must always be indifferent: "One of them is the reader's personal biography, the other is the history of the house of which the room is part" (ERE, 8).

These become the temporal grounds on which he thinks he can recast and recuperate the inherited tradition of philosophical dualism.

> As "subjective" we say that the experience represents; as "objective" it is represented. What represents and what is represented is here numerically the same; but we must remember that no dualism of being represented and representing resides in the experience per se. . . . Its subjectivity and objectivity are functional attributes solely, realized only when the experience is "taken," i.e., talked of, twice, considered along with its two differing contexts respectively, by a new retrospective experience, of which that whole past complication now forms the fresh content. (ERE, 13)

The problem of perspective—how to paint the "world pictures" from the modern, neo-Kantian standpoint of a timeless subject—is now thickened, but not displaced, by the attitude of retrospection. For the world of pure experience "is only virtually or potentially either object or subject." It becomes a purpose, a state of mind, a "reality intended," as we begin acting on it in time, that is, as we begin adding to it by "the doubling of it in retrospection." But even in its simplicity and unity, "the immediate experience in its passing is always 'truth,' practical truth," because it is not yet a state of mind that stands corrected or confirmed by retrospection. For the time being, it is all we have (ERE, 13).

By treating the problem of perspective in this manner, James identifies three orders of truth or reality. There is the "practical truth" residing in the "instant field of the present." There are the truths we learn backward by adding, retrospectively, to the practical truth of immediate experience. And then there is "truth absolute and objective." This third order of truth is final in every sense because its condition is the end of time. So the only truths of which we can speak and be aware are those semiotic artifacts, those provisional, second-order truths, that emerge in the narrative time of historical consciousness and explanation. They do not evade or erase "the immediate experience in its passing"; instead they stand in a developmental relation to this "archaic" origin, organizing and articulating it so that it becomes useful in navigating the future.

Subject-object dualism is, then, a functional distinction that becomes intelligible as a historical phenomenon because it is a historical phenomenon. It is only in retrospect that an experience can be disaggregated: "In its pure state, or when isolated, there is no self-splitting of it into consciousness and what the consciousness is 'of.'" But it does not follow that these divisions of time are falsehoods from which we must flee. James insists instead that they are the conditions of the only truths we can know. That is why he claims that his account can preserve dualism by reinterpreting it.

> The dualism connoted by such double-barreled terms as "experience," "phenomenon," "datum," "Vorfindung"—terms which, in philosophy at any rate, tend more and more to replace the single-barreled terms of "thought" and "thing"—that dualism, I say, is still preserved in this account, but reinterpreted, so that, instead of being mysterious and elusive, it becomes verifiable and concrete. It is an affair of relations, it falls outside, not inside, the single experience considered, and can always be particularized and defined. (*ERE*, 13, 7)

So the resolution of the ambiguity residing in *The Principles* was not as radical as Dewey supposed in 1940; for modern subjectivity and its attendant dualisms do not simply vanish from this account. James does of course object to the neo-Kantian version of the subject. In his view, it was both unnecessary as a bulwark of selfhood or morality against the encroachments of experience and incapable of serving as such in its "thoroughly ghostly condition." But we should not confuse his farewell to this Owl of Minerva with a farewell to owls. He wants to get beyond modern subjectivity by annulling and preserving it; that is why he refuses to treat it as the unfortunate mistake of his unenlightened predecessors. As usual, James is trying to find the middle ground on which he can reconcile "previous truth and novel fact"; as always, he finds that space in time, between now and then.

In the second of the essays collected under the rubric of radical empiricism, "A World of Pure Experience," he explores the same area; in doing so, he completes the critique of modern subjectivity inaugurated in "Does Consciousness Exist?" and introduces the metaphors as well as the arguments that would reappear in *Pragmatism*. James concludes, for example, by claiming that a philosophy of pure experience is analogous to a mosaic, because the spaces between the pieces are no less important parts of the composition than the pieces themselves: "Life is in the transitions as much as in the terms connected; often, indeed, it seems to be there more emphatically." For the passage beyond a given moment will change the significance of earlier moments. "These relations of continuous transition experienced are what make our experiences cognitive. . . . When one of them terminates a previous series of them with a sense of fulfillment, it, we say is what those other experiences 'had in view.' The knowledge, in such a case, is verified, the truth is 'salted down.'" But verification is unusual because it constitutes an ending, not a transition: "Mainly, however, we live on speculative investments, or on our prospects only. But living on things in posse is as good as living in the actual, so long as our credit remains good. It is evident that for the most part it is good, and that the universe seldom protests our drafts." The metaphor works here, at the conclusion of an argument about the centrality of time in self-knowledge, because, as Ezra Pound once noted, credit is the future tense of money. "In this [commercial] sense," James observes, "we at every moment can continue to believe in an existing beyond" (*ERE*, 42–43).

He keeps stopping to summarize, to emphasize that historical time is the key to his argument. For example, "According to my view, experience as a whole is a process in time, whereby innumerable particular terms lapse and are superseded by others that follow upon them by transitions which, whether disjunctive or conjunctive in content, are themselves experiences, and must in general be accounted at least as real as the terms which they relate." Indeed James insists that timeless knowledge is impossible if not inconceivable because "every later moment continues and corroborates an earlier one": "In this continuing and corroborating, taken in no transcendental sense, but denoting definitely felt transitions, lies all that the knowing of a percept by an idea can possibly contain or signify. . . . Knowledge of sensible realities thus comes to life inside the tissue of experience. It is made; and made by relations that unroll themselves in time" (*ERE*, 31–32, 29).

"A World of Pure Experience" recalls, amplifies, and completes the argument of "Does Consciousness Exist?" by showing that our departure from neo-Kantian "rationalism" does not deliver us unto a "humian type of empiricism." James knew that David Hume was one of the first philosophers to write as if the enunciation of ethical principles and the analysis of historical circumstances were not antithetical enterprises—as if the goal of philosophy was to understand the relation between the universal and the particular, not to assume that one was the primary reality from which the other could be deduced. But he also knew that Hume's project failed because it could not go far enough, and became a way of denying the significance of universals as such, that is, of treating the whole as the simple sum of its parts. "Empiricism is known as the opposite of rationalism," James observes dryly, because it "lays the explanatory stress upon the part, the element, the individual, and treats the whole as a collection and the universal as an abstraction." Radical empiricism fulfills the promise of Hume's project, then, by treating the perceived relations or transitions between the moments or parts of experience as if they were themselves real, true, and vital. "To be radical, an empiricism must neither admit into its construction any element that is not directly experienced, nor exclude from them any element that is directly experienced. For such a philosophy, the relations that connect experiences must themselves be experienced relations, and any kind of relation experienced must be accounted as real as anything else in the system" (*ERE*, 34, 22).

As James annuls and preserves the legacy of Kant in "Does Consciousness Exist?" so he preserves and annuls the legacy of Hume in "A World of Pure Experience." He argues that the Kantian/rationalist recourse to "trans-experiential [i.e., supra-historical] agents of unification, substances, intellectual categories and powers, or selves," was the inevitable reaction to—the "natural result" of—an empiricism in which "conjunctive relations" between discrete experiences did not appear as "fully coordinate" with the more obvious discontinuities. Insofar as empiricists continue to "insist most on the disjunctions," and accordingly cannot recognize the semiotic activity that unifies or integrates the parts of experience as itself a form of experience, a more or less rationalist, neo-Kantian retort to Hume is both plausible and necessary. But insofar as empiricists do recognize such activity as a directly experienced element of life, they will have superseded Hume and made the rationalist invocation of extra-temporal agency—for example, "consciousness"—implausible and unnecessary. Radical empiricism "does full justice to conjunctive relations," as James put it, "without, however, treating them as rationalism always tends to treat them, as being true in some supernal way, as if the unity of things and their variety belonged to different orders of truth and vitality altogether" (*ERE*, 23).

If the whole is the sum of its parts by this account, the parts now include the relations between them; and these relations—the "relations that unroll themselves in time"—determine the meanings of the parts by plotting their cognitive positions. It follows that the elements, moments, or terms of experience cannot be detached from their relations to one another, and that the whole, of which they are virtual, possible, and pending parts, defines or constitutes them as such. So the universal is something we experience, as a lived relation—it is a concrete and intrinsic dimension of the particular, not a metaphysical abstraction or heuristic device that we must superimpose on our everyday realities. For it emerges in time, and only in time (*ERE*, 24).

James is, then, claiming that the vicissitudes of time are the necessary condition of the self's integrity as well as knowledge. And he is fully aware of how extraordinary that claim must sound to those educated by the Western philosophical tradition. "The conjunctive relation that has given most trouble to philosophy is the co-conscious transition, so to call it," he notes, "by which one experience passes into another when both belong to the same self." Individuals change with time, of course, but that is no reason, James suggests, to insist that the self is only an agenda of appetites, a "bundle of sensations" (as Hume put it), a perfectly discontinuous and externally determined object that is incapable of moral judgment. For it is change as such—the experience of transition from one state to another—that makes the articulation of "conjunctive relations" between the parts of experience possible and necessary: "Personal histories are processes of change in time, and the change itself is one of things immediately experienced. 'Change' in this case means continuous as opposed to discontinuous transition. But continuous transition is one sort of conjunctive relation" (*ERE*, 25).

James now puts all his cards on the table, and announces that he is proposing to revise the agenda and the history of philosophy. He wants to make it the study of these changes, these transitions, that mobilize, or rather become, the forces of unity or integrity in our selves; he wants to rewrite philosophy as history. "To be a radical empiricist means to hold fast to this conjunctive relation [or 'continuous transition'] of all others, for this is the strategic point, the position through which, if a hole be made, all the corruptions of dialectics and all the metaphysical fictions pour into our philosophy." If we know that the integrity of the self resides in and flows from its experience of time, of change, of development, we have no reason either to depend on suprahistorical "agencies of union"—God, "consciousness," subjectivity, whatever—for the groundwork of truth and morality, or to assume that the habitat of the self-determining moral personality must be something other than historical time (*ERE*, 25).

"To be a radical empiricist" is also to stay focused on the incomplete present, the middle ground where previous truth and novel fact mingle, where the transitions we undergo and apprehend are "like a thin line of flame advancing across the dry autumnal field." On this restless frontier, "we live prospectively as well as retrospectively," and so we experience, as a matter of course, that semiotic suture of past and present and future that James calls a conjunctive relation. But that lived experience is precisely what metaphysics has repressed and mutilated: "The plain conjunctive experience has been discredited by both schools, the empiricists leaving things permanently disjoined, and the rationalists remedying the looseness by their absolutes or substances." The "higher principles of disunion"— the metaphysical fictions of ordinary empiricism—are here abjured, but so, too, are the higher principles of unearned unification, the foundational "agencies of union" on which rationalism thrives (*ERE*, 26–27).

So these essays recast the history of philosophy, and set the stage for pragmatism, in two ways. First, they demonstrate that the debate between rationalism and empiricism presupposes agreement on the discontinuities inscribed in modern subjectivity: "The plain conjunctive experience has been discredited by both schools." In this sense, James shows that the tradition, or the continuum, of modern Western philosophy consists of conflicts over the implications of these discontinuities, and that this tradition, so understood, makes the conflicts of the eighteenth and twentieth centuries commensurable. Second, these essays demonstrate that it is only from the standpoint of James's proposed departure that the tradition in question becomes intelligible—and remains useful—as a continuum of conflicts over the core issues of subjectivity. He preserves the received tradition, in short, by producing a new narrative in which traditional conflicts are explained and annulled. He does not so much break with the past as rewrite it.

The critique of modern subjectivity—of the Cartesian ego—is now complete; for James has shown that the integrity of the self requires not abstention from but immersion in pure experience. By his account, the fall into time and space and desire is the necessary condition of a self-determining moral personality, because it elicits and establishes "conjunctive relations" through which we can apprehend our development in time as continuity, and can project ourselves into a future that is consistent with our pasts. We find our selves, he suggests, only insofar as we find evidence of our being in the world at hand. So he has changed the subject in every sense. But again, James has neither ignored nor repudiated modern subjectivity and its attendant dualisms; he has instead contained them within his more inclusive account.

This is an achievement that José Ortega y Gasset could, and perhaps should, have appreciated. He is the philosopher who insisted that "our newest concept has the obligation to explain the old ones, it must demonstrate that portion of truth which they contained," and who declared, in 1928, that "our era both needs and wants to move beyond modernity," the historical moment whose "basic principle" was the Cartesian "idea of subjectivity." He is also the close reader of Heidegger who hoped that the conceptual movement beyond modernity was already under way in his own thinking, which was of course shaped by a three-year stint in Marburg: "But suppose that this idea of subjectivity which is the root of modernity should be superseded, suppose it should be invalidated in whole or in part by another idea, deeper and firmer. This would mean that a new climate, a new era, was beginning."[13]

Ortega sounds very much like Donald Davidson in announcing the end of the Cartesian ego, the "demise of the subjective." But Whitehead, citing James, had written the same obituary four years before Ortega lectured in Madrid and sixty years before Davidson predicted the murder of modern philosophy. Meanwhile Dewey, also citing James, kept writing similar death notices. Why, then, do we take Ortega's reading of Heidegger—and Davidson's periodization of the subjective—for granted? Why do we foreground Heidegger and bracket James, as, for example, Anthony Giddens does in a chronologically perverse passage: "William James echoes aspects of Heidegger's view when he says of time: 'The literally present moment is a purely verbal supposition, not a position; the only present concretely realized being the 'passing moment' in which the dying rearward of time and its dawning future mix their lights.'"[14]

It is not as if Ortega was unaware of pragmatism—in view of Edmund Husserl's affiliation with William James, Carl Schmitt's fascination with pluralism, Georg Simmel's Nietzschean reading of American thought, Max Scheler's critique of Husserl, James, and Dewey, and, finally, Martin Heidegger's familiarity with pragmatism, such ignorance was practically impossible in the Germany that educated him. Indeed, in *What is Philosophy?*, the lectures of 1928–29, Ortega cited Scheler to suggest that pragmatism represents the "amiable cynicism which is characteristic of the Yankees" and the "imperialism of physics," both of which elevated the "material interests" of the nineteenth-century middle class to the height of philosophical concern. Pragmatists, by this accounting, claim that "truth is the intellectual precipitate of practical utility." They are utilitarians after all, mere positivists at best; for pragmatism "is, in effect, the practice that supplants all theory."[15]

And yet Ortega also suggested that "in pragmatism, and especially in its audacity and ingenuity, there is something profoundly true, even though it be centrifugal." He doesn't bother to explain this cryptic dictum, which is buried in a footnote. So I will try hereafter to exhume the truth it contains, first by reference to early critics of pragmatism, and then by reference to later theories of the end of modernity. In doing so, I hope to unearth a genealogical alternative to the romanticism that Heidegger indulges. Throughout this archaeological excursion, I will accept the correlation of "America," pragmatism, and capitalism that is posited by their critics at home and abroad.[16]

I begin with Oswald Spengler's metaphorical reduction of "America" to the amorphous yet gigantic figure of finance capital—the future of the West—because it reiterates Nietzsche's equation of economic calculation with thinking as such, and because it informs the philosophical accounting of pragmatism to be found in the works of Ortega, Heidegger, and Horkheimer as well as their American counterparts among the so-called Young Intellectuals of the 1920s. Like Edward Bellamy and Thorstein Veblen, Spengler distinguished between "bodily money," that is, stamped coin, and "relational money," that is credit, a "wholly intangible" but highly effective way of controlling the supply of goods—credit was a Faustian "form of thought" which already "presse[d] victoriously upon industry to make the productive work of entrepreneur and engineer and labourer alike its spoil." He identified the latter form of "thinking in money" with the irresistible Roman abstractions that had destroyed classical culture and with the ubiquitous American idioms that were now creating an equally coarse civilization: "What is here described as Civilization, then, is the stage of a Culture at which tradition and personality have lost their immediate effectiveness, and every idea, to be actualized, has to be put into terms of money." The rise of America signified the decline of the West, the transition from culture to civilization—"After Madrid, Paris, London, come Berlin and New York"—and it was able to enforce this transition because it epitomized "high finance," the wholly intangible, but again highly effective, claims of capitalist credit on the future of all things, all goods, all souls.[17]

Spengler correlated that decline, that transition, with the appearance of a "strong-minded, completely non-metaphysical man." Once upon a time he had appeared as the Roman intellect, the man who had suffocated the Athenian soul. Now he appeared as the bearer of "a specifically megalopolitan philosophy that was not speculative but practical, irreligious, social-ethical." Now he appeared as that new man, the ugly American who could visit but never comprehend the monuments of Western intellectual accomplishment: "the mob of parvenu tourists from Rome gaped at the works of the Periclean age with as little understanding as the American globetrotter in the Sistine Chapel at those of Michelangelo."[18]

Long before Cornel West claimed that American intellectuals had "evaded" philosophy as such, Ortega followed Spengler's lead in excluding "America" from the Western tradition of metaphysical speculation. But so, too, did Heidegger. In the 1930s, first in *An Introduction to Metaphysics* (1935), then in "The Age of the World Picture" (1938), he exempted both "America" and pragmatism from this tradition, and on the same material grounds Spengler and Ortega had stipulated. The "darkening of the world" he described in his introduction was both a historical fact and a philosophical question. The fact was Nietzsche's discovery that reality was "evaporating" along with the regulative concepts of metaphysics as Europe receded from the world stage; the question was "Does Nietzsche speak the truth?" Heidegger's answer was yes, of course: Europe had "fallen out of being"— it had forgotten or renounced its "spiritual destiny"—because it was "squeezed" between the equivalent extremes of Russia and America. "From a metaphysical point of view, Russia and America are the same," he declared, in a Weberian reprise of Spengler's original dictum, "the same dreary technological frenzy [and] the same unrestricted organization of the average man" now dominated the headquarters of both capitalism and communism. From a metaphysical point of view, "America," like Russia, was invisible because it had not yet risen above the quotidian concerns determined by a "mass division of labor," by the material demands of modern-industrial life. It had not yet "fallen out of being" because it had not yet attained, or even attempted, any metaphysical equilibrium. So it could not address the "spiritual decline of the earth" that Europe embodied.[19]

In the later "Age of the World Picture," Heidegger correlated pragmatism with the "non-metaphysical man," the intellectual athlete, with whom Spengler had associated ancient Roman and modern American tourists. In remarking on the appearance of "the gigantic," by which he meant the new role of "extension and number" in planning and calculating and adjusting every dimension of human life—these were cultural processes through which "the quantitative becomes a special quality and thus a remarkable kind of greatness"—Heidegger rejected the commonplace equation of "the gigantic" and "America" on the grounds that "'Americanism' is something European," that is, an invention of Western metaphysics, whose essence was the technology of the subjective (the *subiectum*): "It is an as-yet-uncomprehended species of the gigantic, the gigantic that is itself still inchoate and does not as yet originate at all out of the complete and gathered metaphysical essence of the modern age." Like Ortega, his student, Heidegger identified pragmatism as a metaphysical laggard or outlaw—an exception, in any case, to every philosophical rule: "The American interpretation of Americanism by means of pragmatism still remains outside the metaphysical realm." Here he recalled remarks made in a lecture of 1921, when he had mentioned the mobility and plurality of truth under the sign of pragmatism without praising or criticizing it as a philosophical position, that is, without reducing it to relativism.[20]

For Spengler, Ortega, and Heidegger, "America" appears, then, as both the horizon of the extra-metaphysical and the intellectual limit of "Europe" because it represents commerce, utility, technology, and (the future tense of) money—the universalization of the commodity form over there makes it the exception from the other shore. Their critical counterparts and successors are even more emphatic because they note that pragmatists inhabit the state of mind specific to what Gyorgy Lukacs, the student of Weber whom Heidegger read closely, called "reification": they represented themselves and their ideas in the grotesque idiom of commerce, utility, technology, and (the future tense of) money. As early as 1908, for example, Bertrand Russell reminded his genteel readers that William James's "contentions"—these sophistries cannot attain the dignity of genuine philosophical argument—"are never supported by 'fine writing'; he brings them into the market-place, and is not afraid to be homely, untechnical, and slangy." In 1926, Lewis Mumford, who was probably the most ferocious homegrown critic of pragmatism, similarly noted the "persistent use of financial metaphors" in pragmatic poetics: "the very words James used to recommend pragmatism should make us suspicious of its pretensions."[21]

Max Horkheimer, who, like Mumford, drew on Spengler and Ortega—also Scheler and Heidegger—in addressing pragmatism, fully agreed with this assessment. In *Eclipse of Reason* (1947), one of several Frankfurt School manifestoes of the 1940s that would prove quite influential in the United States as late as the 1970s and 80s, Horkheimer suggested that the "philosophical pedigree" of pragmatism was dubious at best because the language of its inventors merely echoed "the reifying mechanisms of the anonymous economic apparatus":

> In an analysis of William James's *Pragmatism* [the reference here is to *Essays in Experimental Logic* (1916)], John Dewey comments upon the concepts of truth and meaning. Quoting James, he says: "True ideas lead us into useful verbal and conceptual quarters, as well as directly up to useful sensible termini. They lead to consistency, stability, and flowing intercourse." An idea, Dewey explains, is "a draft drawn upon existing things and [an] intention to act so as to arrange them in a certain way. From which it follows that if the draft is honored, if existences, following upon the actions, rearrange or re-adjust themselves in the way the idea intends, the idea is true."

Truth is something that happens to an idea, as James put it in *Pragmatism*. Truth in this sense is always contractually impending—it is not visible and effective or lawful and enforceable until the bargaining parties have enacted what they originally promised to do. No wonder Horkheimer concluded that pragmatism "reflects with an almost disarming candor the spirit of the prevailing business culture."[22]

As Spengler, Ortega, and Heidegger were clearly correct to sense that the intellectual exfoliation of "America" in the form of pragmatism had framed a new, extra-metaphysical horizon, so Mumford and Horkheimer were clearly correct to draw our attention to the monetary metaphors that James and Dewey invariably use when they are most interested in convincing us that their post-metaphysical notion of truth is better than what is already available in the marketplace of ideas. In 1891, for example, Dewey claimed that "[e]very judgment a man passes on life is perforce, his 'I bet,' his speculation. So much of his saved capital of truth he invests in his judgment: 'The state of things is thus and so.'" James was equally playful in the essays on radical empiricism, and again in the lectures of 1906 and 1907 that became *Pragmatism*. Here the metaphors of money, banking, and credit do carry the weight of philosophical argument. As we have seen, he suggested in "A World of Pure Experience" that verification is an unusual moment in the development of knowledge because "we live on speculative investments, or on our prospects only"; the future tense of modern life is "as good as living in the actual," he added, "so long as our credit remains good."[23]

In the pivotal chapter 6 of *Pragmatism*, truths become the provisional representations of moments that do not yet exist "out there" in the "real world," in which speculation therefore becomes the normal procedure of what is called thinking, and in which crisis is signaled by a generalized demand for immediate verification—redemption in cash—of the symbolic tokens of truth: "Truth lives, in fact, for the most part on a credit system. Our thoughts and beliefs 'pass,' so long as nothing challenges them, just as bank-notes pass so long as nobody refuses them. But this all points to direct face-to-face verification somewhere, without which the fabric of truth collapses like a financial system with no cash-basis whatever. You accept my verification of one thing, I yours of another. We trade on each other's truth."[24]

James refers repeatedly to the cash value of words in *Pragmatism,* as if there is a bottom line—a foundation of truth, a point of rest—in the ledger that records our intellectual transactions; in a similar vein he also cites "our general obligation to do what pays." Yet he emphatically rejects the notion that the function of what is called thinking is to copy or represent a fixed, external reality and, by implication, the idea that money is only a means of exchange, that is, an immaterial set of symbols that necessarily corresponds to discrete objects "out there" in the "real world" already constituted by the products of labor (or, alternatively, by Nature). James is instead claiming that money, as redefined by the credit economy of modern, corporate business enterprise, is an appropriate metaphor for mind, language, and thought. For example: "You must bring out of each word its practical cash-value, set it at work within the stream of your experience. It appears less as a solution, then, than as a program for more work, and more particularly as an indication of ways in which existing realities may be changed" (*P,* 31–32).

We may well notice that the "cash value" of language resides in the surplus—not the equivalence or the equilibrium—it produces. And we may also notice that this surplus must be reinvested if it is to make a difference, that is, if it is to bear more interest in the future by changing "existing realities." But again, Mumford, Horkheimer, and the others were clearly correct to suggest that pragmatism was a way of "thinking in money." The question is not whether financial metaphors dominate the vocabulary that James and Dewey use to explain the meaning of truth; the question is what we should make of their pragmatic appropriation of the language of credit, the future tense of money.

Our answer will depend on what we want from philosophy and where we stand on the end of modernity. If we think that philosophy must remain faithful to the general traits of our common experience, and so must become an interpretation of historical circumstances that are apparent to everyone, even the least reflective of us, then we will agree with Heidegger in insisting that all metaphysical problems are "fundamentally historical" because it is only in philosophy "that essential relations to the realm of what is take shape." We will want philosophers to explain our existence, not ignore or denounce it because it is too brief and too banal—too crowded with the "material interests" of the middle class—to be worthy of serious thought. And we will want historians to keep an Emersonian eye on the "barbarism and materialism" of our own times. As Heidegger himself put it in commenting on Spengler: "If the past is to be disclosed authentically in terms of what it is, we will have to avoid bringing in questions that ignore the present historical situation."[25]

But what if we know that the end of modernity occurs when "reification" makes a mere prostitute of the man of letters (Lukacs); when the "crisis of humanism" is experienced and articulated as the death of the author, the "demise of the subjective," the end of metaphysics (Heidegger, Rorty, Davidson, Foucault, Derrida); when the world becomes only a fable because we realize we have measured its value "according to categories [aim, unity, truth] that refer to a purely fictitious world" (Nietzsche); when the "fact of credit, of worldwide trade, of the means of transportation" uproots all "former means of obtaining homogenous, enduring characters" (Nietzsche); when the universalization of the commodity form under corporate auspices makes exchange value the measure of use value, and thus guarantees that "individuality loses its economic basis."²⁶ Then what?

Then it is only through nihilism—the ability to make truth claims in the absence of "the subject" or the homogeneity of "character" or the modern individual, and the will to believe in the absence of all authenticity or "objective reality" or "non-human truth"—that philosophy can remain faithful to the general traits of our common experience, and become an interpretation of historical circumstances that are apparent to everyone, even the least reflective of us. "The most extreme form of nihilism," Nietzsche suggested, "would be the view that every belief, every considering-something-true, is necessarily false because there is no true world." Karl Lowith, Gianni Vattimo, and many other writers have of course identified Heidegger as the most effective bearer of this news from nowhere. I want to suggest instead, in argument with Vattimo, that pragmatism is the most extreme, and thus the most productive, form of nihilism; that Nietzsche need not appear as its origin or sponsor or spirit; and that Heidegger is more useful than original in the demolition of metaphysics, which nihilism, in the form of pragmatism, claims as its purpose.²⁷

Bertrand Russell, whose periodization of Western philosophy surely inspired Spengler, explained how pragmatism amounts to an extreme form of nihilism in two brilliant strokes. First he showed that pragmatism treats the truth as a built environment, an artificial edifice created by plural human purposes and languages, rather than as the singular, self-evident residue of a unitary human experience: "In order to understand the pragmatic notion of truth [its 'central doctrine'], we have to be clear as to the basis of fact upon which truths are supposed to rest. Immediate sensible experience, for example, does not come under the alternative of true and false. 'Day follows day,' says James, 'and its contents are simply added. The new contents themselves are not true, they simply come and are. Truth is what we say about them.'" Again, all we have are those semiotic artifacts, those provisional, second-order truths that emerge in the narrative time of historical consciousness and explanation. The one true world—"truth absolute and objective"—would appear only at the end of days.²⁸

Then Russell reduces James's "will to believe" to Nietzsche's "will to power" by equating the effect of their exclusion of "non-human truth" from the settlement of philosophical (and political) debates. "The worship of force, as we find it in Nietzsche, is not to be found in the same form in William James," he acknowledges, but goes on to hedge his bet: "Nevertheless, the excessive individualism of the pragmatic theory of truth is inherently connected with the appeal to force." Russell here confuses consequential yet benign action—for example, a scientific experiment—with deadly military force ("ironclads and Maxim guns"); even so, his explanation of this oft-repeated equation between Nietzsche and James reveals the transcendent source of its enduring appeal: "If there is a non-human truth

. . . there is a standard outside the disputants, to which, we may urge, the dispute ought to be submitted; hence a pacific and judicial settlement of disputes is at least theoretically possible. If, on the contrary, the only way of discovering which of the disputants is in the right is to wait and see which of them is successful, there is no longer any principle except force by which the issue can be decided."[29]

Russell is right to suggest that the (epistemological) alternatives to the pragmatist conception of truth—which lives "on a credit system" that turns every hypothesis into a wager on the shape of the future—require a body of fact that is independent of human purposes and languages. And he is right to suggest that pragmatists can't imagine such a non-human truth, not even when they measure the consequences of the hypothesis called God. But they would not agree with the conclusion that truths, so conceived, are unattainable without an application of force (unless "force" is defined as purposeful action). From their standpoint, "a standard outside the disputants," whoever they may be, already exists in the cultural tradition we call the common law, where revelation—non-human truth— is still inadmissible evidence; in the contentious mechanics of modern politics, where truth becomes "what we say about them"; and in the credit economy of corporate capitalism, where we trade on each other's truths.

In short, pragmatists accept the end of modernity in all its slippery, surreal manifestations, including, as their critics make clear, the universalization of the commodity form. In that sense, they are more accomplished nihilists than either Nietzsche or Heidegger. Let me draw on Vattimo's apology for nihilism to defend this claim. To begin with, he suggests, it is the "mode of thought beyond metaphysics" permitted by the death of God and the dissolution of the "highest values"—that is, by the rendition of Being as value, or, more specifically, "the reduction of Being to exchange-value." Nihilism treats the result of this reduction, which entails an inescapable "logic of permutability," as mere fact, the place to begin thinking, rather than as the obvious occasion for mourning or critique or accusation: "Being is completely dissolved in the discoursing of value, in the indefinite transformations of universal equivalence."

Nihilism thus avoids the "pathos of authenticity" that animates the cultural/ political tradition informed by phenomenology, Marxism, existentialism, and now mysticism—the tradition whose adherents still dream of awakening from the nightmare of wage labor and restoring "an ideal zone of use-value," where work is artisanal and artistic, that is, the unforced activity of a self-mastering individual, and where, accordingly, "the reduction of Being to exchange-value" is impossible. Nihilism thus adjourns modern subjectivity by simply acknowledging what Horkheimer and his adherents must keep mourning, that "individuality loses its economic basis." It accepts, as mere facts, the demise of poiesis and the completion of proletarianization under corporate auspices, which together make alienated, abstract social labor—the universalization of the commodity form— the general trait of our common experience.[30]

Pragmatism is the extremity of nihilism so conceived. It endorses the "social self" that attends the rise of "corporateness," mass society, and consumer culture, for example, just as it embraces the semiotic confusions and possibilities specific to a credit economy. "Money was the sign of real commodities," Edward Bellamy explained in 1887, in a book that both James and Dewey knew well, whereas "credit was but the sign of a sign." With their "persistent use of financial metaphors" at the moment of philosophical truth, that lament was translated into a warrant for intellectual innovation, a vote for the logic of permutability.[31]

By Vattimo's own accounting, then, neither Nietzsche nor Heidegger is as accomplished a nihilist as James or Dewey. There was no principle of hope in Nietzsche's assessment of the "universal haste" with which the "total extermination and uprooting of culture" was being transacted. In *Untimely Meditations,* as in *The Will to Power,* he correlated this catastrophe with the barbarism embedded in what we would recognize as modern, corporate capitalism: "The waters of religion are ebbing, and they are leaving behind swamps or ponds; the nations are again separating from one another in the most hostile manner . . . ; the edified classes and states are being swept along by a money economy which is enormously contemptible. Never was the world more a world, never was it poorer in love and good. . . . Everything, contemporary art and science included, serves the coming barbarism." But an ideal zone of use-value might still wait for us, Nietzsche hints, somewhere inside those imaginary gates that exclude the contemptible barbarism of exchange-value.[32]

Vattimo acknowledges that the early Heidegger of *Being and Time* (1927) similarly indulged the "need to go beyond exchange-value, in the direction of a kind of use-value that can be kept free of the logic of permutability." But he also claims that the later Heidegger—he of "The Letter on Humanism" (1946) and "The Question Concerning Technology" (1955)—was able to connect "the crisis of humanism to the end of metaphysics as the culmination of technology and the moment of passage beyond the world of the subject/object opposition." Vattimo argues further that the resulting *critique* of the subject is the most promising theoretical means by which "the liquidation of the subject at the level of social existence may be given a meaning that is not merely a destructive one." Here the function of nihilism is to convince us that neither our intellectual agendas nor our political purposes should be reduced to a protest against proletarianization, in the quaint manner of the Frankfurt School. According to Vattimo, such "resistance to the attacks launched against man's humanity—still defined in terms of subjectivity and self-consciousness—by the rationalization of social labour" ignores two salient features of our common experience at the end of modernity. First, the rationalization/proletarianization of social labor "has created the historical and social condition for the elimination of the subject." Second, the "moment of passage beyond the world of the subject/object opposition" coincides, in historical time and aesthetic codes, with a philosophical, psychological, literary, and more broadly artistic acknowledgment that "this same subject does not merit a defence."[33]

Vattimo's conclusion should serve as a warning to those who would pin their democratic hopes on reviving craftsmanship, reinstating modern subjectivity, and thus rearming each individual's intrinsic agency as against the corporate-industrial bureaucracies that rationalize social labor and universalize the commodity form. "If the Heideggerian analysis of the connection between metaphysics, humanism and technology is a valid one," he notes, "then *the subject that supposedly has to be defended from technological dehumanization is itself the very root of this dehumanization,* since the kind of subjectivity which is defined strictly as the subject of the object is a pure function of the world of objectivity, and inevitably tends to become itself an object of manipulation."[34]

And yet the *later* Heidegger was no less fearful of the logic of permutability attending the rationalization of social labor than was the early Heidegger; that is, he was no less fearful than Nietzsche or Horkheimer of the subject's "liquidation." In "The Question Concerning Technology," for example, what was cast as "the gigantic" in "The Age of the World Picture" (1938) now auditions as "the rule of Enframing, which demands that nature be orderable as standing-reserve"—in other words, be assembled as a set of interchangeable parts and treated as a manipulable mass of inert objects: "Yet when destining reigns in the mode of Enframing, it is the supreme danger. . . . As soon as what is unconcealed no longer concerns man even as object, but does so, rather, exclusively as standing-reserve, and man in the midst of objectlessness is nothing but the orderer of the standing-reserve, then he comes to the very brink of a precipitous fall; that is, he comes to the point where he himself will have to be taken as standing-reserve."

Heidegger makes a strong case for poiesis—work guided by craftsmanship, not the sluggish routine of the assembly line—as the key constraint on the rule of Enframing, indeed as the only activity that might prevent the petrification of human being itself in the silent warehouse of the standing-reserve: "As a destining, [Enframing] banishes man into that kind of revealing which is an ordering [thus producing the standing-reserve]. Where this ordering holds sway, it drives out every other possibility of revealing. Above all, Enframing conceals that revealing which, in the sense of poeisis, lets what presences come forth into appearance." So the truth as such is at stake in the revolt of poeisis against the rule of Enframing: "Thus the challenging Enframing not only conceals a former way of revealing, bringing-forth, but it conceals revealing itself and with it that wherein unconcealment, i.e., truth, comes to pass." In sum, the techno-metaphysical urge called Enframing "blocks poeisis," and thereby "threatens man with the possibility that it could be denied to him to enter into a more original revealing and hence to experience the call of a more primal truth."[35]

This "idealization of artisanal and artistic production," as Vattimo names the inevitable effect of "humanistic" alternatives to nihilism, is absent from early pragmatist texts, mainly because their authors were uninterested in rediscovering or reappropriating the humanistic ideal—that is, the centrality of "the" subject as against an increasingly invasive externality. The apparent loss of human subjectivity in the universalization of the commodity form looked, from their nihilist standpoint, like the transformation of selfhood in accordance with the socialization of private property and goods production under the organizational aegis of the corporation. They called the result of that transformation the "social self," but they did not assume or argue, in the manner of the Frankfurt School and its myriad American students, that this new version of subjectivity amounted to the "other-directed individual" (Riesman); the "authoritarian personality" (Adorno, Horkheimer); the "managed self" (Lears); or the white-collared prey of mass politics (Mills). Instead they found reasons to believe in the democratic promise of "America" outside that ideal zone of use value where artisanal and artistic production take place, and inside the more common and more commodified experience of abstract social labor under corporate capitalism. In this sense, the original pragmatists remained faithful to the general traits of our experience—but they never relinquished their democratic hopes.[36]

In fact, by taking for granted what Nietzsche and Heidegger understood as the obvious evidence of barbarism (or danger) and the intellectual occasion for accusation, these pragmatists enlarged the domain of democracy to include civil society (where markets and commodities reign) as well as state-centered politics. For example, Jane Addams proposed, on pragmatic grounds, to transpose the key principle of political obligation—consent—from the justification of republican government to the pacification of the capital-labor relation, thus making distributive justice ("social ethics," as she called it) an issue in the "private sector." George Herbert Mead, a close reader of Addams and a close friend of Dewey's, understood the necessity of this move because he recognized the dispersal of power from the state to society—the breakdown of the modern distinction between private and public spheres—which followed from the rise of corporations able to administer prices and regulate markets. "The functions of government, as an institution, are merging with equal rapidity into the industrial world which it is supposed to control," he argued, and this new conjuncture "point[ed] to the passing of functions which are supposed to inhere in the government into activities that belong to the community simply through its organization apart from government."[37]

And long before Walter Lippmann, a student of James at Harvard, suggested that the "trust movement" was "sucking the life out of property"—thus accomplishing what no revolutionary was attempting in America or anywhere else— Henry Carter Adams, another close friend of Dewey's, argued that the kind of "social production" enabled by the new corporations had radically redefined private property; by the same token, it had redefined the modern individual, whose identity had derived from his relation to such property since the eighteenth century: "To deny the fact of social production, and thus preclude a development in the idea of property, is not only unfortunate, but there is no justification for it in the nature of the case. Individualism does not consist in living in isolation, but rather in dwelling in a society of recognized interdependencies. Its development is marked by the regress of self-sufficiency and the progress of association."[38]

But John Dewey himself, the most attentive reader of James, was always the farthest outpost of pragmatic nihilism. In his view, the appearance of a corporate-industrial credit economy was anything but a cause for mourning—when comparing the philosophical merits of the Scholastic and the Speculator early in his career, for example, he chose the Speculator, who treated the Standard Oil Trust as his model of epistemological comportment. That commitment to the contingency of credit as the uncertain measure of truth, and that acknowledgment of corporate personality as the probable arbiter of truth animated all his subsequent thinking. Dewey also accepted the modern-industrial division of labor as the condition of moral community. The central idea of his first major work, *Outlines of a Critical Theory of Ethics* (1891), was the notion that, like morality, "self, or individuality, is essentially social." He demonstrated the idea by reference to the work of the proletarian, not the artisan: "The term 'moral community' can mean only a unity of action, made what it is by the cooperating activities of diverse individuals. There is unity in the work of a factory, not in spite of, but because of the division of labor. Each workman forms the unity not by doing the same that everybody else does, or by trying to do the whole, but by doing his specific part."[39]

Over the next three decades, Dewey developed a social ethics in the terms he derived from James's *Principles*—that is, by acknowledging "the entire uselessness of an ego outside and behind" the scene of acting or thinking. To do so, he understood, was "to substitute a working conception of the self for a metaphysical definition of it," and thus to treat the agency of the individual as the effect of acting on and being in the world. In this sense, Dewey was treating the moral capacity of an individual as if it were something like a linguistic capacity: it was realized and refined—in a word, created—in specific, often spontaneous transactions through which individuals adapted themselves to inherited conventions they could not circumvent without making themselves unintelligible; and yet there was plenty of room for innovation, variation, and deviation in the development of that capacity. As he put it in 1901, "all morality is social in its content." But as his citation of James in the *Essays in Experimental Logic* (1916) would suggest, the new content of the social was the credit economy of corporate capitalism.[40]

In the 1920s, Dewey returned again and again to the reconstruction of subjectivity—in contemporary parlance, the "demise of the subjective"—determined by the increasing "corporateness" of American society, most pointedly in "The Historic Background of Corporate Legal Personality" (1926), an essay for the *Yale Law Journal,* and in *Individualism Old and New* (1929), a collection of pieces originally published in the *New Republic.* "The root difficulty in present controversies about 'natural' [persons] and associated bodies [corporations]," he declared in the earlier essay, "may be that while we oppose one to the other, or try to find some combining union of the two, what we really need to do is overhaul the doctrine of personality which underlies both of them." It was necessary, in other words, to jettison the "popular and philosophical notions of the [natural] person" because they informed "an anarchic and dissolving individualism." As Heidegger was struggling to explain both the appeal and the idiocy of the transcendental ego in the phenomenological explorations that would become *Being and Time,* so Dewey was trying, in a different intellectual register, to explain both the appeal and the irrelevance of the "natural person"—the "man of reason" who had served for three centuries as the *sujet de droit* of modern jurisprudence as well as the presupposition of metaphysical, theological, and vernacular arguments about the sources of subjectivity—in an epoch defined by associated bodies or corporate personalities.[41]

In *Individualism Old and New,* Dewey was more explicit. "The need of the present," he announced, "is to apprehend the fact that, for better or worse, we are living in a corporate age." The "crisis of culture" he noted was a result, in part, of American intellectuals' inability to accept that new age as mere fact. They still indulged "the habit of opposing the corporate and collective to the individual," and they couldn't seem to understand that "the shift that makes the older individualism a dying echo is more marked as well as more rapid in this country" than in Europe. In a chapter titled "The United States, Incorporated," Dewey explained that shift:

> There is no word which adequately expresses what is taking place. "Socialism" has too specific political and economic associations to be appropriate. "Collectivism" is more neutral, but it, too, is a party-word rather than a descriptive term. Perhaps the constantly increasing role of corporations in our economic life gives a clue to a fitting name. The word may be used in a wider sense than is conveyed by its technical legal meaning. We may then say that the United States has steadily moved from an earlier pioneer individualism to a condition of dominant corporateness. . . . Associations tightly or loosely organized more and more define the opportunities, the choices and the actions of individuals.[42]

Such associations had meanwhile redefined the social content of the political; at the very least they had reduced the relative importance of state-centered, policy-oriented electoral politics, and had demoted the rugged, entrepreneurial individual—the independent, omnicompetent citizen of nineteenth-century lore—to class clown. "We repeat over and over that man is a social animal," Dewey complained, "and then we confine the significance of this statement to the sphere in which sociality usually seems least evident, politics." Modern political theory, which treated self-determining citizens, independent individuals all, as the discrete building blocks of republican government, was practically useless in a corporate age: "Groupings for promoting the diversity of goods that [we] share have become the real social units. They occupy the place which traditional theory has claimed either for mere isolated individuals or for the supreme and single political organization [the state]."[43]

Dewey refused to light out for the territory beyond corporate-industrial capitalism, beyond the general traits of our common experience—he had already evacuated the ideal zone of use-value where artisanal and artistic production still prevail, and where "direct democracy" is still enacted in the academic imagination of the university senate. He thought that the older, "pioneer" individualism was a residual malady and insisted that "some kind of socialism" was the obvious cure: "A stable recovery of individuality waits upon the elimination of the older economic and political individualism, an elimination which will liberate imagination and endeavor for the task of making corporate society contribute to the free culture of its members. Only by economic revision can the sound element of the older individuality—equality of opportunity—be made a reality." In short, he refused to indulge the "pathos of authenticity" that comes with the territory still occupied by the American Adam.[44]

So it is unnerving to find Dewey's best biographer, Robert Westbrook, heading for this territory, this same old frontier on which the anti-corporate petite bourgeoisie—the once and future middle class—still roams freely. The presiding spirit of Westbrook's *Democratic Hope: Pragmatism and the Politics of Truth* (2005), and of a cognate historical work by Robert Johnston, is Christopher Lasch, whose *True and Only Heaven* (1991), the last book he saw through production before his untimely death, was an enthusiastic endorsement of "artisans against innovation"—that is, an impassioned plea to reinstate the nineteenth-century principle "that property ownership and the independence it confers are absolutely essential preconditions of citizenship." Lasch was self-consciously restating Herbert Croly's question of 1914: "How can the wage-earners obtain an amount or a degree of economic independence analogous to that upon which the pioneer democrat could count?" So are Westbrook and Johnston, and, for that matter, so are the many other writers who have defended the "local knowledge" of bourgeois society and proprietary capitalism against the large-scale sins of corporate capitalism, from James Weinstein and Philip Scranton to Mark Kann and Teresa Brennan, from William Leach and Jackson Lears to Gretchen Ritter and Elizabeth Sanders. Unlike Dewey's, their answers to Croly's question are uniformly nostalgic for the historical moment of bourgeois society, when property ownership conferred political independence upon individuals and work was the theater in which character was created.[45]

For all of them are in search of a "free social space"—this is the phrase coined by Lawrence Goodwyn, Lasch's favored historian of American populism—which might put us beyond the scope of the commodity form as it appears under corporate-industrial auspices, as the universalization of exchange value even unto one's capacity to produce value through work. And all of them want to resettle the ideal zone of use-value where artisanal and artistic production still prevail, "making a revival of craftsmanship," as Lasch puts it, "the prerequisite of a democratic culture." Westbrook, for example, insists that Dewey "retained an abiding respect for artisanal labor, and in *Art and Experience* (1934) called for preserving its rewards in modern work." He also suggests that we need to resuscitate the "petty-bourgeois radicalism" that Johnston studies with such care, and, accordingly, to "take a closer look at the merits of the antimonopoly tradition."[46]

So the "pathos of authenticity" has become the ethical norm of neo-pragmatism, just as it has become the ethical norm of recent historiography, and perhaps even the ethical norm of party politics. This pathos derives from our inability to give up the ghost of modern subjectivity, and more poignantly, from the recent intellectual effort to revive it by means of a "middle-class radicalism" that promises to restore the "one true world" that would redeem our hopes and deliver us from evil. On the Right that promise consists of a renewed commitment to church, family, and tradition; on the Left it consists, for now, of a renewed commitment to the "movement culture" of the Populist Moment or the Progressive Era or the 1960s. Either way, the globalized commodity form—the universalization of exchange value—appears as the cancer to be irradiated by the ethical authenticity, genuine selfhood, and self-mastering individuality that "direct democracy" requires.

But the early pragmatists, James and Dewey if no one else, understood that the universalization of exchange value made the inherited bourgeois/pioneer/artisanal individuality an endangered species, and welcomed its impending extinction—what we now call "the demise of the subjective" or "the death of the author"—as a result. They were not interested in authenticity of any kind because they knew there was neither a true world apart from "what we say about it"— every truth was a bet on the future that had paid off—nor a genuine self prior to the scene of acting and thinking. They were nihilists. Instead of retreating to the ideal zone of use-value where craftsmanship is the prerequisite of democracy, we should follow their lead, and, in good pragmatist fashion, see what happens.

NOTES

1. See James Livingston, *Pragmatism, Feminism, and Democracy: Rethinking the Politics of American History* (New York: Routledge, 2001), chapters 3, 6.

2. The terms of this argument are drawn from Gianni Vattimo, *The End of Modernity: Nihilism and Hermeneutics in Postmodern Culture*, trans. Jon R. Snyder (Baltimore, Md.: Johns Hopkins University Press, 1988) and from my first attempt to decipher Jamesian metaphors, *Pragmatism and the Political Economy of Cultural Revolution, 1850–1940* (Chapel Hill: University of North Carolina Press, 1994).

3. On the question of modern subjectivity, see Livingston, *Pragmatism, Feminism, and Democracy*, chapters 1–3.

4. See Donald Davidson, "The Myth of the Subjective," reprinted in *Relativism: Interpretation and Confrontation*, ed. Michael Krausz (Notre Dame, Ind.: Notre Dame University Press, 1989), pp. 159–72, here 160, 166, 163.

5. Ibid., 162, 161, 163.

6. See John P. Murphy, *Pragmatism: From Peirce to Davidson* (Boulder, Colo.: Westview Press, 1990), pp. 95–98; Rorty quoted from his introduction, "Pragmatism as Anti-Representationalism," pp. 1–6, here 5. On James's preparations for defending the "'pure experience' hypothesis," see Notebooks 10, 11, 12 in the William James Papers (bMSAm 1092.9), Houghton Library, Harvard University; of these 256 pages, all except the last ten date from 1895–98. See also John J. McDermott's indispensable introduction to the Harvard University Press edition of *Essays in Radical Empiricism*, pp. xi–xlviii.

7. Alfred North Whitehead, *Science and the Modern World* (1925; New York: Mentor, 1948), p. 143.

8. In volume 3 of Jo Ann Boydston, ed., *John Dewey: The Middle Works*, 15 vols. (Carbondale: Southern Illinois University Press, 1976), there are at least five articles from 1905 and 1906 in which Dewey invokes James's authority. "The Realism of Pragmatism" first appeared in 1905, is reprinted in *Middle Works* 3: 153–57, and is here quoted from 156. On Dewey's work in the 1920s and '30s, see Livingston, *Pragmatism, Feminism, and Democracy*, chapters 2–3; and Robert Westbrook, *John Dewey and American Democracy* (Ithaca, N.Y.: Cornell University Press, 1991), pp. 275–487.

9. John Dewey, "The Vanishing Subject in the Psychology of James," *Journal of Philosophy* 37 (1940): 589–99, quoted from pp. 599, 596, 598–99.

10. On the return of the repressed, see Norman O. Brown, *Life against Death: The Psychoanalytical Meaning of History* (Middletown, Conn.: Wesleyan University Press, 1959); on the narrative politics of this return, see Jean Laplanche, *Life and Death in Psychoanalysis*, trans. Jeffrey Mehlman (Baltimore, Md.: Johns Hopkins University Press, 1976). On "desublimation," see Herbert Marcuse, *Eros and Civilization* (Boston: Beacon Press, 1955); on "deterritorialization," see Gilles Deleuze and Felix Guattari, *Anti-*

Oedipus: Capitalism and Schizophrenia, trans. Robert Hurley, Mark Seem, and Helen Lane (Minneapolis: University of Minnesota Press, 1983). The "society of the spectacle" is of course the locution of the Situationist International: see Guy Debord, *The Society of the Spectacle* (1967), trans. Donald Nicholson-Smith (New York: Zone Books, 1995), and the remarkable collection, *Situationist International Anthology,* trans. and ed. Ken Knabb (Berkeley, Calif.: Bureau of Public Secrets, 1981).

11. On this difficult birth of the modern subject, see, for example, Walter J. Ong, *The Presence of the Word* (New Haven, Conn.: Yale University Press, 1967); Norman Bryson, *Vision and Painting: The Logic of the Gaze* (New Haven, Conn.: Yale University Press, 1983), chapters 3–6; Norbert Elias, *The Civilizing Process,* 2 vols., trans. Edmund Jephcott (New York: Pantheon, 1978), vol. 1, pp. 51–217, and vol. 2, pp. 91–225, 270–300; Klaus Theweleit, *Male Fantasies,* 2 vols., trans. Stephen Conway, Erica Carter, and Chris Carter (Minneapolis: University of Minnesota Press, 1987), 1: 300–363. Heidegger was, I think, trying to understand the obstetrics involved when he pondered the implications of Dilthey's "historical worldview"—as he put it in 1925, "The possibility of theoretical research arises here only through a certain reorientation. I can reorient myself by detaching my circumspection from my own concerns and allowing it to become merely a kind of looking around, i.e., [theory]. This move toward the autonomy of sight is the real source of any science." From "Wilhelm Dilthey's Research and the Struggle for a Historical Worldview," in *Martin Heidegger, Supplements: From the Earliest Essays to Being and Time and Beyond,* ed. John Van Buren (Albany: SUNY Press, 2002), 147–76, here 164.

12. On these anxieties and their incorporation into the assumptions, methods, and conclusions of modern science, see Hannah Arendt, *The Human Condition* (Chicago: University of Chicago Press, 1958), chapter 6; E. A. Burtt, *The Metaphysical Foundations of Modern Science,* rev. ed. (Garden City, N.Y.: Doubleday, 1955); and Hans Blumenburg, *The Genesis of the Copernican World,* trans. Robert M. Wallace (Cambridge, Mass.: MIT Press, 1987).

13. José Ortega y Gasset, *What Is Philosophy?* trans. Mildred Adams (New York: Norton, 1960), pp. 227, 183, 149.

14. Anthony Giddens, *Central Problems in Social Theory* (Berkeley and Los Angeles: University of California Press, 1979), pp. 3, 261n4. Giddens here cites the 1943 Longmans edition of *A Pluralistic Universe,* but surely he knew that the first edition appeared in 1909, almost twenty years before the publication of *Being and Time.*

15. Ortega y Gasset, *What Is Philosophy?* pp. 44, 41, 64. On Simmel, Scheler, Heidegger, and the intellectual earthquake pragmatism caused in Germany after 1908, see Hans Joas, *Pragmatism and Social Theory* (Chicago: University of Chicago Press, 1993), pp. 94–121. On Husserl's affiliation with James, see Bruce W. Wilshire, *William James and Phenomenology: A Study of "The Principles of Psychology"* (Bloomington: Indiana University Press, 1968), pp. 120–22; John Wild, *The Radical Empiricism of William James* (Garden City, N.Y.: Doubleday, 1969), pp. 128, 143–44, 160–61, 389–90; and esp. James M. Edie, *William James and Phenomenology* (Bloomington: Indiana University Press, 1987), pp. 19–25, 34–36, 46–48, 67–72. On Schmitt's novel use of pluralism in rethinking sovereignty—his translator declares that "the Anglo-Saxon theory of pluralism was unknown in Germany until Schmitt called attention to it"—see Carl Schmitt, *The Concept of the Political,* trans. George Schwab (1932; New Brunswick: Rutgers University Press, 1976), pp. 37–45. There are many suggestive references to pragmatism in Hubert Dreyfus, *Being-in-the-World: A Commentary on Heidegger's "Being and Time,"* *Division I* (Cambridge, Mass.: MIT Press, 1991)—see, for example, pp. 5–7, 67, 70, 80, 85, and notes 5, 11, 12 at pp. 347–48—and in Rudiger Safranski, *Martin Heidegger: Between Good and Evil,* trans. Ewald Osers (Cambridge, Mass.: Harvard University Press, 1998)—see, for example, pp. 34, 45–50, 123–25, 154–56, 299, 366.

16. *What Is Philosophy?* p. 44n7.

17. Oswald Spengler, *The Decline of the West,* 2 vols., trans. Charles Francis Atkin-

son (1918; New York: Knopf, 1926–28), vol. 2, pp. 477–92, 505–506; vol. 1, pp. 32–33. For Nietzsche's equation of economic calculation and thinking as such, see *On the Genealogy of Morals*, trans. Walter Kaufmann and R. J. Hollingdale (1887; New York: Vintage, 1967), pp. 65–70. See otherwise Edward Bellamy, *Looking Backward: 2000–1887* (1887; New York: New American Library, 1960), chapter 22, and Thorstein Veblen, *The Theory of Business Enterprise* (New York: Scribner's, 1904).

18. Spengler, *Decline of the West*, vol. 1, pp. 32–34.

19. See Cornel West, *The American Evasion of Philosophy* (Madison: University of Wisconsin Press, 1987), for the exceptionalist thesis in full flower. As Heidegger suggested that "Americanism" is a European invention (see note 21 below), so I would suggest that American exceptionalism is, too. Quoted remarks from Martin Heidegger, *An Introduction to Metaphysics*, trans. Ralph Manheim (1935; New Haven, Conn.: Yale University Press, 1959), pp. 37–38, 45–47.

20. Heidegger, *Introduction to Metaphysics*, p. 46; "The Age of the World Picture," in *The Question Concerning Technology and Other Essays*, trans. William Lovitt (1938; New York: Harper & Row, 1977), pp. 115–54, here 135, 153. The remarks on pragmatism in Heidegger, *Gesamtausgabe*, Band 61: Wintersemester 1921/22 (Frankfurt: Victorio Klostermann, 1985), p. 135, are mentioned by Dreyfus, *Being-in-the-World*, p. 342n7; translation from the German courtesy of Andrew J. Livingston.

21. On Lukacs, "reification," and the now routinized critique of consumer culture from the standpoint of the Frankfurt School, see Livingston, *Pragmatism, Feminism, and Democracy*, chapter 1; compare Safranski on Heidegger's use of Weber and Lukacs in his first postwar lecture (1919), in *Martin Heidegger*, pp. 89–98. See otherwise Bertrand Russell, "William James's Conception of Truth," in *Philosophical Essays* (1910; New York: Routledge, 1994), pp. 112–30, here 115; Lewis Mumford, *The Golden Day: A Study in American Culture and Experience* (New York: Horace Liveright, 1926), pp. 188–92.

22. Max Horkheimer, *Eclipse of Reason* (1947; New York: Seabury Press, 1974), pp. 40–42, 52. The strange and debilitating effects of the Frankfurt School's eager reception in American cultural criticism are traced in Livingston, *Pragmatism and Political Economy*, pp. 80–83, 323–25n40; Paul R. Gorman, *Left Intellectuals and Popular Culture in Twentieth-Century America* (Chapel Hill: University of North Carolina Press, 1996), pp. 176–85; and Wilfred McClay, *The Masterless: Self and Society in Modern America* (Chapel Hill: University of North Carolina Press, 1994), pp. 194–222.

23. John Dewey, "The Scholastic and the Speculator" (1891–92), in *John Dewey: The Early Works*, 5 vols., ed. Jo Ann Boydston (Carbondale: Southern Illinois University Press, 1969), vol. 3, pp. 145–54, here 153; William James, "A World of Pure Experience," in *Essays in Radical Empiricism*, pp. 42–43. It is worth noting here that in the aftermath of the financial revolution in the eighteenth century, the Renaissance notion of Fortuna gave way to the "personification of Credit as an inconstant female figure." See Hannah Fenichel Pitkin, *Fortune Is a Woman: Gender and Politics in the Thought of Nicolo Machiavelli* (Berkeley and Los Angeles: University of California Press), chapter 6, esp. pp. 144, 153, 169; and J. G. A. Pocock, *The Machiavellian Moment: Florentine Political Thought and the Atlantic Republican Tradition* (Princeton, N.J.: Princeton University Press, 1975), chapters 13–15, esp. pp. 426, 437, 448, 452.

24. "Pragmatism's Conception of Truth," Lecture 6 of *Pragmatism* (pp. 95–113). James agreed with Bertrand Russell that this was the "pivotal" lecture: see *The Meaning of Truth: A Sequel to Pragmatism* (*MT*), pp. 3–10, 78–89, 99–119.

25. Heidegger, *Introduction to Metaphysics*, p. 43; "Dilthey and the Struggle for a Historical Worldview," *Supplements*, p. 174; see also "The Concept of Time in the Science of History," ibid., pp. 49–60, esp. 57. Here is Emerson's formulation of 1842: "We have yet had no genius in America, with tyrannous eye, which knew the value of our incomparable materials, and saw, in the barbarism and materials of the times, another carnival of the same gods whose picture he so admires in Homer; then in the Middle

Age; then in Calvinism." "The Poet," in *Selections from Ralph Waldo Emerson,* ed. Stephen E. Whicher (Boston: Houghton Mifflin, 1957), pp. 222–41, here 238.

26. Gygory Lukacs, "Reification and the Consciousness of the Proletariat" (1923), in *History and Class Consciousness,* trans. Rodney Livingstone (Cambridge, Mass.: MIT Press, 1971), pp. 83–222; Martin Heidegger, *Being and Time* (1927), trans. (New York: Harper and Row, 1962), Division I; Richard Rorty, *Philosophy and the Mirror of Nature* (Princeton, N.J.: Princeton University Press, 1979), part 3; Davidson, "The Myth of the Subjective"; Michel Foucault, "What Is an Author?" in *Language, Counter-Memory, Practice,* trans. Donald F. Bouchard and Sherry Simon (Ithaca, N.Y.: Cornell University Press, 1977), pp. 113–38; Jacques Derrida, "Violence and Metaphysics," in *Writing and Difference,* trans. Alan Bass (Chicago: University of Chicago Press, 1977), pp. 79–153; Friedrich Nietzsche, *The Will to Power* (1883–88), trans. Walter Kaufmann and R. J. Hollingdale (New York: Vintage, 1967), pp. 43–44; Horkheimer, *Eclipse of Reason,* p. 141. This roster could of course be expanded, for example to include Ludwig Wittgenstein, David Riesman, and C. Wright Mills, but my point, I trust, is made.

27. See Nietzsche, *The Will to Power,* p. 14; Karl Lowith, *Martin Heidegger and European Nihilism,* trans. Gary Steiner, ed. Richard Wolin (New York: Columbia University Press, 1995), pp. 31–134, 173–208; and Vattimo, *End of Modernity,* pp. 19–30.

28. Russell quoting James, "William James's Conception of Truth," p. 117. For the Spenglerian connection, see pp. 65–66, 108.

29. Russell, "William James's Conception of Truth," p. 109. On the importance of "The Will to Believe" in Russell's interpretation or pragmatism, see pp. 81–86.

30. Vattimo, *End of Modernity,* pp. 1–47. When I say "and now mysticism" here, I have in mind both the rediscovery of Wittgenstein's notion of the mystical and the new interest in James's "spooky side"; the latter can be sampled in Robert Westbrook's *Democratic Hope: Pragmatism and the Politics of Truth* (Ithaca, N.Y.: Cornell University Press, 2005), for example at pp. 68–69, where he criticizes me for evading the irrational or inexplicable dimensions of Jamesian thinking: "Above all, Livingston ignores what philosopher Richard Gale has nicely termed the 'spooky side' of James's latter-day search for the self." Above all? This would be laughable if it were not so earnestly proffered as a critique of my "fanciful" interpretations of pragmatism.

31. Bellamy quoted and discussed in Livingston, *Pragmatism and Political Economy,* pp. 146–54.

32. Nietzsche quoted and discussed in Wolin, "An Introduction" to Lowith, *Heidegger and European Nihilism,* pp. 1–28, here 16–17.

33. Vattimo, *The End of Modernity,* pp. 22, 26–27, 45–46.

34. Ibid., p. 46.

35. Heidegger, "The Question Concerning Technology," in *The Question,* pp. 3–35, here 26–27, 30, 28.

36. See David Riesman, *The Lonely Crowd* (New Haven, Conn.: Yale University Press, 1950); Theodor Adorno et al., *The Authoritarian Personality* (New York: Harper, 1950); T. J. Jackson Lears, "The Ad Man and the Grand Inquisitor: Intimacy, Publicity, and the Managed Self in America, 1880–1940," in *Constructions of the Self,* ed. George Levine (New Brunswick: Rutgers University Press, 1992), pp. 107–42; and C. Wright Mills, *White Collar* (New York: Oxford University Press, 1951).

37. See Jane Addams, "A Modern Lear" (1894), reprinted in *The Social Thought of Jane Addams,* ed. Christopher Lasch (Indianapolis: Bobbs-Merrill, 1965), pp. 105–23; G. H. Mead, "The Working Hypothesis in Social Reform," *American Journal of Sociology* 5 (1899): 367–71.

38. Walter Lippmann, *Drift and Mastery* (1914; Madison: University of Wisconsin Press, 1985), pp. 45–47; Henry Carter Adams, "Economics and Jurisprudence" (1896) in *Two Essays by H. C. Adams,* ed. Joseph Dorfman (New York: Columbia University Press, 1954), pp. 137–62, here 147.

39. Young John Dewey quoted and discussed in Livingston, *Pragmatism and Political Economy*, pp. 187–96.

40. Old John Dewey quoted and discussed in ibid., pp. 76–83.

41. See ibid., pp. 174–75.

42. John Dewey, *Individualism Old and New* (1929; New York: Capricorn Books, 1962), pp. 49, 82, 36.

43. See Livingston, *Pragmatism, Feminism, and Democracy*, pp. 51–55, 79–82.

44. Dewey, *Individualism Old and New*, p. 72.

45. Westbrook, *Democratic Hope*, cited above at note 33; Robert Johnston, *The Radical Middle Class: Populist Democracy and the Question of Capitalism in Progressive Era Portland, Oregon* (Princeton, N.J.: Princeton University Press, 2003), e.g., at pp. 11–12, 323nn36–37; Christopher Lasch, *The True and Only Heaven: Progress and Its Critics* (New York: Norton, 1991), pp. 16, 223, 207. See otherwise James Weinstein, *The Corporate Ideal in the Liberal State* (Boston: Beacon Press, 1968); Philip Scranton, *Proprietary Capitalism: The Textile Manufacture at Philadelphia, 1800–1885* (Philadelphia: University of Pennsylvania Press, 1983), and sequels culminating in *Endless Novelty: Specialty Production and American Industrialization, 1865–1925* (Princeton, N.J.: Princeton University Press, 1997); Mark E. Kann, *Middle Class Radicalism in Santa Monica* (Philadelphia: Temple University Press, 1986); Teresa Brennan, *History after Lacan* (New York: Routledge, 1993); William Leach, *Land of Desire: Merchants, Power and the Rise of a New American Culture* (New York: Vintage, 1993); Jackson Lears, *Fables of Abundance: A Cultural History of Advertising in America* (New York: Basic, 1994); Gretchen Ritter, *Goldbugs and Greenbacks: The Antimonopoly Tradition and the Politics of Finance in America* (New York: Cambridge University Press, 1997); and Elizabeth Sanders, *Roots of Reform: Farmers, Workers, and the American State, 1877–1917* (Chicago: University of Chicago Press, 1999).

46. Lasch, *True and Only Heaven*, p. 346; Westbrook, *Democratic Hope*, pp. 135–36, 136n49. I can't agree with Westbrook's characterization of *Art as Experience* here, not any more than I can accept his "spooky" rendition of pragmatism. Dewey wanted to reconstruct the relation between means and ends in wage labor, not turn all workers into artisans; that is why he was an advocate of "industrial democracy" rather than "pioneer individualism" and proprietary capitalism: see *Art as Experience* (1934; New York: Perigree Books, 1980), chapter 9, and James Livingston, "War and the Intellectuals: Bourne, Dewey, and the Fate of Pragmatism," *Journal of the Gilded Age and Progressive Era* 2 (2003): 431–50.

9. Active Tension

·
·
·
·

Linda Simon

James's insistence on the relationship between an individual's philosophy and his temperament urges us to ask, first of all, how can we understand the connection of pragmatism to James's own "essential personal flavor" (*P*, 24)? And second, if pragmatism is not idiosyncratic to James but applicable and appealing to others, as well, then how does it account for the myriad varieties of individual perspectives, needs, and yearnings that James says characterize humanity? How does it provide a method of solving problems that fosters a sense of community?

Because the definitions of pragmatism that we can infer from James's many writings about experience, knowledge, truth, and mind are various and protean, understanding pragmatism itself is a slippery project. And so is pinning down the quicksilver personality that was James. While we can generalize about some facets of his temperament, other qualities were contradictory. As he admitted, he had many selves, some manifested publicly, some only privately, some hidden, some evolving. His identity as a public intellectual was not necessarily consistent with his identity as a father and husband; nor were his pragmatic ideas about religion and spirituality necessarily consistent with his ideas about political and civic life. Nevertheless, it is possible to begin with a working definition of pragmatism and, similarly, a working definition of William James.

Let's define pragmatism as a method of solving metaphysical debates and of making decisions in a changing world. This world is unstable, unfixed, undetermined, and yet there is a reality that we can know through our own experiences. Through actions and practices we test our ideas by paying attention to their consequences for us and for others. What is the effect of holding one idea rather than another? How do our ideas contribute to the world we are creating by our interactions, decisions, and behavior? These are questions to which a pragmatist responds. For James, pragmatism had a particular relevance to religion, and offered a way to reconcile science with metaphysics (*P*, 31). It served, he said, as "a happy harmonizer of empiricist ways of thinking, with the more religious demands of human beings" (*P*, 39). It allowed for the possibility of God.

Let's define James, as he reveals himself in *Pragmatism,* as a restless spirit who resists the imposition of any authority on what he wants to believe. He wants to be able to make decisions according to his own values and needs, and yet he recognizes that personal desires can create a world of self-serving individuals who do not care about communal life. He defines himself as a combination of a tender-minded person who is romantic, religious, free-willist, and at the same time a tough-minded person who is empiricist, pluralistic, and skeptical. As a radical pragmatist, if he is one, he sees himself as "a happy-go-lucky anarchist sort of creature" for whom truth "grows up inside of all the finite experiences" (*P*, 124–32). He knows that who we are shapes what we see, what we attend to, and he urges us to be self-conscious about the assumptions that we hold so that we remain open to novelty. Concepts are limiting; even language is limiting to the free-spiritist James.

At the same time that he wants to live in a changing world of concrete experience, he also yearns for spiritual affirmation; he believes that religion can serve as both a moral guide and a refuge: "a place," he writes, "of escape from the crassness of reality's surface" (*P*, 23). He yearns to believe that there is a meaning in the universe that transcends the material and that this transcendent meaning endures even after material things decay. But James is focused on real experience; he is delighted by living. When he turns to religion or to "rationalistic philosophy that indeed may call itself religious," he discovers that it "keeps out of all definite touch with concrete facts and joys and sorrows" (*P*, 17). This separation distresses him, and, he believes, distresses many of his contemporaries, too.

James apparently includes himself when he notes that there is "a decidedly empiricist proclivity" in his own time. People want facts, they want science, but they also want religion, and they think that empiricism is not religious enough, nor is religion empiricist enough (*P*, 14–15). Increasingly, he sees, a "naturalistic or positivistic feeling" has privileged science, and a focus on nature has diminished human importance. "The romantic spontaneity and courage are gone," he complains; "the vision is materialistic and depressing" (*P*, 15). How is it possible, he asks, for one to hold a belief in both the material and the immaterial? Pragmatism makes it possible.

Pragmatism allows the mind to interact with the material world, with concrete facts, and with live problems. But this interaction with the concrete and the new need not be discomfiting: in solving problems, pragmatism allows a person to make decisions consistent with past beliefs—including belief in the unseen and ineffable—and also to formulate new beliefs consistent with the individual's temperament. "A new opinion counts as 'true,'" James writes, "just in proportion as it gratifies the individual's desire to assimilate the novel in his experience to his beliefs in stock. . . . When old truth grows, then, by new truth's addition, it is for subjective reasons" (*P*, 36). Indeed, James believes, "*our fundamental ways of thinking about things are discoveries of exceedingly remote ancestors, which have been able to preserve themselves throughout the experience of all subsequent time"* (*P*, 83; emphasis in original). This enduring way of thinking is what we call *common sense:* it is a culturally shared inheritance.

The pragmatist, then, has three important qualities: he or she is an active agent, a decider, an embracer of the new, eager to participate in the spontaneous events of an evolving universe. The pragmatist is an individual endowed with self-knowledge, cognizant of the beliefs and desires that are consistent with his or her temperament. And the pragmatist is part of a community that shares an inheritance passed down through history.

The James who wrote *Pragmatism* in 1906, though, at the age of sixty-four and at the end of a successful career as a professor, writer, and lecturer, was not the James who, in his twenties, was attracted to the ideas of John Stuart Mill (to whom James dedicated *Pragmatism*), Charles Renouvier, and James's friend Charles Sanders Peirce. Pragmatism did not begin in 1906, nor even in 1898 with James's lecture "Philosophical Conceptions and Practical Results." Its roots can be found in James's earliest philosophical writings, and his aspirations toward pragmatism can be seen in his personal letters to family and friends. These sources also help us to understand why pragmatism was attractive to a man of his temperament.

As a young man, James was anything but decisive, and he was frustrated by his weaknesses. He struggled with his father to affirm his own interpretation of his personality and, broadly speaking, his vocation. The ongoing argument that James had with his father about the nature of reality and selfhood precipitated a crisis that James Livingston usefully calls "an epistemological crisis": specifically, James needed to answer the question "how can I tell what is going on here?"[1] This crisis manifested itself physically and philosophically.

Henry James Sr., enlightened by Swedenborg, denigrated involvement with worldly matters in favor of metaphysical engagement. He exhorted his children not to train for a career or profession, but simply "to be." This burden fell most onerously upon William, the eldest child, who Henry hoped would follow in his direction as a moral theorist and religious philosopher. William was to aspire to a rarefied spirituality that called for self-abnegation and subservience to God. While William wanted to please his father and earn his esteem, he felt drawn to projects that his father scorned. When he was eighteen, he saw himself as an artist, sensitive to intense and pure spiritual impressions that he received from art. His father argued against this possibility, claiming, as William interpreted it in an 1860 letter to Henry James, that an individual would risk being "degraded" by "intercourse with art" because art would distract him from intellectual, philosophical, and moral concerns (*CWJ*, IV, 38). William gave up art, unsure of his talents and worried that his father might be right, and turned first to science, studying chemistry at the Lawrence Scientific School, and then to medicine. For his first thirty years, at least, his vocational indecisions played out in somatic problems: bad back, eye strain, digestive troubles, and general fatigue. He was, in short, neurasthenic, suffering from weak nerves.

In 1867, when he was twenty-five and a medical student at Harvard, his symptoms became so severe that he went to Germany to try to regain his strength and health. There, he received a letter from his father, again criticizing his philosophical views, this time because he was enmeshed in science. Science, Henry wrote in 1867, exerted a "temporary blight . . . upon your metaphysic wit." William was mired, his father continued, in a "scientific or puerile stage of [intellectual] progress" because he believed "in some universal quantity called Nature" that made "the idea of creation . . . idle & superfluous" to him (*CWJ*, IV, 205). William confessed difficulty in understanding his father, but guessed, he said, that his father meant this: "[Y]ou give the creature a natural consciousness, with which he identifies himself and thus becomes alienated, aware of an opposition in him to the creator. This opposition under the influence of Religion becomes hateful to him, a recoil from his natural consciousness takes place, and with it the true creation, to which what has preceded is merely subsidiary, takes place, but a spontaneous movement of return to the Creator being originated" (*CWJ*, IV, 219–20).

William, though, rejected this abnegation of selfhood and its implication of social withdrawal. On the contrary, he wrote to his friend Thomas Ward in 1868, "*Every thing* we know & are is through men." In moments of doubt and depression, he told Ward, he felt sustained by "the thought of my having a will, and of my belonging to a brotherhood of men possessed of a capacity for pleasure & pain of different kinds. . . . [W]e can by our will make the enjoyment of our brothers stand us in the stead of a final cause, and through a knowledge of the fact that that enjoyment on the whole depends on what individuals accomplish, lead a life so active, and so sustained by a clean-conscience as not to need to fret much." Each individual may contribute to the good of humanity through art, philosophy, medicine, social change, or even business. Through such contributions, "when you have added to the property of the race, even if no one knows your name, yet it is certain that without what you have done, some individuals must needs be acting now in a somewhat different manner. You have modified their life, you are in *real* relation with them, you have in so far forth entered into their being" (*CWJ*, IV, 248–49). There is both yearning and optimism in this statement, and yet James still was haunted by his father's perspective on reality and his assessment of his son's intellectual capacities. William's proclamation that he believed in his own will was undermined by his father. His own contribution, he disclosed to friends, necessarily would be weak—a small "nick," he told Thomas Ward—because *he* was weak. He could not read for long hours because his eyes would strain. His weak back made laboratory work impossible, and the practice of medicine, too. His most debilitating physical symptom was a persistent feeling of fatigue, of lack of energy, of lassitude. In 1869, recuperating from a bout of depression, he wrote to a friend, Catherine Havens, that at last he could begin to feel his "old vital powers begin distinctly to 'wiggle' within me, as if to say with the immortal D. Webster, 'we aint dead yet'" (*CWJ*, IV, 367). James knew, then, the difference between enervation and aliveness, between numbness and the "wiggle" that seemed so preferable and yet so unattainable.

Certain as he was about his temperament, he struggled with the question of its origin and potential for change. In the mid-nineteenth century, temperament was considered largely inherited—constitutional—and although it might be managed, still one was what one was. James's father also suffered from intermittent depressions, alleviated, he claimed, by his embracing of Swedenborgianism. Many other relatives were alcoholics: Henry James wrote in his autobiography that even as boys, he and William had a "sense of 'dissipation' as an abounding element in family histories"; their father often told them stories of relatives who, despite "brilliant promise and romantic charm, ended badly, as badly as possible."[2] Again and again, we see in William's letters to his friends testimony to his conviction that his energies were limited, his mind and body fragile, and his fate doomed.

His brother Bob, he thought, shared his weaknesses, and James advised Bob in 1870 that for such blighted men as they, life could offer no alternative but to "sit it out patiently to the end and see what it all amounts to" (*CWJ*, IV, 405). Indecision plagued him, efforts to engage in life exhausted him. And yet there were moments when he was forced to make a decision, and these moments, we will see, proved exhilarating. He simply could not sit and wait, however much he advised Bob to do so; he simply had to take part in the energetic world of change and progress. We can see a crucial instance of his temperament at work when, in 1876, at the age of thirty-four, he fell in love, something that seems to have happened to him, rather than something that he actively initiated. Earlier, in 1869, when his brother Bob had become engaged, William wrote advising against it. "After all," he reminded Bob, "what results from every marriage is a part of the next generation, and feeling as strongly as I do that the greater part of the whole evil of this wicked world is the result of infirm health, I account it as a true crime against humanity for anyone to run the probable risk of generating unhealthy offspring." He himself, he told Bob, would never marry, so as not to inflict upon his child the "dorsal trouble" that raged in his blood (*CWJ*, IV, 389). It is not surprising, then, that when James himself faced the decision whether or not to marry, his earlier vow generated deep distress. He felt an enormous responsibility not only to his future wife, but to his potential heirs.

In one of the tortured letters that he sent in 1877 to Alice Howe Gibbens during their courtship, James tried to define his temperament. Apparently, the two had agreed to a "mutual transparency" that would enable them to know one another better, and for James, this effort meant revealing what he thought was a well-hidden self. As he explained to Alice, a man's character was "the particular mental or moral attitude, in which, when it came upon him, he felt mostly deeply and intensely alive & active. At such moments," he told Alice, "there is a voice inside which speaks & says '*this* is the real me!'" Once we can see what elicits this intense feeling of aliveness, James said, we can predict in what circumstances the individual will be successful and happy, or, in other circumstances, frustrated and desolate. For James, this

characteristic attitude . . . always involves an element of active tension, of holding my own as it were, & *trusting* outward things to perform their part so as it make it a full harmony, but without any *guarantee* that they will. Make it a guarantee,— and the attitude immediately becomes to my consciousness stagnant and stingless. Take away the guarantee, and I feel . . . a sort of deep enthusiastic bliss, of bitter willingness to do and suffer anything, which translates itself physically by a kind of stinging pain inside of my breast-bone . . . and which, although it is a mere mood or emotion to which I can give no form in words, authenticates itself to me as the deepest principle of all active & theoretic determination, which I possess. (*CWJ*, IV, 571)

This moment of tension, then, this moment of thrilling aliveness, was generated when he had to make a decision for which the outcome was in question. Not knowing the outcome, taking a chance, was so intensely blissful as to be painful.

The word that recurs most frequently in this letter is *active,* used three times, once as an adjective describing his own feelings, once modifying the noun *tension* and once *determination.* Pragmatism demands activity, celebrates novelty, and reflects a confidence in one's own authority; as a philosophy, it generates excited tension because the results of decisions are not known. Those results, though, necessarily will be affirming of one's desires to the extent that each individual recognizes those desires. Self-knowledge, then, is the basis of pragmatism.

Asking about one's own stake in settling one or another question is essential for the pragmatist, and James celebrated individual difference. While introspection afforded him insights into his own personality, his work as a psychologist underscored his conviction that other minds remained essentially unknowable. "No thought," he wrote in *The Principles of Psychology,*

ever comes into direct *sight* of a thought in another personal consciousness than its own. Absolute insulation, irreducible pluralism, is the law. . . . It seems as if the elementary psychic facts were not *thought* or *this thought* or *that thought,* but *my thought,* every thought being *owned.* Neither contemporaneity, nor proximity in space, nor similarity of quality and content are able to fuse thoughts together which are sundered by the barrier of belonging to different personal minds. . . . [T]he breach from one mind to another is perhaps the greatest breach in nature. (*PP,* I, 221, 231)

For James, what he saw as inescapable solitariness was at the same time regrettable (we are each essentially alone and unknowable) and celebratory (we are each independent, autonomous, and self-possessed). Still, however unbridgeable we might imagine the breach from one mind to another, James was confident that pragmatism could serve as a means of solving conflicts and promoting social cohesiveness. Certainly he underscored his philosophy with a conviction that all humans share some common needs, such as the need to be respected for his or her individuality.

Individual integrity and autonomy was a source of anxiety in the mid to late nineteenth century, not only for James, but widely in American culture. People feared invasion of body, mind, and nation; they felt tensions generated by new means of communications; they worried about a personal sense of fragmentation.

James was not alone in feeling that "our empirical future feels to us unsafe, and needs some higher guarantee" (*P*, 61). There were many reasons for this feeling. Immigrants thronged the nation, and an increasingly heterogeneous population, it seemed to many people, threatened to erode shared values, and even to foment anarchy. It was one thing for James—a Harvard professor—to joke about himself as an anarchist in the pages of his philosophy, but it was a far different thing to read about anarchists on the front pages of the *New York Times* or the *Chicago Tribune*. As America entered the world stage, fierce debate arose about our foreign policy: isolationist? interventionist?

Communities were at risk, as were minds and bodies. A few diseases raged recurringly—diphtheria, cholera, tuberculosis—and a newly proposed germ theory presented a scenario in which the body was vulnerable to invasion by microbes. Personal consciousness, too, was a problem; the idea of a singular, integrated personality competed with the idea of a fragmented, multiple construction of self. James's essay "The Hidden Self" was one among many considerations of layered identity by philosophers, psychologists, physicians, and novelists. Robert Louis Stevenson's *Dr. Jekyll and Mr. Hyde* and Oscar Wilde's *The Picture of Dorian Gray* portrayed horrifying tales of evil selves potentially alive within anyone. To treat mental illnesses, including the astoundingly large number of people who claimed to suffer from multiple personalities, physicians began using the psychological case history as a tool in diagnosis, from which there emerged a new vocabulary of talking about one's inner life. Both physicians and patients needed to find words to ensure a shared understanding of what suffering felt like. Psychological research focused not only on investigation of pathology, but on areas such as telepathy and modes of communication between minds. Many psychologists, James foremost among them, believed in the veracity of mediums, which, like telepathy, supported the notion that one mind could enter another. Mind reading was a popular form of entertainment. And yet James, who investigated mediums for the American Society for Psychical Research, also claimed that minds were impenetrable.

New technologies of communication—the telegraph and the telephone—assaulted the senses and, some physicians said, contributed to the epidemic of neurasthenia, of which James was hardly the only sufferer. These technologies fostered communication, but also the invasion of one's personal space and time. Neurasthenia afflicted "brain workers" in great numbers, and experiments in treatment led, soon enough, to the "talking cure"—James tried this—and psychoanalysis. In fiction, no doubt reflecting cultural anxieties, the theme of vampirism recurred. In Henry James's fiction, though, as in his brother's philosophy, the possibility of knowing another person always is thwarted. Characters are misunderstood; some resist another's attempt to understand; others elect solitude rather than risk intimacy. Each individual, William James believed, is "intensely odd" (*P*, 24), and yet he proposed that pragmatism could respond both to that oddness and to humanity's shared "common sense."

The word *novelty* is central to James's philosophies, reappearing as *varieties* in his massive collection of testimony, *The Varieties of Religious Experience*. "Free-will," he wrote in *Pragmatism,* "pragmatically means *novelties in the world,* the right to expect that in its deepest elements as well as in its surface phenomena, the future may not identically repeat and imitate the past" (*P,* 60). Free will implies difference, and yet for all the celebration and affirmation of diverse perceptions, angles of vision, and experiences, James concedes that most people comprise a mixture of tough- and tender-minded characteristics, much like himself. He believes, also, that the readers to whom he addressed his ideas shared significant social and cultural traits: they were educated, affluent, conversant with scientific ideas; and most important, as he argued in *Varieties,* he believed that others, like him, longed for the protectiveness of a God to stave off the fear of annihilation and felt suspicious that science negated the possibility of that God. "A world without a God in it to say the last word, may indeed burn up or freeze," James wrote, "but we then think of him as still mindful of the old ideals and sure to bring them elsewhere to fruition; so that, where he is, tragedy is only provisional and partial, and shipwreck and dissolution not the absolutely final things." Materialism, on the other hand, "means simply the denial that the moral order is eternal, and the cutting off of ultimate hopes; spiritualism means the affirmation of an eternal moral order and the letting loose of hope" (*P,* 55). Pragmatism offered a future of promise not only because it accounted for novelty, but because it allowed for God: "spiritualistic faith in all its forms deals with a world of *promise,*" James said, "while materialism's sun sets in a sea of disappointment" (*P,* 56).

Despite the differences in individual temperament, then, James asserted that all people shared something vital: the desire to feel faith in the spiritual. Just as decisiveness generated feelings of energy and aliveness, so, too, faith "not only incites our more strenuous moments, but it also takes our joyous, careless, trustful moments, and it justifies them." To those who worried that the existence of God can never be proven—that believers necessarily would seem naive or gullible—James countered that we can "enjoy" God without proving his existence simply through the satisfaction of belief. "I myself," he wrote, "believe that the evidence for God lies primarily in inner personal experiences" (*P,* 56). To those who held that Darwinian theory precluded belief in a "grand designer," James responded that "[t]he mere word 'design' by itself has, we see, no consequences and explains nothing. It is the barrenest of principles. The old question of *whether* there is design is idle. The real question is *what* is the world, whether or not it have a designer—and that can be revealed only by the study of nature's particulars" (*P,* 58). Still, for James and, he was certain, for others like him, belief in a designer could yield "a certain pragmatic benefit. . . . 'Design,' worthless tho it be as a mere rationalistic principle set above or behind things for our admiration, becomes, if our faith concretes it into something theistic, a term of *promise.* Returning with it into experience, we gain a more confiding outlook on the future. If not a blind force but a seeing force runs things, we may reasonably expect better issues" (*P,* 58–59).

Again and again, James suggested that the result of belief was not merely a sense of personal peacefulness but a positive force for the moral life of the community. Belief implied shared ethics, a shared sense of the value of human life.

The return to life can't come about by talking. It is an *act*; to make you return to life, I must set an example for your imitation, I must deafen you to talk, or to the importance of talk, by showing you, as Bergson does, that the concepts we talk with are made for purposes of *practice* and not for purposes of insight. Or I must *point*, point to the mere *that* of life, and you by inner sympathy must fill out the *what* for yourselves. . . . Our thoughts determine our acts, and our acts redetermine the previous nature of the world. (*APU,* 131, 143; italics in original)

Although belief in God emerges as James's most urgent question in *Pragmatism,* generations of readers have taken the tenets of pragmatism, its implications for knowing truth and making decisions, and its richness as a methodology as relevant to civic life. Surely James seems to imply this, and yet even here, how pragmatism works, and for whom it works, is problematic. Because pragmatism invites each individual to change the world through decisions and actions, it seems to be not only a way to solve philosophical disputes, but also a way to foster a liberal, democratic community characterized by the civic courage of which James professed to be so fond.

In our own time, pragmatism often is defined as expediency—whatever works, or whatever decision seems to benefit most people over the special interests of a few is labeled as pragmatic. A pragmatic politician is decisive, looking at consequences of decisions rather than making decisions according to some high-minded theoretical position. Pragmatism in politics is not always associated with liberalism, and yet James, with his championing of the individual over the corporate, his protests against bigness in all things, his idiosyncratic interests in psychical research and alternative medicine—all these predilections have caused James to be labeled a liberal. But as he admitted, new facts are assimilated in the context of held beliefs, and the result sometimes privileges held beliefs. To see James's pragmatism in action, then, we might look at his response to a much-publicized and controversial event that called upon public intellectuals to take a stand: the aftermath of the Haymarket riot in Chicago in 1886.

On May 3, workers at the International Harvester company in Chicago were picketing for a shortened workday—shortened, that is, to eight hours—when a fight broke out between strikers and strikebreakers. The police intervened, and in the upheaval that ensued, six strikers were killed and many more were injured. The next day, the militant labor group Black International organized a protest rally in Haymarket Square. When the police tried to disperse the crowd, disaster again struck: this time, a bomb exploded, a policeman was killed, and a riot squad rushed in, resulting in hundreds of injured participants. The event certainly was not unusual for the time—hundreds of strikes disrupted daily life each year, and the labor problem was a common topic in newspapers and magazines, such as the *Nation* and the *North American Review,* that James wrote for and read. This event, because of its violence, made the threat of anarchy prominently visible. German and Eastern European terrorists, Americans widely believed, were intent on traumatizing, undermining, and irreparably injuring the nation.

In response to the violence, the police rounded up what by then were the usual suspects: ten German and Polish activists, of whom eight were indicted. The trial was widely reported in newspapers across the country. Readers knew that although the grand jury at first wanted to indict them for conspiracy rather than murder, the judge insisted on the charge of murder. Although during jury selection many jurors admitted that they already had made up their mind about the defendants' guilt, these jurors were allowed to serve. Irregularities abounded, and yet the trial proceeded, the jury found the men guilty, and they were sentenced to death by hanging. Newspaper articles appeared daily chronicling the arrest, the jury selection, the trial, and the sentencing. Lawyers for the accused repeatedly claimed that their clients were being tried for what they believed, rather than what they actually did. The presiding judge admitted this: these anarchists had advocated violence, and, the *New York Times* reported, "there was no question that the explosion was the result of their teaching, their plotting, their incitement, and their preparations for such a mode of attack." They needed to be held up as examples to others who incited violence: "[T]he value of the case is in the demonstration that men cannot teach murder as a means to any end whatever and escape responsibility for the crimes traceable directly to their teachings."[3] Many political liberals—including James's wife, Alice; his sister-in-law Mary; his brother-in-law, William Mackintyre Salter, head of the Ethical Culture Society in Chicago; and his friend William Dean Howells—took up the cause of gaining clemency for men who, they believed, were sentenced for their political beliefs and not guilty of throwing a bomb. Salter protested vigorously, and in the fall of 1887, asked James to sign a petition to Illinois's Governor Oglesby supporting the condemned men.

What kind of universe did Salter live in? A universe where free speech prevailed; where an oppressed working class could avail themselves of the right to assembly. Where big business would not crush the men and women who made those businesses profitable. Where trials were based on evidence and murder meant murder and not speaking about murder. Salter's actions to protest the men's condemnation voted for that kind of universe. James, though, to the disappointment of everyone involved, refused to sign the petition.

"When you're not sure, dont [sic] act," he told Salter. Despite the publicity that surrounded the case, despite daily newspaper coverage of the riot, the arrests, the selection of the jury, the testimony, and the sentencing, James said that he could not form a personal opinion for lack of evidence. He would need to see original documents, and even with them, he was not sure he would have enough information. Several of his lawyer-friends—Oliver Wendell Holmes, John Gray, and John Ropes among them—agreed that the lawyers for the defendants probably had done their job; the case probably had been tried fairly. Like James, they claimed not to know the facts.

It was not the facts that James believed were important, in any case, but the "policy" that the sentence represented. "It is very hard to forecast consequences," he wrote to Salter in 1887; "and all that is said about making martyrs and embittering the working classes fails to affect me, if the men be guilty." With this "if," James left open the possibility that the men were, indeed, not guilty; but their guilt or innocence was not as important to him as the "policy" of setting an example to other activists.

> The simplest forecast I can make seems to me as plausible as any other; and that is this, that when people have allowed themselves to play with fire for an indefinite time in the way of violent declamation, so that at last they feel quite irresponsible, the quickest and best way to teach them that it is no playing matter, and to make them feel responsible, is to make a few of them suffer all the consequences. Hereafter, every one will be warned by the execution that if he joins such a society, he does it with knowledge of the risk. (*CWJ*, VI, 284–86)

This decision and justification raises a question regarding pragmatism: is James invoking "policy" the same way he might invoke the "ethical system" that he thinks works against pragmatism? Is he bringing to this case preconceptions— "dogmas" or "doctrines"—that make it impossible for him to consider facts? Is he taking the "attitude of looking away from first things, principles, 'categories,' supposed necessities; and looking towards last things, fruits, consequences, facts" (*P*, 32)? Or is he making a decision that feels right because it is consistent with previously held and comfortable beliefs?

Besides wanting the execution to set an example, James brings up another "general principle": the inadvisability of trying a case by public opinion once it has received judgment in court "by the responsible powers." For these reasons, James feels justified in withholding his name. But there is another reason, even more troubling in the context of James's purported belief in civic courage and engagement: "Nothing," he assures Salter, "is expected of the likes of me, so no construction can be put upon it if nothing comes from me." This statement, from a man who wanted others to believe in an unfinished universe, a world recreated with every personal action, seems particularly contradictory of pragmatism. How could James suddenly decide, as he wrote in the letter to Salter, that "it is incredible that my signature should weight an atom either way" (*CWJ*, VI, 284–86) when he underscores every human's authority to make the world?

I bring up this example because it feels analogous to our own concerns about freedom, repression, the threat of terrorism, and the role of political and moral leadership in a time of vulnerability not unlike James's. I bring it up because the word "pragmatism" recurs frequently when we talk about politics, sometimes as praise for someone's actions, sometimes damning. We, like James, live in a time when efforts to understand other minds, especially the minds of our adversaries, generate frustration. If we agree with James that the most important thing we can learn about an individual is his or her view of the universe, how can we ascertain that view when, as James also asserts, to do so would require that we bridge the greatest breach in nature—that between two minds? Pragmatism, as James sometimes presents his ideas, seems to offer us a way to transcend differences and ask ourselves, and one another: What beliefs sustain our community? What personal actions support the common good? At the same time, James's life and work urge us to ask some unsettling questions: Does each of us count? Is it inconceivable that our "vote" matters at all? Is it possible to sustain a collective belief in moral goodness? Can we ever know enough "facts" to make reasonable decisions? What is the role of a public intellectual in our own time? All these questions emerge from *Pragmatism* and persist, unanswered, one hundred years later.

NOTES

1. James Livingston, "Hamlet, James, and the Woman Question," *Raritan* 17, no. 2 (Fall 1997): 53.
2. Henry James, *Autobiography*, ed. Frederick W. Dupee (1913; Princeton, N.J.: Princeton University Press, 1941), p. 29.
3. *New York Times,* October 10, 1886, p. 8 (ProQuest Historical Newspapers).

10. Reflections on the Future of Pragmatism

Ruth Anna Putnam

James said that pragmatism is a new name for some old ways of thinking. Taking pragmatism as a way of thinking, an attitude toward one's self, the physical and social world in which one happens to live, and toward, or at any rate in, philosophy, I maintain that pragmatism has survived, though often not under that name, and, perhaps audaciously that it will survive, though perhaps, again, not under that name. In any case, I am no more audacious than James himself, who, on January 2, 1907, wrote to his friend Théodore Flournoy,

> I want to make you all enthusiastic converts to "pragmatism" (—something not necessarily connected at all with "radical empiricism") on which I gave 8 Lowell lectures to a fine audience in Boston this winter (these are the lectures which I shall repeat in N.Y.). I didn't know, until I came to prepare them, how full of power to found a "school" and to become a "cause," the pragmatistic idea was. But now I am all aflame with it, as displacing all rationalistic systems,—all systems in fact with rationalistic elements in them—and I mean to turn the lectures into a solid little cube of a book which I hope to send you by next October, and which will, I am confident, make the pragmatic method appear, to you also, as the philosophy of the future. Every sane and sound tendency in life can be brought in under it. (*CWJ*, XI, 299)

While I don't believe that pragmatism is or should be a "school" or that it is or will be a philosophy in the sense of a system, I do believe that the pragmatic attitude is so fruitful, both in philosophy and in life, that it will continue to have its enthusiastic proponents.

Pragmatists, by which I mean those who have this attitude (or at least some of its key features), take themselves to be agents in the world rather than spectators; that is, experiencing is not a passive receiving of impressions but an interacting of an organism with its environment. Sometimes acting predominates on the side of the organism—the organism does something to the physical or social environment; at other times, undergoing predominates—the organism is being done to by the environment; at yet other times, there seems to be activity on both sides. Contrary to the older empiricists as well as twentieth-century analytic philosophers, pragmatists do not restrict "experience" to sense experience; enjoying and suffering, feeling angry or afraid, making an effort, and so on, are also experiences. Moreover, as James points out repeatedly, we experience relations. But this last detail does not concern us here. In what follows I hope to make clear how the agent point of view shows itself in various aspects of the pragmatic attitude, precisely in those aspects that are of enduring value.

Pragmatism as Public Philosophy

Since we are celebrating the centenary of James's *Pragmatism,* I shall draw attention particularly to features of the pragmatic attitude emphasized by James. The very fact that *Pragmatism* was given as lectures to large audiences, most members of which were not philosophers, signifies, I believe, that pragmatism is more than an academic philosophy. Thus, it is important to notice that both James and Dewey, and later Rorty and West were/are public philosophers addressing matters of public concern in language and venues accessible to the public. Indeed Dewey wrote, "Philosophy recovers itself when it ceases to be a device for dealing with the problems of philosophers and becomes a method, cultivated by philosophers, for dealing with the problems of men."[1] I believe Dewey meant, and in any case I mean, that philosophy needs to avoid a scholastic self-absorption in self-generated problems. Taking the agent point of view "evades" that sort of philosophizing; I borrow the term from Cornel West.

Philosophy deals most immediately with the problems of human beings when philosophers apply philosophical thinking to areas of human activity other than philosophy itself. Dewey's *Democracy and Education* (1916) is an early example. Indeed I see the influence of pragmatism in the proliferation of philosophies-of-(some field or other) even when that influence is not acknowledged. But I rejoice when I see explicit references to pragmatism, for example, in works by Elizabeth Anderson and Larry Hickman.

Pragmatism as Meliorism

When, in his first lecture, James read the anarchist Morrison I. Swift's descriptions of the horrors of abject poverty, it must have seemed to his audience that James was crossing a border, the border between philosophy and journalism, or perhaps between philosophy and sociology. Of course, it would be absurd to claim that James in these lectures sought for a solution to the problem of poverty, or that he developed a philosophy of poverty, or of journalism. He read these excerpts to make his audience vividly aware of facts that created for him, and he believed for his audience, an intellectual problem. He characterized the problem as a desire for a philosophy that would "combine both things, the scientific loyalty to facts and willingness to take account of them, the spirit of adaptation and accommodation, in short, but also the old confidence in human values and the resultant spontaneity whether of the religious or of the romantic type." And he responds, "I offer the oddly named thing pragmatism as a philosophy that can satisfy both kinds of demand. It can remain religious like the rationalisms. But at the same time, like the empiricisms, it can preserve the richest intimacy with facts" (P, 17 and 23). The facts that were particularly relevant were those concerning human poverty and other evils, and the religion that James found intolerable was Absolute Idealism, or indeed any religion that posited an all-knowing, all-powerful God and tried to deny the reality of evil. The "solution" James finally offered in the last lecture was, he admitted, not required by pragmatism, but, he insisted, "My own pragmatism offers no objection" (P, 142). He called this solution "meliorism." It consists of three propositions:

1: The world is not perfect, or evil is real.
2: The future is not determined; human beings cooperating can make the world better.
3: A finite deity is their helper, *primus inter pares,* in this endeavor.

I shall, in what follows, consider propositions 1 and 2 to constitute meliorism and the addition of 3 to give specifically theistic meliorism. A finite deity is James's solution, or rather evasion, of the problem of evil. Or, one might say that James replaced the intellectual problem of evil, the problem whether evil is "real" (a problem from the spectator's point of view), with the practical problem, the problem of how to alleviate evil (a problem from the agent's point of view). The second and third propositions are metaphysical hypotheses; I shall say more about James's attitude to them below.

Meliorism, with or without the third proposition, is a view that has never been more desperately needed than today. James contrasted meliorism, characterized as "the salvation of the world is possible," with the two views that the salvation of the world is either impossible or assured. I am not sure what James meant by "salvation," but we might plausibly mean halting global warming before it destroys human life or civilization. We know that it will take human effort, both on the individual and on the national and international level, to achieve salvation in this sense. And, as James also pointed out, individual effort needs to be motivated by a trust that others will make a like effort.

I hasten to add that meliorism should not be understood only globally. More limited problems also require cooperation based on a belief that things can be improved and that others will also pitch in. Examples are easy to come by. Again, as above, much more needs to be said, but that too is not my task here. There is, for example, a vast literature on problems of coordination, on trust, and on free-riders. This literature may serve as an example of the point made above that public problems ("real world problems") may give rise to academic problems and benefit from the resulting academic inquiries. The cooperation that meliorism requires and assumes to be forthcoming again calls for cross-disciplinary inquiries, whether on the model of bio-medical ethics or on that of philosophy of law. These fields that transgress boundaries between traditional disciplines will, I believe, continue to flourish because they provide two requisites for successful cooperation: an exchange not just of opinions but of viewpoints (I shall return to this point below) and a venue in which to make explicit both shared and clashing values and to work on a resolution of value conflicts. On this, too, I shall say more below.

Pragmatism as a Method of Settling Metaphysical Disputes

According to James, pragmatism is a philosophy; it is a method of settling metaphysical disputes; it is an attitude; and it is a theory of truth (*P*, 23, 28, 31, and 32–33). I shall ignore pragmatism as a theory of truth; other contributors to this volume have devoted ample attention to it. And since pragmatism is not a philosophical "system," not a set of propositions, it is a philosophy precisely in the sense of being an attitude, a way of life, in particular a way of dealing with problems. We have seen how James dealt with the problem of evil, but he said of his solution not that pragmatism required it but merely that his pragmatism offered no objection. Yet he held that pragmatism is a method of settling metaphysical disputes, namely, by using the pragmatic maxim, or, as he also called it, the principle of Peirce. I do not intend to discuss the different formulations of the maxim provided by Peirce and James, nor the different uses to which they meant to put the principle. I do not believe that the pragmatic maxim, at least in James's understanding of it, is one of those features of pragmatism that have survived or will be revived. But James's initial formulation of the maxim is an example of the agent point of view applied to metaphysical disagreements. James wrote, "[T]o develop a thought's meaning, we need only determine what conduct it is fitted to produce: that conduct is for us its sole significance" (*P*, 29). If I were to criticize the maxim or James's version of it, I would have to quote what James added, but my purpose here is not polemical. I merely wish to point out that James's emphasis on conduct follows naturally from the agent point of view. If then one asks, concerning competing metaphysical hypotheses, what differences in conduct a belief in one and in the other would be likely to produce, then our choice of one or the other will be a moral choice. James believed, for example, that belief in a deterministic universe would lead to a debilitating pessimism or to a subjectivism that would inevitably lead to "a nerveless sentimentality or a sensualism without bounds" (*WB*, 132). His moral revulsion leads him to indeterminism and thus to the second proposition of meliorism.

Perhaps James is right, perhaps what seem to be metaphysical questions are, at bottom, moral questions. But at the beginning of the twenty-first century moral disagreements loom as large as, if not larger than, metaphysical disagreements. Reducing metaphysical to moral disagreements does not seem to me a promising strategy if our goal is agreement. Consider, for example, the question whether a human fetus is a human being. It is quite clear what conduct is permissible or prohibited if the answer is negative or positive. But since there is no agreement on the moral question—indeed the disagreement is heated precisely because it is a moral disagreement—James's method, James's use of the pragmatic maxim, is useless, although in his defense one might point out that his question—what conduct is it fitted to produce?—has the merit of revealing why the protagonists argue so passionately about the metaphysical status of the fetus. Perhaps such clarity can be helpful.

Pragmatism as an Attitude

Leaving the maxim aside, leaving the very idea of settling meta-physical disputes aside, let us take a look at James's characterization of the pragmatic attitude. "The attitude of looking away from first things, principles, 'categories,' supposed necessities; and of looking toward last things, fruits, con-sequences, facts" (*P*, 32). Frankly, I find this quite vague. Surely, in every inquiry some things (principles or supposed necessities) are taken for granted; surely, we cannot think without thinking about kinds of things (categories); surely, there is nothing wrong with an inquiry into causes (first things). What James wants to say is that pragmatists are not dogmatic. What is taken for granted in one inquiry may well be called into question in another. Pragmatists qua pragmatists do not seek absolutely first things; they agree with biologists who study the evolution of the species but do not take what they discover as evidence for or against an intel-ligent designer. But, as we saw above, pragmatism does not bar religious inquiries; it merely asserts that they are not scientific, a view shared by many scientists, both atheistic and theistic. The categories James rejects are neither the classifica-tions of common sense nor those of science; he questions Kantian categories and objects to rote thinking, for example, racist or xenophobic thinking. The positive aspects of the pragmatist attitude mentioned by James are basically aspects of the attitude of any scientist; I feel quite safe in saying that they are alive and well among scientists and a large majority of the general population. It behooves us to ask what it means for a philosopher to have the pragmatist attitude, for the claim James and I make is that the attitude will prevail in philosophy. The answer to that question is, I believe, found in the remark of Dewey's quoted above that philosophy must deal with the problems of human beings. Philosophy must not be a refuge from our problems; it must help us to see them clearly. If pragmatism does that, and if at times the problems seem overwhelming, one may expect that at those times pragmatism might suffer an eclipse. Others have suggested that the optimism that is an inseparable part of Meliorism, the faith in the possibility of progress, seems too facile at such times. I am not quite convinced of either of these explanations. For those of us who were graduate students in the fifties, the excitement that various types of analytic philosophers brought to our campuses was irresistible. I speak here autobiographically. One studied with Reichenbach and Carnap and listened to lectures by Austin and by various students of Witt-genstein. And yet, almost simultaneously, one was awakened (some more than others, some sooner, some later) from one's analytic slumbers by Quine's "Two Dogmas of Empiricism." And from some of our teachers we learned something about pragmatism, seeds that lay dormant for a while and then began to sprout.

I am not competent, nor would this be the place, to write the history of the re-awakening of pragmatism. My little autobiography is meant to acknowledge the perspective from which I predict the resilience of pragmatism. I am inclined to think that if one can claim that post-Holocaust depression caused the eclipse of pragmatism, then one can also claim that the social ferment of the civil rights movement and, a short while later, second-wave feminism caused pragmatism's revival. Because one hopes, with good reason, that there will be social ferment for a long time to come; one hopes, with equal reason, that the pragmatic attitude will stand in fruitful interaction with that ferment.

Pragmatism as Pluralism

I have digressed. My task is to present features of the pragmatist temper of mind that I believe will continue to stand us in good stead. Pragma-tists hold that human beings are social not only in the sense that, because we are slow to mature, we need others to nurture us; not only in the sense that almost all of us need human companions to keep our sanity; not only in the sense that human knowledge is so vast and interrelated that each of us must rely on the experience, inventiveness, and testimony of numerous others past and present; but, pragmatists hold, in the sense that one's very self and self-conception are to a very significant extent the result of one's social environment. For example, whether one thinks of oneself as a philosopher and a mother or as a mother who teaches philosophy depends in part on whether one is valued as a philosopher or as a mother or as both by one's peers; it depends in part on the social status of philosophers and that of mothers in one's community; and it depends only partly on one's own estimation of one's abilities as a mother and as a philosopher and one's devotion to these roles.

Human beings are, in contemporary feminist language, "situated," and, in turn, what one comes to believe as the result of one's experience is influenced by one's situation. A believing participant in a religious rite has an experience that differs radically from that of an uninvolved spectator, and that differs from the experience of an anthropologist who knows what the rite means to the believers. Thus, in this sense also, knowledge is (largely) social, and so is morality. Indeed, morality too is social in more than one sense: it deals with relations between hu-mans; it is objective, according to James, because humans care for each other; it is handed down to each of us as customary morality, though we are able, Dewey emphasizes, by reflection, to modify that morality. Here I merely want to point out that though we are situated—we cannot help that—we are not condemned to relativism. We can become conscious of what our situation is and that it colors our perceptions just as others' different situations color theirs. If so, if we rec-ognize the inevitability of multiple perspectives, we are pluralists in one of the senses in which James is a pluralist. He writes, in the preface to *Talks to Teachers on Psychology and to Students on Some of Life's Ideals,*

> According to [the pluralistic or individualistic] philosophy the truth is too
> great for any one actual mind, even though that mind be dubbed "the Absolute," to

know the whole of it. The facts and worths of life need many cognizers to take them in. There is no point of view absolutely public and universal. Private and uncommunicable perceptions always remain over, and the worst of it is that those who look for them from the outside never know where.

And James continues,

> The practical consequence of such a philosophy is the well-known democratic respect for the sacredness of individuality—is, at any rate, the outward tolerance of whatever is not itself intolerant. These phrases are so familiar that they sound now rather dead to our ears. Once they had a passionate inner meaning. Such a passionate inner meaning they may acquire again if the pretensions of our nation to inflict its own inner ideals and institutions vie et armis upon Orientals should meet with a resistance as obdurate as so far it has been gallant and spirited. Religiously and philosophically, our ancient national doctrine of live and let live may prove to have a far deeper meaning than our people now seem to imagine it to possess. (*TT*, 4–5)

Because I believe that pluralism is one of pragmatism's greatest contributions to philosophy—the other being its wide notion of experience—I want to look at this quotation with some care. But first, and by the way, I need to mention that James considered himself a pluralist in more than one sense. As already mentioned, he rejected determinism, holding that a plurality of futures are open to us. He also held, it is spelled out in detail in the chapter on Common Sense, that each of us is able to understand what we experience in at least three ways: the commonsense way of thinking, the scientific way, and the philosophic way. In fact, I would say that there are more than three ways, but it is doubtful that there is an unambiguous way of counting ways of thinking (or vocabularies or conceptual systems).

In any case, the pluralism asserted in the preface to *Talks to Teachers* and illustrated and elaborated in "On a Certain Blindness in Human Beings" and "What Makes a Life Significant" refers not to the plurality of general perspectives open to each of us but to the plurality of points of view that we severally occupy. This is a more radical "situatedness" than that emphasized by some feminists, by Marxists, or by critical legal theorists and others who point to social perspectives of dominance and oppression based on gender, class, or race. It is no accident that James calls this aspect of his philosophy "pluralistic or individualistic," for he points to the plurality of individual points of view. Concerning each of these he makes two points: (1) it is limited, no one can take in the whole universe, or indeed very much of even his or her near environment; (2) it adds something to the picture, and thus each person is worth listening to. And here it is important to note that the picture includes both "the facts and worths" of life. If we then ask what conduct pluralism is fitted to produce, it is, as James says, respect, or at the very least tolerance, for the alien point of view. That means being willing to hear what the other has to say, which, in turn, means creating institutions that make it possible for the other to speak and to be heard. But it means more than the institutions of a political democracy—universal suffrage, frequent elections, and majority rule. It means more even than a commitment to rights of individuals or to liberty, equality, and fraternity. It is, Dewey said, "[A] way of life, social and individual," and he elucidated: "The key note of democracy as a way of life may be expressed, it seems to me, as the necessity for the participation of every mature human being in formation of the values that regulate the living of men together—which is necessary from the standpoint of both the general welfare and the full development of human beings as individuals."[2] Recognizing that each human being has something worthwhile and unique to contribute to the "formation of values" that regulate our living together seems more important than ever. We can no longer confine our attention to our compatriots or to our co-religionists. Our compatriots belong to many different faith communities or to none. Our co-religionists are found in many nations. Pluralism, in the sense of respect for diverse views and values, is desperately needed in the contemporary world. But what exactly is involved in respecting the alien view? Must we succumb to a debilitating relativism? The agent point of view both requires a refutation of relativism and provides, I believe, the means for that refutation.

It must be pointed out, first, that the other's "take" on things may simply enrich ours, may increase our understanding and appreciation of the situation we share. Or the other may flatly contradict what we believe to be the case, and then further investigation may be called for—this happens frequently in science. At other times it may be clear to most of us that the other is plainly mistaken—the earth just is not flat. And yet, time and again in the history of science what "only a mad man would believe" became accepted scientific opinion. What is at stake in these kinds of cases is the pragmatist commitment to fallibilism, and there is work here for philosophers, for that notion is far from clear. Nothing much seems to hang on disputes between those who accept the scientific consensus and those who do not, except when the latter have the power of religion or of the state on their side. The present dispute between teachers of biology who teach the theory of evolution and proponents of "intelligent design" who seek "equal time" raises this issue once again and calls for a pluralist analysis. My own pragmatist "solution" is to point out that the theory of evolution is a scientific theory while the hypothesis of intelligent design is a religious, that is, a philosophical hypothesis. Hence the former belongs in science but not in philosophy classes, and the latter in philosophy but not in science classes. I mentioned earlier that multiple perspectives are available to each of us; students having attended both classes need not be confused if they have also studied pragmatism. They will understand that just as the good Bishop Berkeley did not eat ideas for breakfast, so no scientific prediction or explanation follows from a theological premise.

But James spoke not only of the facts but also of the "worths" of things, and when values clash, matters become considerably more complicated. While philosophers when they think about ethics tend to exaggerate the ease with which scientific disagreements can be settled, one can hardly say that they exaggerate the seriousness of moral disagreements and the difficulty of resolving them. Pragmatists by emphasizing pluralism seem to be committed to moral relativism, insofar as morality is social, or to rank subjectivism insofar as one's morality is shaped by one's own reflection. But this is not so. Here again the agent point of view comes to the fore. We act to realize our values (in pursuit of our goals, to honor our commitments, etc.), and we evaluate the results of our actions. In ethics as in science, we learn from experience and we learn from other people's experiences. The flourishing of modern science was in large measure due to the democratization of scientific inquiry. In ethics the democratization of inquiry presupposes the democratization of the public, the establishment of venues and institutions that include those whose voices are rarely heard and even less taken account of. The suggestion that those whose voices are weak should band together to shout in unison comes easily to mind. Labor Unions, the NAACP, the League of Women Voters, the Sierra Club, and the like are cases in point, yet that list itself is quite variegated. One must also remember—for James this was of great importance—that the members of such organizations are individuals who differ widely and importantly in other respects, and these differences need also to be respected. There is need here for philosophical inquiry as well as for political action. Pluralism and fallibilism can, I hope, protect us from going down too many blind alleys. Here again everything substantial must remain unsaid. I am suggesting that in a world of ever-increasing diversity in even its smallest social units there is an ever-increasing need for the respect and tolerance James advocated under the rubric of pluralism.

There is then much work for pluralist philosophers. They may articulate the concerns of a group that needs to be heard, as feminist philosophers do. They may address specific issues in political philosophy or the philosophy of law. They may clarify the basic notions of pluralism: point of view or situation, respect and tolerance, the idea of putting oneself in another's shoes, and so on. Finally, pragmatist philosophers, precisely because they are pluralists, must transcend the boundaries of so-called schools of philosophy. Thus, although the major present-day pragmatists were trained in one version or another of Anglo-American analytic philosophy, they turned their attention, sooner or later, not only to pragmatism but from within pragmatism to one or another strain of so-called continental philosophy. I shall only mention Richard Rorty's interest in Heidegger and Hilary Putnam's interest in Levinas.

I mention these tasks for pragmatists in the expectation that they will be taken up. If so, we need not worry about the continuance of pragmatist philosophizing; James's faith and mine in the future of pragmatism will be vindicated.

NOTES

1. John Dewey, "The Need for a Recovery of Philosophy," *John Dewey: The Middle Works, 1899–1924*, vol. 10, ed. Jo Ann Boydston (Carbondale: Southern Illinois University Press, 1980 [1917]), p. 46.

2. John Dewey, "Democracy and Educational Administration," *John Dewey: The Later Works, 1925–1953*, vol. 11, ed. Jo Ann Boydston (Carbondale: Southern Illinois University Press, 1987 [1937]), pp. 217–18.

11.   Looking toward Last Things: James's
·   Pragmatism beyond Its First Century
·
·
·   JOHN J. STUHR

In "What Pragmatism Means," William James told his audience, and later his readers, that his pragmatism would be a "conquering destiny" (*P*, 30). In 1907, the year *Pragmatism* was published, he told his brother, Henry, that he would not be surprised if a decade later his pragmatic philosophy appeared "epoch-making" and something "quite like the protestant reformation," explaining that he had no doubt at all about the "definitive triumph" of its "general way of thinking" (*CWJ*, III, 339). He even spelled out the stages by which he expected this would happen: Pragmatism first would be considered absurd, then admitted to be true but trivial, and finally declared an insightful invention earlier created by others and commonly known all along (*P*, 95).

More than a century later, has it turned out that James was right?

And does it matter? If so, how? And for whom?

Pragmatism as Method, Theory of Truth, and Temperament

It is not possible to determine whether James was right, or whether this matters at all, unless we know what he meant. This is one of the lessons taught by Peirce, James, Dewey, and other pragmatists (and other philosophers too): the truth of a claim cannot be determined if the meaning of that claim is not clear. So, what does James mean by "pragmatism?" Moreover, what does it mean for any philosophy's general way of thinking to be a "definitive triumph," to be a "conquering destiny" (*P*, 30), or to be "epoch-making?"

What is pragmatism? James characterized it in three related but distinct ways. First, it is, he said, a new name for a way or method of thinking that makes it possible to settle otherwise interminable metaphysical disputes by tracing the practical meaning of beliefs and, so, determining what practical difference it would make if one rather than others were true (*P*, 28). Pragmatism is a method.

Now, when James's pragmatism is understood as a method, it is important to recognize that James does not claim it is a method for settling *all* disputes. Any resolution or any settling of an experiential or practical dispute, whether trivial or important, requires evidence, experiment and its results, and practical inquiry. How many scholarly books are in my office? Does a particular hiker one afternoon walk continuously in a rough circle from the north to the east to the south and then to the west of a squirrel in a tree near camp? Does drinking coffee regularly cause elevated blood pressure? What colors were dinosaurs? Would increasing the federal tax on petroleum products stimulate greater conservation and/or development of alternative energy sources and technologies? If you finish reading this essay and carefully think about it, will you understand James's pragmatism much, much better than if you do not? Pragmatism, as James well knew, does not all by itself provide answers to questions like these. It is not an armchair philosophy. It holds that this kind of question or dispute cannot be settled without experience, practical consequences, active investigation, experimentation, and inquiry.

James's pragmatism, as he carefully explained, is a method for settling only "metaphysical" disputes. What are "metaphysical" disputes? James provided no concise definition, but his examples make clear that metaphysical disputes are disputes about the meaning of some particular notion. For example, what does it mean for a book to be a "scholarly" book? What does it mean for a hiker to "go around" a squirrel on a tree? What does it mean to drink coffee "regularly?" What does it mean to say an action is "good?"[1] What does it mean for "God" to "exist?" What does it mean to "carefully think about" a chapter or a book or a philosophy? In settling "metaphysical" disputes by making clear the practical, experiential meaning of the notions involved, James's pragmatism makes it possible, subsequently, to engage in practical, experiential inquiry. Until the practical meaning—the "cash-value"—of an idea is clear, no amount of practical inquiry can determine the truth or falsity of beliefs that include and make use of this idea. As Peirce recognized, making our ideas clear does not by itself fix belief and remove doubt, but the former is a necessary precondition of the latter. As James put it, with his pragmatic method, "science and metaphysics would come much nearer together, would in fact work absolutely hand in hand" (*P*, 31). In this way, pragmatism, as a method, is "a program for more work" and "an indication of the ways in which existing realities may be *changed*": "Pragmatism unstiffens all our theories, limbers them up and sets each one at work" (*P*, 32). As a method, then, James's pragmatism does not pretend to settle all disputes. Instead, it simply provides a means to clarify the meaning of beliefs so that they become instruments, so that their results can be determined, and so that they can be put to a practical test, the test of experience—that is, our plural experiences. In so doing, James's pragmatism connects theory to practice and breathes life into the very meaning of ideas and beliefs.

Second, James wrote that pragmatism is not only a method but is also a theory of truth. What theory of truth? The theory that (famously or, for persons allergic to "anti-intellectual tendencies," infamously) holds that beliefs are true insofar as "*they help us get into satisfactory relation with other parts of our experience,*" insofar as "we can ride" on them and be led or carried "prosperously from any one part of our experience to any other part," insofar as they are "a smoother-over of transitions" and successfully marry "old opinion to new fact" (*P*, 35). When a belief works this way, James explained that it "makes itself true, gets itself classed as true" (*P*, 36), and becomes true. The practical difference between true and false ideas is that true ideas can be assimilated, validated, and corroborated. They can be verified, and their verity, thus, is this process of verification, of truth-making (*P*, 97). This is the pragmatic meaning of truth, the practical consequence of holding a true, as opposed to false, belief. It is the result of unstiffening traditional theories of truth: "Purely objective truth, truth in whose establishment the function of giving human satisfaction in marrying previous parts of experience with newer parts played no role whatever, is nowhere to be found" (*P*, 37). This account of truth is the result of breathing life into the truth of beliefs: "Truth independent; truth that we *find* merely; truth no longer malleable to human need; truth incorrigible, in a word . . . means only the dead heart of the living tree, and its being," "means only that truth also has its paleontology and its 'prescription,' and may grow stiff with years of veteran service and petrified in men's regard by sheer antiquity" (*P*, 37). Pragmatism is a theory of truth.

Now, when James's pragmatism is understood as a theory of truth, it is important to recognize that this pragmatic theory of truth is just a part of an epistemology that is itself just one branch of a larger pragmatic account of values. To fail to recognize this point is to fail almost entirely to understand James's philosophy. And it is probably to find strange or mistaken that insofar as a belief is "profitable to our lives" and, thus, has "cash-value," James, for this reason, calls the belief true (*P*, 42). Nonetheless, James set forth his view very clearly and directly, writing: "truth is *one species of good.*" Contrary to long-petrified divisions within philosophy, truth is not "a category distinct from good, and co-ordinate with it." Instead, truth is a subset of good; epistemology is a subset of ethics. James continued: "*The true is the name for whatever proves itself to be good in the way of belief*" (*P*, 42). It is "*only the expedient in the way of our thinking, just as 'the right' is only the expedient in the way of our behaving*" (*P*, 106).

If epistemology is a subset of politics and if truth is a species of good, as James held, what is the good? Contrary to the image of James as happy individualist, his pragmatic ethics is a thoroughgoing social philosophy fully attuned to struggles for solidarity and to the tragic dimension of life. Noting that goods have "no absolute natures, independent of personal support" but instead "are objects of feeling and desire, which have no foothold or anchorage in Being, apart from the existence of actually living minds" (*WB*, 150), James held that values are pluralistic in two respects. First, there are many different sentient beings and cultures with (not only shared but also) different feelings and desires and standpoints and experiences. There are equally real, plural goods, and there is, for James no "abstract moral order in which the objective truth resides" in some goods rather than others (*WB*, 148). Because "*the essence of good is simply to satisfy demand*" (*WB*, 153), and because there are many different demands, there are many different goods. Accordingly, we live not in a moral universe but, instead, a social pluri-verse of values. No individual consciousness enjoys the prerogative of obliging others to conform to its rule, no single moralist rightly rules (*WB*, 147, 155). By understanding goods as relations and in noting that "the elementary forces in ethics are probably as plural as those of physics are" (*WB*, 153), James developed what amounts to relativity theory in philosophy—his pragmatism, radical empiricism, and pluralism—more or less at the same time as Albert Einstein, the William James of physics, developed relativity theory in physics.

In addition, values are pluralistic in a second sense. Each individual has multiple, crisscrossing, conflicting feelings and desires and experiences. The fulfillment or actualization of any one is at once the loss or destruction of other possible goods, other objects of other desires. James wrote that this is a "tragic situation": "There is always a *pinch* between the ideal and the actual which can only be got through by leaving part of the ideal behind. . . . Some part of the ideal must be butchered. . . . It is a tragic situation . . ." (*WB*, 153–54). This is not a view of tragedy as incidental to the lives of some. It is a view of tragedy as intrinsic and irreducible to the realization of any good by anyone at any time.

This tragic, social account of the moral life is, finally, pragmatic. It counsels action and turns from theory to practice. Rather than pretending to justify in theory one set of values—including the set of values that are truths—above or against all others, James advised "*invent some manner* of realizing our own ideals which will also satisfy the alien demands—that and that only is the path of peace" (*WB*, 155)! Rather than claiming the prerogative to oblige others to think as one wants (*WB*, 147) or seeking to theorize into submission all views different from one's own, this philosophy directs us to struggle to change the conditions that sustain current conflict and dispute and to try to create new conditions that can support something better for all. James asked: "What closet-solutions can possibly anticipate the results of trials made on such a scale" (*WB*, 157)? He answered: "From this unsparing practical ordeal no professor's lecture and no array of books can save us" (*WB*, 162)—though lecturing and book-writing professors continue to pretend otherwise. This surely is a strenuous path: hard work on behalf of ideals that cannot be realized in full and might not even be realized in part.

Third, this highly strenuous character of pragmatism—that is, the strenuous character of living pragmatically as distinct from the not-very-strenuous character of theorizing about or studying pragmatism—points to another main way James described pragmatism. Pragmatism, like all philosophies, James claimed, is a particular "attitude" (*P*, 31), a "temperament" (*P*, 11–15), a "dumb willingness and unwillingness" of interior character (*WB*, 162), a "vision" and "expression" of "intimate character" (*APU*, 14), trust in and "loyalty" to one's own experience and world (*APU*, 10), a personal "feeling" of the whole universe and "total push and pressure of the cosmos" (*P*, 24, 9), "our more or less dumb sense of what life honestly and deeply means" (*P*, 9). Different philosophies, for James, are just different "modes of feeling the whole push, and seeing the whole drift of life, forced on one by one's total character and experience, and on the whole *preferred*—there is no other truthful word—as one's best working attitude" (*APU*, 14–15). Philosophies, then, are not fundamentally matters of doctrine, reason, and theory; they are matters of habit, mood, and practice. Pragmatism is a temperament.

What is the temperament of pragmatism? James answered: "*The attitude of looking away from first things, principles, 'categories,' supposed necessity; and of looking towards last things, fruits, consequences, facts*" (*P*, 32). From the standpoint of the dualisms of traditional philosophy, pragmatism may appear as attunement to the temporal rather than the eternal, the future rather than the past, the particular rather than the universal, the fallible rather than the infallible, the vague rather than the certain, differences rather than identity, relations rather than absolutes, the many rather than the one, experience rather than reason, the concrete rather than the abstract, action rather than speculation, feeling rather than logic, and this actual world rather than some other one postulated or logically possible. And although James often made use of these contrasts—very frequently railing against the absolute, the rational, the monistic, the intellectual, and the already complete, for example—his pragmatic attitude of looking to experience does not engage these dualisms, at least on traditional terms. Rather, in the pragmatic attitude, traditional dualisms are undercut wholesale and wholly bypassed. In the hands of James, supposed metaphysical dualisms are cashed out as functional distinctions with practical meanings within experience; they become not real or unreal, but rather useful or useless for particular purposes of particular persons. Because pragmatism itself is a theory, the pragmatic attitude or temperament is not simply an anti-theory attitude. Instead, it is an attitude that, in looking to last things and concrete experiences, produces and is produced by theory reconstructed by pragmatic method. The pragmatic attitude is not an attunement, feeling, preference that can be mapped onto traditional dualisms so differently attuned.

To look, as pragmatism suggests, toward last things is messy. First, it is messy because experience—both the looking and the thing looked at, the how and the what of experience—is incomplete, always unfinished, always under way, always renewing (for better and/or worse). Second, it is messy because experience is always plural. Just as James claimed that "truth" is just "a class-name for all sorts of definite working-values in experience" (*P*, 38), experience is a class name for all sorts of particular experiences—plural experiences—of particular beings with particular perspectives and standpoints at particular times and places. "Looking toward last things" is a class name for lots of different lookings and lots of different things looked at, none of which has the prerogative to be definitive or final. For this "pluralistic pragmatism," James wrote, "truth grows up inside of all the finite experiences": "Nothing outside of the flux secures the issue of it. It can hope salvation only from its own intrinsic promises and potencies" (*P*, 125). Finally, third, looking toward last things is messy also because it is not primarily or wholly a matter of language or knowledge. For James, life as lived is different from life reflected, represented, and communicated. For James, individuality outruns all classification (*APU*, 7), but knowledge is classification. Living is concrete, but its representation is abstraction. Percepts conceptualized are transformed, not mirrored. Accordingly, to be attuned to last things, fruits, consequences, and facts is to be attuned, by means of language and knowledge, to experience that is irreducibly other than language and knowledge. Pragmatism, for James, is a philosophy of experience—and not a philosophy of language, narrative, or vocabularies. The pragmatic attitude is a mode of feeling and not merely a mode of knowing, narrating, or communicating. Pointing to this, and focusing always on experiences rather than vocabularies, James observed: "There is no complete generalization, no total point of view, no all-pervasive unity, but everywhere some residual resistance to verbalization, formulation, and discursification, some genius of reality that escapes from the pressure of the logical finger, that says 'hands off,' and claims its privacy, and means to be left to its own life" (*EP*, 189–90).

Philosophies as Triumphs

Now, what does it mean for a philosophy—whether James's pragmatism or some other philosophy—to be a "definitive triumph," a "conquering destiny," or "epoch-making?" In order to determine whether or not James's account of method, truth, and temperament is a triumph—whether or not more than a century after *Pragmatism* we now live in an epoch of pragmatism—these notions of a philosophy's "triumph," "destiny," and "epoch-making" must be made clear.

To the extent that different philosophies understand differently the meaning of "triumph" by a philosophy, it is difficult to provide this clarity in a non-question-begging manner. For example, does "triumph" in, and by, a philosophy mean that this philosophy identifies and expresses universal, eternal, objective truths? Or does it mean instead that such a philosophy produces what James called "the sentiment of rationality" (*WB*, 57–89)? Or does it mean that a philosophy is a key factor in bringing about some cultural upheaval or maintaining some status quo? Or does it mean that the philosophy provides proof, valid argument, justification, or overwhelming evidence for all of the major claims it makes? Or does the triumph of a philosophy mean that this philosophy reaffirms some faith or banishes some doubt? Or does it mean that lots and lots of people believe it (for the duration of its triumph and epoch)—or that they poll each other and produce a ranking that puts this philosophy at the top? Or might a philosophy be triumphant if only a select few believe it? Does it mean that people who believe it report their lives happier, healthier, wealthier, more loving, otherwise more satisfied, or more meaningful that those who do not hold this philosophy? Or does it mean that belief in a philosophy delivers to its believers knowledge of eternal life? Or does the triumph of a philosophy mean that it nurtures successfully a strenuous mood and the willingness to endure immediate hardships in pursuit of a distant ideal? Or does it mean something else?

If the meaning of a philosophy's "triumph" is relative to, and a function of, some particular philosophy and its temperament, what then is the pragmatic meaning of a philosophy's "triumph?" What does, or would, it mean for pragmatism to "triumph" on its own terms?

It means this. First, if pragmatism is understood as a method for settling metaphysical disputes, it would be "triumphant" to the extent that it works—that is, to the extent that it actually settles, or makes possible the settlement of, metaphysical disputes. Does James's pragmatic method allow us to settle traditional, otherwise interminable metaphysical disputes? A method for doing X is successful on its own terms to the extent that it makes possible achievement of X.

Second, if pragmatism is understood as a theory of truth, it is "triumphant" to the extent that this theory is true—that is, to the extent that this theory is verified, corroborated, marries old opinion and new fact, puts us in satisfactory relation with other parts of our experiences, and works. The pragmatic test for the truth of the pragmatic theory of truth is the same test as that for the truth of any belief. To triumph, this theory must pass its own test.

Third, if pragmatism is understood as a temperament or attitude or intimate mood, pragmatism is "triumphant" when it illuminates the universe in a manner that suits this pragmatic temperament (*P*, 11), a manner that is not "out of plumb and out of key and out of 'whack'" (*P*, 25) but rather impressive to this temperament, a manner in which this temperament feels at home (*APU*, 10), a manner that produces feelings of "ease, peace, rest" (*WB*, 57), all-pervading fluency and "intimacy," and defines "the future *congruously with our spontaneous powers*" (*WB*, 57, 75, 70).

Evaluating Pragmatism

So, in the more than one hundred years since *Pragmatism* was published, has James's pragmatism proven itself triumphant and epoch-making? Has the pragmatic method shown itself to work and, as a result, been widely employed? Has the pragmatic theory of truth proven itself true and, as a result, been widely adopted? And, has the pragmatic temperament found itself increasingly at home in the world articulated by *Pragmatism,* and found itself, increasingly the temperament of the epoch, both funding and funded by the times in which we live?

Like most things in life, the verdict appears mixed. Metaphysical disputes surely did not come to an end in 1907—despite theorists since that time who have proclaimed an end to metaphysics or taken up "post-metaphysical" thinking in fields from philosophy to architecture, ecology, and political theory. Debates about the nature of God, reality, knowledge, goodness, and beauty continue—in the academy, on the street, and even in some camping parties in the mountains. Moreover, pragmatism seems not to have brought metaphysical sides or opponents together. Instead, it frequently seems to be just an additional side—and so more "divider" than "uniter." If there were Platonists and Aristotelians and Cartesians and Kantians, and Hegelians before James published *Pragmatism,* it seems there still are all those and now some Jamesians too. Of course, this does not in any way demonstrate that the pragmatic method does not work. It merely indicates that the pragmatic method often is not employed. Nonetheless, on the surface, at least, the evidence does not seem entirely to support the view that pragmatism has become something quite like the Protestant Reformation. And, so far, at least, there are no hotel rooms with nightstands stocked with a copy of *Pragmatism* in the top drawer.

The verdict appears much the same concerning the pragmatic theory of truth. The "Ph.D. Octopus" (*ECR,* 67–73) that James diagnosed early now has a near–death grip on much of education (including professional philosophy) and much of life, and it produces confident and clever scholars (some following in the footsteps of Moore or Russell, some following Horkheimer or Adorno, and some following Santayana or Royce) armed with tidy arguments (with inconspicuous premises) against the pragmatic theory of truth. Of course, the presence of these critics, here again, does not in any way demonstrate that the pragmatic theory of truth is not true. It only shows that even if the oldest truths are plastic (*P,* 37), as James claimed, still many persons who keep a tight and traditional grip on these oldest truths are not equally plastic. Moreover, supposed alternative accounts of truth that abstract truth from practical interests are alternatives to pragmatism only insofar as they are abstract and have "nothing to do with our experiences": "There never was a more exquisite example of an idea abstracted from the concretes of experience and then used to oppose and negate what it was abstracted from" (*P,* 108–109). Nonetheless, after more than a century, the pragmatic theory of truth seems to be more at the stage of being considered absurd or the stage of being admitted as correct but trivial than is at the stage of being broadly held and broadly viewed as insightful. Conquering destiny and "mission accomplished?" No, not yet at least.

This same mixed verdict and anything but fully positive picture emerges when pragmatism is understood as a temperament or attitude. As James recognized, there are many persons whose vision is not pragmatic, who do not find pragmatism to be their vision of their experience and world, who do not feel and prefer pragmatism's pluralistic universe. James's pragmatism is not what life honestly means to them, and it is not their deepest preferred working attitude. Their lives are not attuned to the whole push of pragmatism: that reality is unfinished; that finite sentient beings contribute to the ongoing remaking of it and its ideals (including truth); that the success or failure of this remaking is found in practical consequences in plural, concrete experiences—in last things rather than first principles; and, that this is strenuous work with no guarantee of even passing success—success that always carries with it real loss and tragedy. Even cheerleaders for pragmatism must admit that one hundred years after *Pragmatism,* this temperament is not the omnipresent or even characteristic temperament of our times. There are pragmatists, but there are many, many absolutists, fundamentalists, rationalists, and monists. The century after James has been marked by at least as many efforts to eliminate, frustrate, ignore, or silence demands other than one's own as by the invention, urged by James, of ways to realize both one's own and alien demands. It has been marked by many points of view claiming to be the one, total point of view.

Does this mixed verdict on the pragmatic method, theory of truth, and temperament show that James was wrong? Friends of James may be inclined to try to make this verdict less mixed. They might point out, for example, that there are persons who in their theories do not endorse pragmatism but who in their lives affirm and make use of it. To be a pragmatist on pragmatism's own terms, they might add, is a matter of practice and not just theory.² Fair enough: There may be persons, practices, and aspects or chunks of culture that are pragmatic before, or without ever, being recognized, theorized, or self-reflected as pragmatic. Friends of James might also stress James's pluralism and his recognition that there are a multiplicity of temperaments—such that his pragmatism is not rendered false just because it does not resonate with persons with different temperaments. Again, fair enough: a philosophy may be a "conquering destiny" without conquering every mind, and no philosophy ever has viewed the mere existence of non-believers to be sufficient evidence of its own falsity or failure.

Even granting these points, however, it is not clear that pragmatism has been triumphant to the degree that James, or some of his rhetoric, projected. There are persons who reject pragmatism in practice as well as theory. And there continue to be many of them. It is tempting, therefore, to conclude that in *Pragmatism* James did not establish the truth of pragmatism—simply because James's pragmatism is neither preached nor practiced by so many persons.

This conclusion would be a mistake and a thorough misunderstanding of James's philosophy and its importance.

This is the key point here: James's pragmatism, as he recognized, is not something that can be established (one way or the other) by, and in, theory or abstraction alone. *Pragmatism,* the lectures and book, is not an attempt (whether triumph or failure) to prove the truth of pragmatism. It is not a successful proof of the truth of pragmatism and it is not a failed proof of the truth of pragmatism. For James, book chapters, journal articles, and lectures do not and can not prove the truth or falsity of a philosophy—pragmatism or any other philosophy. Instead, truth or falsity is located and found in last things, fruits, consequences, facts, in concrete experiences of leading, marrying, cashing out, satisfying, riding on, and corroborating, in feelings, preferences, fluencies and intimacies, attunements.

In *Pragmatism,* James did not provide a theoretical, abstract proof of the truth of pragmatism. Instead, he showed that merely theoretical, abstract arguments and objections do not and cannot constitute proof of the falsity of pragmatism. Against these critics, James argued that pragmatism is a live hypothesis for experience and that there is no theoretical case against it. James made this point repeatedly. Here is one particularly clear example:

> Pragmatism, pending the final empirical ascertainment of just what the balance of union and disunion among things may be, must obviously range herself upon the pluralistic side. Some day, she admits, even total union, with one knower, one origin, and a universe consolidated in every conceivable way, may turn out to be the most acceptable of all hypotheses. Meanwhile the opposite hypothesis, of a world imperfectly unified still, and perhaps always to remain so, must be sincerely entertained. This latter hypothesis is pluralism's doctrine. Since absolute monism forbids its being even considered seriously, branding it as irrational from the start, it is clear that pragmatism must turn its back on absolute monism, and follow pluralism's more empirical path. (*P,* 79)

If pragmatism is to be known false, for James, it must be shown false—shown false in, and by, somebody's concrete experience. James's message to his audience members is that if his pragmatism fits their experience and is verified, validated, and corroborated in that experience, then they need not worry that there is some valid abstract argument that disproves or outlaws in theory what they find to be so in practice.

James swept aside all the would-be theoretical objections and "pretended logic" (*P*, 142) to pragmatism and established pragmatism as an empirical hypothesis or experiential possibility waiting on last things, waiting on the experiences of his audiences, waiting on you and what you want (*P*, 17). He did this by recasting philosophical disputes not primarily as disputes of reason (as though some philosophers just need to re-take a logic or critical thinking course or enroll in a remedial calculus tutorial) but as differences of temperament and vision (in which different persons have different experiences, none able to legislate for, or against, all others).[3]

This is why James described his objective in *Pragmatism* in language other than the language of "proof" and "argument," the language of "Being," or the language of language itself. James explained his purpose in the language of suggestion and temperament, the language of hypotheses, interests, inspirations, approvals, experienced satisfactions, preferences and feelings, and last things. He did not announce his purpose or objective as demonstration, but, instead, said this sort of thing: "I stand desirous of interesting you in a philosophy" (*P*, 10); "I hope I may end by inspiring you with my belief" (30); "I hope that as these lectures go on, the concreteness and closeness to facts of pragmatism . . . may be what approves itself to you as its most satisfactory peculiarity" (39); and, "I leave it to you to judge" (*P*, 111). James concluded *Pragmatism* by simply stating that persons with a pragmatic temperament may find his pragmatism "exactly what you require" (*P*, 144). And he consistently postponed the justification of his pragmatism (*P*, 39), making clear that any such justification must wait on the experience that followed from its consideration—on whether pragmatism is or is not exactly what is required by concrete experiences.

Pragmatism 2.0

James thought *Pragmatism,* his book, would be "epoch-making" in part because he thought his era already was pragmatic, increasingly populated by persons with a pragmatic temperament that combines "tender-minded" and "tough-minded" orientations and wants a philosophy that combines both (*P*, 17). He sought to inspire that temperament, generalize its philosophy, and make it conscious of itself (*P*, 30). Was James's era pragmatic—with pragmatism triumphant a decade after the publication of *Pragmatism*? More than a century after, is our era today pragmatic? These are sweeping questions, and their answers probably depend on what one chooses to stress and on what John Dewey called "selective emphasis." What is clear enough, however, is that just as James offered no theoretical proof for his pragmatism, there is no point in pretending to do so today. James strove to show that there is nothing in theory that constitutes reason to reject, or to affirm, pragmatism. Accordingly, today the task for Jamesian pragmatists—and here I mean to refer to a kind of life rather than an allegiance in the academy—is to create the cultural conditions that in turn produce experiences that validate pragmatism and further attune that experience itself to its reasonableness and its vision. That would be epoch-making. And it would be, for pragmatism, the moral equivalent of abstract philosophy.

What conditions give rise to a pragmatic temperament? Three points loom largest. First, a pragmatic temperament is melioristic. Distinct from optimism and pessimism, meliorism holds that the salvation of the world is "neither inevitable nor impossible": "It treats it as a possibility, which becomes more and more of a probability the more numerous the actual conditions of salvation become" (P, 137). It holds that the salvation of the world—this-worldly salvation—and the realization of hope may—just may—be possible if we work hard toward these ends. It requires hope and hard work. However, when life is without hope, when there is no ability or no incentive to imagine something better than the way things are and the way things have been, when despair dominates and resignation pervades, and when imagination is ground down, then hope will not be experienced as one's best working attitude, will not be felt in the whole push and drift of life, and will not be part of one's intimate character and temperament. Accordingly, anyone concerned to spread the pragmatic temperament understood as, in part, a melioristic temperament, must be concerned actively to create and spread conditions that foster hope, imagination, and the experience of unrealized possibilities. And while these conditions may in part depend upon acts of individual will to engage in hope, they depend more basically and broadly on the attunements of cultural conditions—including political institutions, economic arrangements, social relations, systems of meaning, and ecological realities. Hope requires not only the will to hope but also the social material conditions of hope. Pragmatism and its temperament depend on both.

Meliorism demands more than hope. It also demands hard work. However, when life evidences chasms that cannot be bridged between one's reach and one's grasp, between means and end, between one's effort and its results, between struggle and achievement, then hard work will not be one's best working attitude, will find no home in one's character, and will not fit one's life. If one's own experience is that one is impotent to make a difference, striving to make a difference—even or especially when advised by a privileged Harvard philosopher to strive to make a difference—looks like a game only for suckers, the more fortunate, and the more powerful. Actions that never seem to pay off have no cash value, and any philosophy addressed to lives filled principally with such actions will seem bankrupt and out of whack. And, of course, there is nothing particularly pragmatic about linking theory and practice in theory but doing nothing to join them in practice. Accordingly, anyone concerned to make triumphant the pragmatic temperament must be concerned to enlarge conditions that forge experienced connections between effort and achievement, thus empowering otherwise relatively powerless persons. Like the conditions of hope, these conditions are cultural and not merely individual. They are matters of social change and cultural revolution, and not merely personal transformation or individual makeover.

Second, a pragmatic temperament is pluralistic, irreducibly pluralistic. Distinct from absolutism and nihilism, pluralism holds that values (including truth) are relations made in experience, and that this experience is always perspectival, always personal, and always partial. James noted: "We say this theory solves it on the whole more satisfactorily than that theory; but that means more satisfactorily to ourselves, and individuals will emphasize their points of satisfaction differently" (*P*, 35). Though many philosophers continue to be eager to show that some one point of view (typically their own) is the Real, True, Good, or Beautiful point of view, no consciousness enjoys the prerogative of obliging others to conform to its rule and point of view, and no person's theory trumps someone else's experience, feelings, and faith in that experience. Pragmatism, then, requires humility. However, when life is marked not only by blindness to the values of the differences of others but also by blindness to this very blindness, when God is experienced as on one side only, and when one's beliefs fully feel absolute, certain, infallible, or final, then pluralistic humility will have little or no resonance, little or no fluency and intimacy, and little or no satisfaction. Accordingly, anyone committed to the growth of the pragmatic temperament must commit to extending the conditions that foster humility and felt opportunity in the face of what is different and even unfamiliar, the determination to invent ways to realize multiple demands, and the realization that this invention must be a process that includes effectively from the start the perspectives of those who make these multiple demands. While there is a role in all this for inspiration and exhortation to live with less self-certainty and less self-centeredness, here too the transformation demanded by pragmatism is fundamentally change in wide-ranging cultural conditions and the moods, habits, and character they educate and produce. Humility does not require quietism or self-effacement. It requires selves committed in action to living without false pride. It requires selves committed to participating not in varieties of colonization but, rather, in work to produce what James called "an ethical republic here below" (*WB*, 150).

Third, this melioristic pluralistic pragmatic temperament is irreducibly a matter of faith—wholly this-worldly faith, but faith nonetheless. Why? James's pragmatism simultaneously holds both of the following: first, that justification of belief is located in last things, that it is a function of consequences and results and outcome; and second, that action is always undertaken in advance of its consequences and results and outcome. No belief about our lives, therefore, can be fully or finally justified in advance of action undertaken on its behalf. And, until there can be no further such action, no justification on behalf of action to date can be full or final. James recognized that his pragmatism, just like any other philosophy, cannot be a final philosophy, a philosophy made up in advance of last things. Accordingly, anyone interested in fostering a pragmatic temperament must work to create conditions that stimulate and sustain before-the-fact melioristic and pluralistic commitments in advance of their after-the-fact consequences.

To do this is to encourage what James called "the strenuous mood," to call forth action on behalf of ideals for which there is no guarantee of realization. It is to call forth action on the parts of those who believe "we might" that is equal in commitment and energy to those who believe "we can" or "we will." The tone of this action cannot be that of "conquering destiny," a phrase that easily appears doubly problematic and even antithetical to pragmatism—a philosophy that (1) denies fate and predeterminism and so understands destinies not at all as pre-destinations but only as eventual outcomes and how things turn out to be for a while, and (2) focuses not on conquest and prerogative but rather on multiplicity, difference, and invention of ways to satisfy otherwise competing demands. In this context, pragmatism, understood as a philosophy, cannot be a conquering destiny. It can be only a hypothesis awaiting verification in experiences of persons temperamentally inclined or disinclined by cultural conditions as much as individual will to experience, or not experience, that verification, leading, working, satisfying, preferring. *Pragmatism,* understood as James's book, may be seen as a conquering destiny to the extent that it successfully rendered obsolete and remote merely theoretical arguments against the possibility of its truth, and so helped stimulate the making of cultural conditions that give rise to broadly pragmatic temperaments. More than a century later (and despite the still-present nostalgia and traditionalism of philosophical flat-earthers who yearn for something more real or at least something more authentic), this appears to be not the Copernican Revolution but, rather, the theoretical quantum leap forward effected by *Pragmatism.*

The pragmatic task is only a little theoretical. It is an unfinished task, and even centuries later it will remain so. As James pointed out, there can be no final conclusion until everything finally has concluded (*EP,* 190). Pragmatism's cash value is not based in, or backed by, any metaphysical or epistemological or moral gold standard or other permanent deposits. It is based on, and in, exchange systems marked by credit, gains and losses, and ineliminable risk. What is that risk? It is life in a world without eternity, permanence, certainty, or absolutes. It is a world that we cannot ultimately represent to ourselves, a world that is not the best of all possible worlds but instead, often less than decent and always tragic. It is a world still, always, in the making, unmaking, and remaking by cooperative activity. This is not a world in which one's fate can be surmounted by scorn, as Camus said of Sisyphus.[4] It is a world without fate or complete maturity and gods or final Enlightenment, a world in which experiences might be changed by hopes, actions, and faiths.

In *Pragmatism,* James strove to show that there is no theoretical reason to reject this worldview. For those who think—who feel, who experience—that he is right, there is little reason to repeat this task. Instead of showing itself possible in theory, the task for pragmatism in its second century is making itself actual in practice. To produce the conditions upon which a pragmatic temperament or attunement depends is an immense task. In a world marked by intolerance, arrogance, self-righteousness, violence, custom, hatred, close-mindedness, fatalism, imperialism, fundamentalism, and absolutism, what James describes—looking toward last things—may seem so out of touch as to be out of reach. Maybe so. This might be so. The last one hundred years have not been one hundred years of pragmatism. It is not likely that the next one hundred will be so. But James's

Pragmatism points in the direction of the work that alone has provided, and can provide now, a basis for hope that the next one hundred years might be increasingly pragmatic. For pragmatists, that is all there is, and that is enough. For persons unsure whether this is enough, the pragmatic meaning of *Pragmatism* is this: Give it a try.

NOTES

1. Note that in "The Moral Philosopher and the Moral Life," James explicitly labels as "metaphysical" all questions about "the very *meaning*" of value words such as "good," "ill," and "obligation" (*WB*, 142, 145).

2. Of course, this also means that there can be persons who claim in their theories to be pragmatists but who affirm a very different philosophy in practice. This is a special danger, perhaps, for dreary disciples of pragmatism who are inclined to say, in effect, "Oh, William James must have thought it all before" (*APU*, 13).

3. For a further development of this point, see my "Only Going So Fast: Philosophies as Fashions," *Journal of Speculative Philosophy* 20, no. 3 (2006): 147–64.

4. Albert Camus, *The Myth of Sisyphus and Other Essays*, trans. Justin O'Brien (New York: Vintage Books, 1955), p. 90.

CONTRIBUTORS

Mark Bauerlein is Professor of English at Emory University, and he recently served as Director of Research and Analysis at the National Endowment for the Arts. His books include *The Pragmatic Mind; Literary Criticism: An Autopsy;* and *The Dumbest Generation: How the Digital Age Stupefies Young Americans and Jeopardizes Our Future.* His reviews and commentaries have appeared in the *Wall Street Journal,* the *Washington Post,* the *Weekly Standard, TLS, Yale Review,* and other national publications.

Richard M. Gale is Professor Emeritus at the University of Pittsburgh. His major research interests are in the problem of time, negation and nonbeing, philosophy of religion, and American pragmatism. His books include *The Language of Time; Problems of Negation and Non-Being; On the Nature and Existence of God; The Divided Self of William James; The Philosophy of William James: An Introduction; On The Philosophy of Religion;* and, most recently, *John Dewey's Quest for Intimacy: The Journey of a Promethean Mystic.*

William J. Gavin is Professor of Philosophy at the University of Southern Maine. He is the author of more than one hundred articles and reviews, many of them dealing with American philosophy, and his books include: *William James and the Reinstatement of the Vague* and *Cuttin' the Body Loose: Historical, Biological, and Personal Approaches to Death and Dying.* He is also editor of *Context over Foundation: Dewey and Marx* and *In Dewey's Wake: Unfinished Work of Pragmatic Reconstruction.* He is a former president of the William James Society.

James T. Kloppenberg, Charles Warren Professor of American History at Harvard University, is author of *Uncertain Victory: Social Democracy and Progressivism in European and American Thought, 1870–1920* and *The Virtues of Liberalism,* and editor, with Richard Wightman Fox, of *A Companion to American Thought.* His current projects include a history of democracy in European and American thought from the ancient world through the nineteenth century and a study of pragmatism in twentieth-century American culture.

James Livingston is Professor of History at Rutgers University. Working in intellectual, literary, and economic history, he has published essays on Shakespeare, Poe, Dreiser, Walt Disney, and Richard Rorty, and books, including *Origins of the Federal Reserve System: Money, Class, and Corporate Capitalism, 1890–1913; Pragmatism and the Political Economy of Cultural Revolution, 1850–1940;* and *Pragmatism, Feminism, and Democracy.* His current project, *The Origins of Our*

Time, illuminates the pre–American Century cultural roots of what is taken for granted in early twenty-first century America.

José M. Medina, Associate Professor of Philosophy at Vanderbilt University, works in philosophy of language and social/political philosophy, with special focus on gender, race, ethnicity, and American philosophy. Drawing on speech act theory and pragmatism, he has articulated a *polyphonic contextualism* that provides a performative account of meaning, identity, and discursive agency. He is the author of many articles on meaning and identity; his books include *Speaking from Elsewhere; Language: Key Concepts in Philosophy;* and *The Unity of Wittgenstein's Philosophy.*

Ross Posnock is Professor of English and Comparative Literature at Columbia University. Specializing in the literature and history of nineteenth- and twentieth-century United States, pragmatism, Henry James, and W. E. B. DuBois, he teaches in the English department and the program in American studies. His books include *The Trial of Curiosity: Henry James, William James, and the Challenge of Modernity; Color and Culture: Black Writers and the Making of the Modern Intellectual; The Cambridge Companion to Ralph Ellison;* and *Philip Roth's Rude Truth: The Art of Immaturity.*

Ruth Anna Putnam is Professor Emerita of Philosophy at Wellesley College. She is editor of *The Cambridge Companion to William James,* and the author of numerous articles on William James, John Dewey, and pragmatism, and essays in ethics and political philosophy. She twice directed NEH Summer Seminars for Secondary School Teachers on the work of Emerson and James.

Linda Simon is Professor of English at Skidmore College. In addition to biographies of Alice B. Toklas, Thornton Wilder, and Lady Margaret Beaufort (the grandmother of Henry VIII), her books include *The Critical Reception of Henry James: Creating a Master; Dark Light: Electricity and Anxiety from the Telegraph to the X-ray;* and *Genuine Reality: A Life of William James.* She also edited the collection *William James Remembered* and serves as general editor of the interdisciplinary online journal *William James Studies.*

John J. Stuhr is Arts and Sciences Distinguished Professor of Philosophy and American Studies and Chair of the Department of Philosophy at Emory University. Focusing on ethics, political philosophy, and contemporary cultural problems, and drawing on both American and European philosophy, his publications include *Genealogical Pragmatism; John Dewey;* and *Pragmatism, Postmodernism, and the Future of Philosophy.* A past president of the Society for the Advancement of American Philosophy, he is Director of the American Philosophies Forum, and co-editor of *Journal of Speculative Philosophy.*

Bruce Wilshire is Emeritus Senior Professor of Philosophy at Rutgers University. His wide-ranging interests include William James, pragmatism, and indigenous American thought (*William James and Phenomenology; William James: The Essential Writings;* and *The Primal Roots of American Philosophy*); the phenomenology and ontology of theater (*Role Playing and Identity*); and education, contemporary culture, violence, and nature (*The Moral Collapse of the University; Wild Hunger: The Primal Roots of Modern Addiction;* and *Get 'Em All, Kill 'Em! Genocide, Terrorism, Righteous Communities*).

INDEX